D1799932

Minor Poems of Michael Drayton

by

Michael Drayton

The Echo Library 2007

Published by

The Echo Library

Echo Library
131 High St.
Teddington
Middlesex TW11 8HH

www.echo-library.com

Please report serious faults in the text to complaints@echo-library.com

ISBN 978-1-40684-072-8

CONTENTS

4

INTRODUCTION

Michael Drayton was born in 1563, at Hartshill, near Atherstone, in Warwickshire, where a cottage, said to have been his, is still shown. He early became a page to Sir Henry Goodere, at Polesworth Hall: his own words give the best picture of his early years here.[1] His education would seem to have been good, but ordinary; and it is very doubtful if he ever went to a university.[2] Besides the authors mentioned in the Epistle to Henry Reynolds, he was certainly familiar with Ovid and Horace, and possibly with Catullus: while there seems no reason to doubt that he read Greek, though it is quite true that his references to Greek authors do not prove any first-hand acquaintance. He understood French, and read Rabelais and the French sonneteers, and he seems to have been acquainted with Italian.[3] His knowledge of English literature was wide, and his judgement good: but his chief bent lay towards the history, legendary and otherwise, of his native country, and his vast stores of learning on this subject bore fruit in the Polyolbion.

While still at Polesworth, Drayton fell in love with his patron's younger daughter, Anne;[4] and, though she married, in 1596, Sir Henry Rainsford of Clifford, Drayton continued his devotion to her for many years, and also became an intimate friend of her husband's, writing a sincere elegy on his death.[5] About February, 1591, Drayton paid a visit to London, and published his first work, the Harmony of the Church, a series of paraphrases from the Old Testament, in fourteen-syllabled verse of no particular vigour or grace. This book was immediately suppressed by order of Archbishop Whitgift, possibly because it was supposed to savour of Puritanism.[6] The author, however, published another edition in 1610; indeed, he seems to have had a fondness for this style of work; for in 1604 he published a dull poem, Moyses in a Map of his Miracles, re-issued in 1630 as Moses his Birth and Miracles. Accompanying this piece, in 1630, were two other 'Divine poems': Noah's Floud, and David and Goliath. Noah's Floud is, in part, one of Drayton's happiest attempts at the catalogue style of bestiary; and Mr. Elton finds in it some foreshadowing of the manner of Paradise Lost. But, as a whole, Drayton's attempts in this direction deserve the oblivion into which they, in common with the similar productions of

---

[1] Cf. Elegy viij, To Henery Reynolds, Esquire, p. 108.
[2] Sir Aston Cokayne, in 1658, says that he went to Oxford, while Fleay asserts, without authority, that his university was probably Cambridge.
[3] Cf. the motto of Ideas Mirrour, the allusions to Ariosto in the Nymphidia, p. 129; and above all, the Heroical Epistles; Dedic. of Ep. of D. of Suffolk to Q. Margaret: 'Sweet is the French Tongue, more sweet the Italian, but most sweet are they both, if spoken by your admired self.' Cf. Surrey to Geraldine, ll. 5 sqq., with Drayton's note.
[4] Cf. Sonnet xij (ed. 1602), p. 42, "Tis nine years now since first I lost my wit.' (This sonnet may, of course, occur in the supposed 1600 ed., which would fix an earlier date for Drayton's beginning of love.)
[5] Elegy ix, p. 113.
[6] Cf. Morley's ed. of Barons' Wars, &c. (1887), p. 6.

other authors, have fallen. In the dedication and preface to the Harmony of the Church are some of the few traces of Euphuism shown in Drayton's work; passages in the Heroical Epistles also occur to the mind.[7] He was always averse to affectation, literary or otherwise, and in Elegy viij deliberately condemns Lyly's fantastic style.

Probably before Drayton went up to London, Sir Henry Goodere saw that he would stand in need of a patron more powerful than the master of Polesworth, and introduced him to the Earl and Countess of Bedford. Those who believe[8] Drayton to have been a Pope in petty spite, identify the 'Idea' of his earlier poems with Lucy, Countess of Bedford; though they are forced to acknowledge as self-evident that the 'Idea' of his later work is Anne, Lady Rainsford. They then proceed to say that Drayton, after consistently honouring the Countess in his verse for twelve years, abruptly transferred his allegiance, not forgetting to heap foul abuse on his former patroness, out of pique at some temporary withdrawal of favour. Not only is this directly contrary to all we know and can infer of Drayton's character, but Mr. Elton has decisively disproved it by a summary of bibliographical and other evidence. Into the question it is here unnecessary to enter, and it has been mentioned only because it alone, of the many Drayton-controversies, has cast any slur on the poet's reputation.

In 1593, Drayton published Idea, the Shepherds Garland, in nine Eclogues; in 1606 he added a tenth, the best of all, to the new edition, and rearranged the order, so that the new eclogue became the ninth. In these Pastorals, while following the Shepherds Calendar in many ways, he already displays something of the sturdy independence which characterized him through life. He abandons Spenser's quasi-rustic dialect, and, while keeping to most of the pastoral conventions, such as the singing-match and threnody, he contrives to introduce something of a more natural and homely strain. He keeps the political allusions, notably in the Eclogue containing the song in praise of Beta, who is, of course, Queen Elizabeth. But an over-bold remark in the last line of that song was struck out in 1606; and the new eclogue has no political reference. He is not ashamed to allude directly to Spenser; and indeed his direct debts are limited to a few scattered phrases, as in the Ballad of Dowsabel. Almost to the end of his literary career, Drayton mentions Spenser with reverence and praise.[9]

It is in the songs interspersed in the Eclogues that Drayton's best work at this time is to be found: already his metrical versatility is discernible; for though he doubtless remembered the many varieties of metre employed by Spenser in

---

[7] Cf. E.H. Ep. 'Mat. to K.J.,' 100 sqq., &c.

[8] Professor Courthope and others. There was some excuse for blunders before the publication of Professor Elton's book; and they have been made easier by an unfortunate misprint. Professor Courthope twice misprints the first line of the Love-Parting Sonnet, as 'Since there's no help, come let us rise and part', and, so printed, the line supports better the theory that the poem refers to a patroness and not to a mistress. Cf. Courthope, Hist. Eng. Poetry, iii. pp. 40 and 43.

[9] Cf. E. and Phoebe, sub fin.; Shep. Sir. 145-8; Ep. Hy. Reyn. 79 sqq.

the Calendar, his verses already bear a stamp of their own. The long but impetuous lines, such as 'Trim up her golden tresses with Apollo's sacred tree', afford a striking contrast to the archaic romance-metre, derived from Sir Thopas and its fellows, which appears in Dowsabel, and it again to the melancholy, murmuring cadences of the lament for Elphin. It must, however, be confessed that certain of the songs in the 1593 edition were full of recondite conceits and laboured antitheses, and were rightly struck out, to be replaced by lovelier poems, in the edition of 1606. The song to Beta was printed in Englands Helicon, 1600; here, for the first time, appeared the song of Dead Love, and for the only time, Rowlands Madrigal. In these songs, Drayton offends least in grammar, always a weak point with him; in the body of the Eclogues, in the earlier Sonnets, in the Odes, occur the most extraordinary and perplexing inversions. Quite the most striking feature of the Eclogues, especially in their later form, is their bold attempt at greater realism, at a breaking-away from the conventional images and scenery.

Having paid his tribute to one poetic fashion, Drayton in 1594 fell in with the prevailing craze for sonneteering, and published Ideas Mirrour, a series of fifty-one 'amours' or sonnets, with two prefatory poems, one by Drayton and one by an unknown, signing himself Gorbo il fidele. The title of these poems Drayton possibly borrowed from the French sonneteer, de Pontoux: in their style much recollection of Sidney, Constable, and Daniel is traceable. They are ostensibly addressed to his mistress, and some of them are genuine in feeling; but many are merely imitative exercises in conceit; some, apparently, trials in metre. These amours were again printed, with the title of 'sonnets', in 1599[10], 1600, 1602, 1603, 1605, 1608, 1610, 1613, 1619, and 1631, during the poet's lifetime. It is needless here to discuss whether Drayton were the 'rival poet' to Shakespeare, whether these sonnets were really addressed to a man, or merely to the ideal Platonic beauty; for those who are interested in these points, I subjoin references to the sonnets which touch upon them.[11] From the prentice-work evident in many of the Amours, it would seem that certain of them are among Drayton's earliest poems; but others show a craftsman not meanly advanced in his art. Nevertheless, with few exceptions, this first 'bundle of sonnets' consists rather of trials of skill, bubbles of the mind; most of his sonnets which strike the reader as touched or penetrated with genuine passion belong to the editions from 1599 onwards; implying that his love for Anne Goodere, if at all represented in these poems, grew with his years, for the 'love-parting' is first found in the edition of 1619. But for us the question should not be, are these sonnets genuine representations of the personal feeling of the poet? but rather, how far do they arouse or echo in us as individuals the universal passion? There are at least some of Drayton's sonnets which possess a direct, instant, and universal appeal, by reason of their simple force and straightforward ring; and

---

[10] Those reprints which were really new editions are in italics.
[11] 1594 ed., Pref. Son. and nos. 12, 18, 28; 1599 ed., nos. 3, 31, 46; 1602 ed., 12, 27, 31; and 1603 ed., 47.

not in virtue of any subtle charm of sound and rhythm, or overmastering splendour of diction or thought. Ornament vanishes, and soberness and simplicity increase, as we proceed in the editions of the sonnets. Drayton's chief attempt in the jewelled or ornamental style appeared in 1595, with the title of Endimion and Phoebe, and was, in a sense, an imitation of Marlowe's Hero and Leander. Hero and Leander is, as Swinburne says, a shrine of Parian marble, illumined from within by a clear flame of passion; while Endimion and Phoebe is rather a curiously wrought tapestry, such as that in Mortimer's Tower, woven in splendid and harmonious colours, wherein, however, the figures attain no clearness or subtlety of outline, and move in semi-conventional scenery. It is, none the less, graceful and impressive, and of a like musical fluency with other poems of its class, such as Venus and Adonis, or Salmacis and Hermaphrodius. Parts of it were re-set and spoilt in a 1606 publication of Drayton's, called The Man in the Moone.

In 1593 and 1594 Drayton also published his earliest pieces on the mediaeval theme of the 'Falls of the Illustrious'; they were Peirs Gavesson and Matilda the faire and chaste daughter of the Lord Robert Fitzwater. Here Drayton followed in the track of Boccaccio, Lydgate, and the Mirrour for Magistrates, walking in the way which Chaucer had derided in his Monkes Tale: and with only too great fidelity does Drayton adapt himself to the dullnesses of his model: fine rhetoric is not altogether wanting, and there is, of course, the consciousness that these subjects deal with the history of his beloved country, but neither these, nor Robert, Duke of Normandy (1596), nor Great Cromwell, Earl of Essex (1607 and 1609), nor the Miseries of Margaret (1627) can escape the charge of tediousness.[12] England's Heroical Epistles were first published in 1597, and other editions, of 1598, 1599, and 1602, contain new epistles. These are Drayton's first attempt to strike out a new and original vein of English poetry: they are a series of letters, modelled on Ovid's Heroides,[13] addressed by various pairs of lovers, famous in English history, to each other, and arranged in chronological order, from Henry II and Rosamond to Lady Jane Grey and Lord Guilford Dudley. They are, in a sense, the most important of Drayton's writings, and they have certainly been the most popular, up to the early nineteenth century. In these poems Drayton foreshadowed, and probably inspired, the smooth style of Fairfax, Waller, and Dryden. The metre, the grammar, and the thought, are all perfectly easy to follow, even though he employs many of the Ovidian 'turns' and 'clenches'. A certain attempt at realization of the different

---

[12] Meres thought otherwise. Cf. Palladis Tamia (1598), 'As Accius, M. Atilius, and Milithus were called Tragediographi, because they writ tragedies: so may wee truly terme Michael Drayton Tragaediographus for his passionate penning the downfals of valiant Robert of Normandy, chast Matilda, and great Gaueston.' Cf. Barnefield, Poems: in diuers humors (ed. Arber, p. 119), 'And Drayton, whose wel-written Tragedies, | And Sweete Epistles, soare thy fame to skies. | Thy learned name is equall with the rest; | Whose stately Numbers are so well addrest.'
[13] Cf. Meres, Palladis Tamia (1598), 'Michael Drayton doth imitate Ouid in his England's Heroical Epistles.'

characters is observable, but the poems are fine rhetorical exercises rather than realizations of the dramatic and passionate possibilities of their themes. In 1596, Drayton, as we have seen, published the Mortimeriados, a kind of epic, with Mortimer as its hero, of the wars between King Edward II and the Barons.[14] It was written in the seven-line stanza of Chaucer's Troilus and Cressida and Spenser's Hymns. On its republication in 1603, with the title of the Barons' Wars, the metre was changed to ottava rima, and Drayton showed, in an excellent preface, that he fully appreciated the principles and the subtleties of the metrical art. While possessing many fine passages, the Barons' Wars is somewhat dull, lacking much of the poetry of the older version; and does not escape from Drayton's own criticism of Daniel's Chronicle Poems: 'too much historian in verse,...His rhymes were smooth, his metres well did close, But yet his manner better fitted prose'.[15] The description of Mortimer's Tower in the sixth book recalls the ornate style of Endimion and Phoebe, while the fifth book, describing the miseries of King Edward, is the most moving and dramatic. But there is a general lifelessness and lack of movement for which these purple passages barely atone. The cause of the production of so many chronicle poems about this time has been supposed[16] to be the desire of showing the horrors of civil war, at a time when the queen was growing old, and no successor had, as it seemed, been accepted. Also they were a kind of parallel to the Chronicle Play; and Drayton, in any case even if we grant him to have been influenced by the example of Daniel, never needed much incentive to treat a national theme.

About this time, we find Drayton writing for the stage. It seems unnecessary here to discuss whether the writing of plays is evidence of Drayton's poverty, or his versatility;[17] but the fact remains that he had a hand in the production of about twenty. Of these, the only one which certainly survives is The first part of the true and honorable historie, of the life of Sir John Oldcastle, the good Lord Cobham, &c. It is practically impossible to distinguish Drayton's share in this curious play, and it does not, therefore, materially assist the elucidation of the question whether he had any dramatic feeling or skill. It can be safely affirmed that the dramatic instinct was nor uppermost in his mind; he was a Seneca rather than a Euripides: but to deny him all dramatic idea, as does Dr. Whitaker, is too severe. There is decided, if slender, dramatic skill and feeling in certain of the Nymphals. Drayton's persons are usually, it must be said, rather figures in a tableau, or series of tableaux; but in the second and seventh Nymphals, and occasionally in the tenth, there is real dramatic movement. Closely connected with this question is the consideration of humour, which is wrongly denied to

---

[14] Cf. id., ibid., 'As Lucan hath mournefully depainted the ciuil wars of Pompey and Cæsar: so hath Daniel the ciuill wars of Yorke and Lancaster, and Drayton the civill wars of Edward the second and the Barons.'

[15] Cf. Elegy viij. 126-8.

[16] Cf. Morley's ed., Barons' Wars, &c., 1887, pp. 6-7.

[17] Cf. Elron, pp. 83-93, and Whitaker, M. Drayton as a Dramatist (Public. Mod. Lang. Assoc. of America, vol. xviij. 3).

Drayton. Humour is observable first, perhaps, in the Owle (1604); then in the Ode to his Rival (1619); and later in the Nymphidia, Shepheards Sirena, and Muses Elyzium. The second Nymphal shows us the quiet laughter, the humorous twinkle, with which Drayton writes at times. The subject is an [Greek: agôn] or contest between two shepherds for the affections of a nymph called Lirope: Lalus is a vale-bred swain, of refined and elegant manners, skilled, nevertheless, in all manly sports and exercises; Cleon, no less a master in physical prowess, was nurtured by a hind in the mountains; the contrast between their manners is admirably sustained: Cleon is rough, inclined to be rude and scoffing, totally without tact, even where his mistress is concerned. Lalus remembers her upbringing and her tastes; he makes no unnecessary or ostentatious display of wealth; his gifts are simple and charming, while Cleon's are so grotesquely unsuited to a swain, that it is tempting to suppose that Drayton was quietly satirizing Marlowe's Passionate Shepherd. Lirope listens gravely to the swains in turn, and makes demure but provoking answers, raising each to the height of hope, and then casting them both down into the depths of despair; finally she refuses both, yet without altogether killing hope. Her first answer is a good specimen of her banter and of Drayton's humour.[18]

On the accession of James I, Drayton hastened to greet the King with a somewhat laboured song To the Maiestie of King James; but this poem was apparently considered to be premature: he cried Vivat Rex, without having said, Mortua est eheu Regina, and accordingly he suffered the penalty of his 'forward pen',[19] and was severely neglected by King and Court. Throughout James's reign a darker and more satirical mood possesses Drayton, intruding at times even into his strenuous recreation-ground, the Polyolbion, and manifesting itself more directly in his satires, the Owle (1604), the Moon-Calfe (1627), the Man in the Moone (1606), and his verse-letters and elegies; while his disappointment with the times, the country, and the King, flashes out occasionally even in the Odes, and is heard in his last publication, the Muses Elizium (1630). To counterbalance the disappointment in his hopes from the King, Drayton found a new and life-long friend in Walter Aston, of Tixall, in Staffordshire; this gentleman was created Knight of the Bath by James, and made Drayton one of his esquires. By Aston's 'continual bounty' the poet was able to devote himself almost entirely to more congenial literary work; for, while Meres speaks of the Polyolbion in 1598,[20] and we may easily see that Drayton had the idea of that work at least as early as 1594,[21] yet he cannot have been able to give much time to it till now. Nevertheless, the 'declining and corrupt times' worked on Drayton's mind and grieved and darkened his soul, for we must remember that

---

[18] Cf. Nl. ij. 127 sqq., p. 172.

[19] Cf. Elegy ij. 20.

[20] Cf. Palladis Tamia: 'Michael Drayton is now in penning, in English verse, a Poem called Poly-olbion, Geographicall & Hydrographicall of all the forests, woods, mountaines, fountaines, riuers, lakes, flouds, bathes, & springs that be in England.'

[21] Cf. Amours (1594), xx and xxiv.

he was perfectly prosperous then and was not therefore incited to satire by bodily want or distress.

In 1604 he published the Owle, a mild satire, under the form of a moral fable of government, reminding the reader a little of the Parlement of Foules. The Man in the Moone (1606) is partly a recension of Endimion and Phoebe, but is a heterogeneous mass of weakly satire, of no particular merit. The Moon-Calfe (1627) is Drayton's most savage and misanthropic excursion into the region of Satire; in which, though occasionally nobly ironic, he is more usually coarse and blustering, in the style of Marston.[22] In 1605 Drayton brought out his first 'collected poems', from which the Eclogues and the Owle are omitted; and in 1606 he published his Poemes Lyrick and Pastorall, Odes, Eglogs, The Man in the Moone. Of these the Eglogs are a recension of the Shepherd's Garland of 1593: we have already spoken of The Man in the Moone. The Odes are by far the most important and striking feature of the book. In the preface, Drayton professes to be following Pindar, Anacreon, and Horace, though, as he modestly implies, at a great distance. Under the title of Odes he includes a variety of subjects, and a variety of metres; ranging from an Ode to his Harp or to his Criticks, to a Ballad of Agincourt, or a poem on the Rose compared with his Mistress. In the edition of 1619 appeared several more Odes, including some of the best; while many of the others underwent careful revision, notably the Ballad. 'Sing wee the Rose,' perhaps because of its unintelligibility, and the Ode to his friend John Savage, perhaps because too closely imitated from Horace, were omitted. Drayton was not the first to use the term Ode for a lyrical poem, in English: Soothern in 1584, and Daniel in 1592 had preceded him; but he was the first to give the name popularity in England, and to lift the kind as Ronsard had lifted it in France; and till the time of Cowper no other English poet showed mastery of the short, staccato measure of the Anacreontic as distinct from the Pindaric Ode. In the Odes Drayton shows to the fullest extent his metrical versatility: he touches the Skeltonic metre, the long ten-syllabled line of the Sacrifice to Apollo; and ascends from the smooth and melodious rhythms of the New Year through the inspiring harp-tones of the Virginian Voyage to the clangour and swing of the Ballad of Agincourt. His grammar is possibly more distorted here than anywhere, but, as Mr. Elton says, 'these are the obstacles of any poet who uses measures of four or six syllables.' His tone throughout is rather that of the harp, as played, perhaps, in Polesworth Hall, than that of any other instrument; but in 1619 Drayton has taken to him the lute of Carew and his compeers. In 1619 the style is lighter, the fancy gayer, more exquisite, more recondite. Most of his few metaphysical conceits are to be found in these later Odes, as in the Heart, the Valentine, and the Crier. In the comparison of the two editions the nobler, if more strained, tone of the earlier is obvious; it is still Elizabethan, in its nobility of ideal and purpose, in its enthusiasm, in its belief and confidence in England and her men; and this even though we catch a

---

[22] Cf. Sonnet vj (1619 edition); which is a dignified summary of much that he says more coarsely in the Moone-Calfe.

glimpse of the Jacobean woe in the Ode to John Savage: the 1619 Odes are of a different world; their spirit is lighter, more insouciant in appearance, though perhaps studiedly so; the rhythms are more fantastic, with less of strength and firmness, though with more of grace and superficial beauty; even the very textual alterations, while usually increasing the grace and the music of the lines, remind the reader that something of the old spontaneity and freshness is gone.

In 1607 and 1609, Drayton published two editions of the last and weakest of his mediaeval poems—the Legend of Great Cromwell; and for the next few years he produced nothing new, only attending to the publication of certain reprints and new editions. During this time, however, he was working steadily at the Polyolbion, helped by the patronage of Aston and of Prince Henry. In 1612-13, Drayton burst upon an indifferent world with the first part of the great poem, containing eighteen songs; the title-page will give the best idea of the contents and plan of the book: 'Poly-Olbion or a Chorographicall Description of the Tracts, Riuers, Mountaines, Forests, and other Parts of this renowned Isle of Great Britaine, With intermixture of the most Remarquable Stories, Antiquities, Wonders, Rarityes, Pleasures, and Commodities of the same: Digested in a Poem by Michael Drayton, Esq. With a Table added, for direction to those occurrences of Story and Antiquities, whereunto the Course of the Volume easily leades not.' &c. On this work Drayton had been engaged for nearly the whole of his poetical career. The learning and research displayed in the poem are extraordinary, almost equalling the erudition of Selden in his Annotations to each Song. The first part was, for various reasons, a drug in the market, and Drayton found great difficulty in securing a publisher for the second part. But during the years from 1613 to 1622, he became acquainted with Drummond of Hawthornden through a common friend, Sir William Alexander of Menstry, afterwards Earl of Stirling. In 1618, Drayton starts a correspondence; and towards the end of the year mentions that he is corresponding also with Andro Hart, bookseller, of Edinburgh. The subject of his letter was probably the publication of the Second Part; which Drayton alludes to in a letter of 1619 thus: 'I have done twelve books more, that is from the eighteenth book, which was Kent, if you note it; all the East part and North to the river Tweed; but it lies by me; for the booksellers and I are in terms; they are a company of base knaves, whom I both scorn and kick at.' Finally, in 1622, Drayton got Marriott, Grismand, and Dewe, of London, to take the work, and it was published with a dedication to Prince Charles, who, after his brother's death, had given Drayton patronage. Drayton's preface to the Second Part is well worth quoting:

'To any that will read it. When I first undertook this Poem, or, as some very skilful in this kind have pleased to term it, this Herculean labour, I was by some virtuous friends persuaded, that I should receive much comfort and encouragement therein; and for these reasons; First, that it was a new, clear, way, never before gone by any; then, that it contained all the Delicacies, Delights, and Rarities of this renowned Isle, interwoven with the Histories of the Britons, Saxons, Normans, and the later English: And further that there is scarcely any of the Nobility or Gentry of this land, but that he is in some way or other by his

Blood interested therein. But it hath fallen out otherwise; for instead of that comfort, which my noble friends (from the freedom of their spirits) proposed as my due, I have met with barbarous ignorance, and base detraction; such a cloud hath the Devil drawn over the world's judgment, whose opinion is in few years fallen so far below all ballatry, that the lethargy is incurable: nay, some of the Stationers, that had the selling of the First Part of this Poem, because it went not so fast away in the sale, as some of their beastly and abominable trash, (a shame both to our language and nation) have either despitefully left out, or at least carelessly neglected the Epistles to the Readers, and so have cozened the buyers with unperfected books; which these that have undertaken the Second Part, have been forced to amend in the First, for the small number that are yet remaining in their hands. And some of our outlandish, unnatural, English, (I know not how otherwise to express them) stick not to say that there is nothing in this Island worth studying for, and take a great pride to be ignorant in any thing thereof; for these, since they delight in their folly, I wish it may be hereditary from them to their posterity, that their children may be begg'd for fools to the fifth generation, until it may be beyond the memory of man to know that there was ever other of their families: neither can this deter me from going on with Scotland, if means and time do not hinder me, to perform as much as I have promised in my First Song:

> Till through the sleepy main, to Thuly I have gone,
> And seen the Frozen Isles, the cold Deucalidon,
> Amongst whose iron Rocks, grim Saturn yet remains
> Bound in those gloomy caves with adamantine chains.

And as for those cattle whereof I spake before, Odi profanum vulgus, et arceo, of which I account them, be they never so great, and so I leave them. To my friends, and the lovers of my labours, I wish all happiness. Michael Drayton.'

The Polyolbion as a whole is easy and pleasant to read; and though in some parts it savours too much of a mere catalogue, yet it has many things truly poetical. The best books are perhaps the xiij, xiv, and xv, where he is on his own ground, and therefore naturally at his best. It is interesting to notice how much attention and space he devotes to Wales. He describes not only the 'wonders' but also the fauna and flora of each district; and of the two it would seem that the flowers interested him more. Though he was a keen observer of country sights and sounds (a fact sufficiently attested by the Nymphidia and the Nymphals), it is evident that his interest in most things except flowers was rather momentary or conventional than continuous and heart-felt; but of the flowers he loves to talk, whether he weaves us a garland for the Thame's wedding, or gives us the contents of a maund of simples; and his love, if somewhat homely and unimaginative, is apparent enough. But the main inspiration, as it is the main theme, of the Polyolbion is the glory and might and wealth, past, present, and future, of England, her possessions and her folk. Through all this glory, however, we catch the tone of Elizabethan sorrow over the 'Ruines of Time';

grief that all these mighty men and their works will perish and be forgotten, unless the poet makes them live for ever on the lips of men. Drayton's own voluminousness has defeated his purpose, and sunk his poem by its own bulk. Though it is difficult to go so far as Mr. Bullen, and say that the only thing better than a stroll in the Polyolbion is one in a Sussex lane, it is still harder to agree with Canon Beeching, that 'there are few beauties on the road', the beauties are many, though of a quietly rural type, and the road, if long and winding, is of good surface, while its cranks constitute much of its charm. It is doubtless, from the outside, an appalling poem in these days of epitomes and monographs, but it certainly deserves to be rescued from oblivion and read.

In 1618 Drayton contributed two Elegies to Henry FitzGeoffrey's Satyrs and Epigrames. These were on the Lady Penelope Clifton, and on 'the death of the three sonnes of the Lord Sheffield, drowned neere where Trent falleth into Humber'. Neither is remarkable save for far-fetched conceits; they were reprinted in 1610, and again, with many others, in the volume of 1627. In 1619 Drayton issued a folio collected edition of his works, and reprinted it in 1620. In 1627 followed a folio of wholly fresh matter, including the Battaile of Agincourt; the Miseries of Queene Margarite, Nimphidia, Quest of Cinthia, Shepheards Sirena, Moone-Calfe, and Elegies upon sundry occasions. The Battaile of Agincourt is a somewhat otiose expansion, with purple patches, of the Ballad; it is, nevertheless, Drayton's best lengthy piece on a historical theme. Of the Miseries of Queene Margarite and of the Moone-Calfe we have already spoken. The most notable piece in the book is the Nimphidia. This poem of the Court of Fairy has 'invention, grace, and humour', as Canon Beeching has said. It would be interesting to know exactly when it was composed and committed to paper, for it is thought that the three fairy poems in Herrick's Hesperides were written about 1626. In any case, Drayton's poem touches very little, and chiefly in the beginning, on the subject of any one of Herrick's three pieces. The style, execution, and impression left on the reader are quite different; even as they are totally unlike those of the Midsummer Night's Dream. Herrick's pieces are extraordinary combinations of the idea of 'King of Shadows', with a reality fantastically sober: the poems are steeped in moonlight. In Drayton all is clear day, or the most unromantic of nights; though everything is charming, there is no attempt at idealization, little of the higher faculty of imagination; but great realism, and much play of fancy. Herrick's verses were written by Cobweb and Moth together, Drayton's by Puck. Granting, however, the initial deficiency in subtlety of charm, the whole poem is inimitably graceful and piquant. The gay humour, the demure horror of the witchcraft, the terrible seriousness of the battle, wonderfully realize the mock-heroic gigantesque; and while there is not the minute accuracy of Gulliver in Lilliput, Drayton did not write for a sceptical or too-prying audience; quite half his readers believed more or less in fairies. In the metre of the poem Drayton again echoes that of the older romances, as he did in Dowsabel. In the Quest of Cinthia, while ostensibly we come to the real world of mortals, we are really in a non-existent land of pastoral convention, in the most pseudo-Arcadian atmosphere in which Drayton ever worked. The metre and the language are, however, charmingly managed. The Shepheards Sirena is a poem, apparently, 'where more is meant than meets the ear,' as so often in pastoral poetry[23]; it is difficult to see exactly what is meant; but the Jacobean strain of doubt and fear is there, and the poem would seem to have been written some time earlier than 1627. The Elegies comprise a great variety of styles and themes; some are really threnodies, some verse-letters, some laments over the evil times, and one a summary of Drayton's literary opinions. He employs the couplet in his Elegies with a masterly hand, often with a deliberately rugged effect, as in his broader Marstonic satire addressed to William Browne; while the line of greater smoothness but equal strength is to be seen in the letters to Sandys and Jeffreys. He is fantastic and conceited in most of the threnodies; but, as is natural, that on his old friend, Sir Henry Rainsford, is least artificial and fullest of true feeling. The epistle to Henery Reynolds. Of Poets and Poesie shows Drayton as a sane and sagacious critic, ready to see the good, but keen to discern the weakness also; perhaps the clearest evidence of his critical skill is the way in which nearly all of his judgements on his contemporaries coincide with the received modern opinions.

In his later years Drayton enjoyed the patronage of the third Earl and Countess of Dorset; and in 1630 he published his last volume, the Muses Elizium, of which he dedicated the pastoral part to the Earl, and the three divine poems at the end to the Countess. The Muses Elizium proper consists of Ten Pastorals or Nymphals, prefaced by a Description of Elizium. The three divine poems have been mentioned before, and were Noah's Floud, Moses his Birth and Miracles, and David and Goliah. The Nymphals are the crown and summary of much of the best in Drayton's work. Here he departed from the conventional type of pastoral, even more than in the Shepherd's Garland; but to say that he sang of English rustic life would hardly be true: the sixth Nymphal, allowing for a few pardonable exaggerations by the competitors, is almost all English, if we except the names; so is the tenth with the same exception; the first and fourth might take place anywhere, but are not likely in any country; the second is more conventional; the fifth is almost, but not quite, English; the third, seventh, and ninth are avowedly classical in theme; while the eighth is a more delicate and subtle fairy poem than the Nymphidia. The fourth and tenth Nymphals are also touched with the sadder, almost satiric vein; the former inveighing against the English imitation of foreigners and love of extravagance in dress; while the tenth complains of the improvident and wasteful felling of trees in the English forests. This last Nymphal, though designedly an epilogue, is probably rather a warning than a despairing lament, even though we conceive the old satyr to be Drayton himself. As a whole the Nymphals show Drayton at his happiest and lightest in style and metre; at his moments of greatest serenity and even gaiety; an atmosphere of sunshine seems to envelope them all, though the sun sink behind a cloud in the last. His music now is that of a rippling stream, whereas in his

---

[23] Cf. Morley's ed. Barons' Wars, &c., p. 8.

earlier days he spoke weightier and more sonorous words, with a mouth of gold.[24]

To estimate the poetical faculty of Drayton is a somewhat perplexing task; for, while rarely subtle, or rising to empyrean heights, he wrote in such varied styles, on such various themes, that the task, at first, seems that of criticizing many poets, not one. But through all his work runs the same eminently English spirit, the same honesty and clearness of idea, the same stolidity of purpose, and not infrequently of execution also; the same enthusiasm characterizes all his earlier, and much of his later work; the enthusiasm especially characteristic of Elizabethan England, and shown by Drayton in his passion for England and the English, in his triumphant joy in their splendid past, and his certainty of their future glory. As a poet, he lacked imagination and fine fury; he supplied their place by the airiest and clearest of fancies, by the strenuous labour of a great brain illumined by the steady flame of love for his country and for his lady. Mr. Courthope has said that he lacked loftiness and resolution of artistic purpose; without these, we ask, how could a man, not lavishly dowered with poetry in his soul, have achieved so much of it? It was his very fixity and loftiness of purpose, his English stubbornness and doggedness of resolution that enabled him to surmount so many obstacles of style and metre, of subject and thought. His two purposes, of glorifying his mistress and his friends, and of sounding England's glories past and future, while insisting on the dangers of a present decadence, never flagged or failed. All his poetry up to 1627 has this object directly or secondarily; and much after this date. Of the more abstract and universal aspects of his art he had not much conception; but he caught eagerly at the fashionable belief in the eternizing power of poetry; and had it not been that, where his patriotism was uppermost, he was deficient in humour and sense of proportion, he would have succeeded better: as it is, his more directly patriotic pieces are usually the dullest or longest of his works. He requires, like all other poets, the impulse of an absolutely personal and individual feeling, a moment of more intimate sympathy, to rouse him to his heights of song. Thus the Ballad of Agincourt is on the very theme of all patriotic themes that most attracted him; Virginian and other Voyages lay very close to his heart; and in certain sonnets to his lady lies his only imperishable work. Of sheer melody and power of song he had little, apart from his themes: he could not have sat down and written a few lark's or nightingale's notes about nothing as some of his contemporaries were able to do: he required the stimulus of a subject, and if he were really moved thereby he beat the music out. Only in one or two of the later Odes, and in the volumes of 1627 and 1630, does his music ever seem to flow from him naturally. Akin to this quality of broad and extensive workmanship, to this faculty of

---

[24] Charles FitzGeoffrey, Drake (1596), 'golden-mouthed Drayton musical.' Guilpin, Skialetheia (1598), 'Drayton's condemned of some for imitation, But others say, 'tis the best poet's fashion...Drayton's justly surnam'd golden-mouth'd.' Meres, Palladis Tamia (1598),' In Charles Fitz-Jefferies Drake Drayton is termed "golden-mouth'd" for the purity and pretiousnesse of his stile and phrase.'

taking a subject and when writing, with all thought concentrated on it, rather than on the method of writing about it, is his strange lack of what are usually called 'quotations'. For this is not only due to the fact that he is little known; there are, besides, so few detached remarks or aphorisms that are separately quotable; so few examples of that curiosa felicitas of diction: lines like these,

> Thy Bowe, halfe broke, is peec'd with old desire;
> Her Bowe is beauty with ten thousand strings....

are rare enough. Drayton, in fact, comes as near controverting the statement Poeta nascitur, non fit, as any one in English literature: by diligent toil and earnest desire he won a place for himself in the second rank of English poets: through love he once set foot in the circle of the mightiest. Sincere he was always, simple often, sensuous rarely. His great industry, his careful study, and his great receptivity are shown in the unusual spectacle of a man who has sung well in the language of his youth, suddenly learning, in his age, the tongue spoken by the younger generation, and reproducing it with individuality and sureness of touch. It is in rhetoric, splendid or rugged, in argument, in plain statement or description, in the outline sketch of a picture, that Drayton excels; magic of atmosphere and colouring are rarely present. Stolidity is, perhaps, his besetting sin; yet it is the sign of a slow, not a dull, intellect; an intellect, like his heart, which never let slip what it had once taken to itself.

As a man Drayton would seem to have been an excellent type of the sturdy, clear-headed, but yet romantic and enthusiastic Englishman; gifted with much natural ability, sedulously increased by study; quietly humorous, self-restrained; and if temporarily soured by disappointment and the disjointed times, yet emerging at last into a greater serenity, a more unadulterated gaiety than had ever before characterized him. It is possible, but from his clear and sane balance of mind improbable, that many of his light later poems are due to deliberate self-blinding and self-deception, a walking in enchanted lands of the mind.

Of Drayton's three known portraits the earliest shows him at the age of thirty-six, and is now in the National Portrait Gallery. A look of quiet, speculative melancholy seems to pervade it; there is, as yet, no moroseness, no evidence of severe conflict with the world, no shadow of stress or of doubt. The second and best-known portrait shows us Drayton at the age of fifty, and was engraved by Hole, as a frontispiece to the poems of 1619. Here a notable change has come over the face; the mouth is hardened, and depressed at the corners through disappointment and disillusionment; the eyes are full of a pathos increased by the puzzled and perturbed uplift of the brows. Yet a stubbornness and tenacity of purpose invests the features and reminds us that Drayton is of the old and sound Elizabethan stock, 'on evil days though fallen.' Let it be remembered, that he was in 1613, when the portrait was taken, in more or less prosperous circumstances; it was the sad degeneracy, the meanness and feebleness of the generation around him, that chiefly depressed and embittered him. The final portrait, now in the Dulwich Gallery, represents the poet as a man of sixty-five; and is quite in keeping with the sunnier and calmer tone of his later poetry. It is the face of one who has not emerged unscathed from the world's conflict, but has attained to a certain calm, a measure of tranquillity, a portion of content, who has learnt the lesson that there is a soul of goodness in things evil. The Hole portrait shows him with long hair, small 'goatee' beard, and aquiline nose drawn up at the nostrils: while the National portrait shows a type of nose and beard intermediate between the Hole and the Dulwich pictures: the general contour of the face, though the forehead is broad enough, is long and oval. Drayton seems to have been tall and thin, and to have been very susceptible of cold, and therefore to have hated Winter and the North.[25] He is said to have shared in the supper which caused Shakespeare's death; but his own verses[26] breathe the spirit of Milton's sonnet to Cyriack Skinner, rather than that of a devotee of Bacchus.

He died in 1631, possibly on December 23, and was buried under the North wall of Westminster Abbey. Meres's[27] opinion of his character during his early life is as follows: 'As Aulus Persius Flaccus is reported among al writers to be of an honest life and vpright conuersation: so Michael Drayton, quem totics honoris et amoris causa nomino, among schollers, souldiours, Poets, and all sorts of people is helde for a man of uertuous disposition, honest conversation, and well gouerned cariage; which is almost miraculous among good wits in these declining and corrupt times, when there is nothing but rogery in villanous man, and when cheating and craftines is counted the cleanest wit, and soundest wisedome.'[28] Fuller also, in a similar strain, says, 'He was a pious poet, his conscience having the command of his fancy, very temperate in his life, slow of speech, and inoffensive in company.'

In conclusion I have to thank Mr. H.M. Sanders, of Pembroke College, Oxford, for help and advice, and Professor Raleigh and Mr. R.W. Chapman for help and criticism while the volume was in the press. Above all, I am at every turn indebted to Professor Elton's invaluable Michael Drayton,[29] without which the work of any student of Drayton would be rendered, if not impossible, at least infinitely harder.

CYRIL BRETT.
ALTON, STAFFORDSHIRE.

---

[25] Cf. E. H. E., pp. 90, 99 (ed. 1737); Elegy i; and Ode written in the Peak.
[26] Elegy viij, ad init.
[27] Palladis Tamia (1598).
[28] Cf. Returne from Parnassus, i. 2 (1600) ed. Arb. p. 11.
[29] Michael Drayton. A Critical Study. Oliver Elton, M.A. London: A. Constable & Co., 1905.

SONNETS

[from the Edition of 1594]

To the deere Chyld of the Muses, and
   his euer kind Mecænas, Ma. Anthony
       Cooke, Esquire

Vovchsafe to grace these rude vnpolish'd rymes,
Which long (dear friend) haue slept in sable night,
And, come abroad now in these glorious tymes,
Can hardly brook the purenes of the light.
But still you see their desteny is such,
That in the world theyr fortune they must try,
Perhaps they better shall abide the tuch,
Wearing your name, theyr gracious liuery.
Yet these mine owne: I wrong not other men,
Nor trafique further then thys happy Clyme,
Nor filch from Portes, nor from Petrarchs pen,
A fault too common in this latter time.
   Diuine Syr Phillip, I auouch thy writ,
   I am no Pickpurse of anothers wit.
          Yours deuoted,
          M. DRAYTON.

Amour 1

Reade heere (sweet Mayd) the story of my wo,
The drery abstracts of my endles cares,
With my liues sorow enterlyned so;
Smok'd with my sighes, and blotted with my teares:
The sad memorials of my miseries,
Pend in the griefe of myne afflicted ghost;
My liues complaint in doleful Elegies,
With so pure loue as tyme could neuer boast.
Receaue the incense which I offer heere,
By my strong fayth ascending to thy fame,
My zeale, my hope, my vowes, my praise, my prayer,
My soules oblation to thy sacred name:
   Which name my Muse to highest heauen shal raise
   By chast desire, true loue, and vertues praise.

Amour 2

My fayre, if thou wilt register my loue,
More then worlds volumes shall thereof arise;
Preserue my teares, and thou thy selfe shall proue
A second flood downe rayning from mine eyes.
Note but my sighes, and thine eyes shal behold
The Sun-beames smothered with immortall smoke;
And if by thee, my prayers may be enrold,
They heauen and earth to pitty shall prouoke.
Looke thou into my breast, and thou shall see
Chaste holy vowes for my soules sacrifice:
That soule (sweet Maide) which so hath honoured thee,
Erecting Trophies to thy sacred eyes;
   Those eyes to my heart shining euer bright,
   When darknes hath obscur'd each other light.

Amour 3

My thoughts bred vp with Eagle-birds of loue,
And, for their vertues I desiered to know,
Vpon the nest I set them forth, to proue
If they were of the Eagles kinde or no:
But they no sooner saw my Sunne appeare,
But on her rayes with gazing eyes they stood;
Which proou'd my birds delighted in the ayre,
And that they came of this rare kinglie brood.
But now their plumes, full sumd with sweet desire,
To shew their kinde began to clime the skies:
Doe what I could my Eaglets would aspire,
Straight mounting vp to thy celestiall eyes.
   And thus (my faire) my thoughts away be flowne,
   And from my breast into thine eyes be gone.

Amour 4

My faire, had I not erst adorned my Lute
With those sweet strings stolne from thy golden hayre,
Vnto the world had all my ioyes been mute,
Nor had I learn'd to descant on my faire.
Had not mine eye seene thy Celestiall eye,
Nor my hart knowne the power of thy name,
My soule had ne'er felt thy Diuinitie,
Nor my Muse been the trumpet of thy fame.
But thy diuine perfections, by their skill,

This miracle on my poore Muse haue tried,
And, by inspiring, glorifide my quill,
And in my verse thy selfe art deified:
    Thus from thy selfe the cause is thus deriued,
    That by thy fame all fame shall be suruiued.

Amour 5

Since holy Vestall lawes haue been neglected,
The Gods pure fire hath been extinguisht quite;
No Virgin once attending on that light,
Nor yet those heauenly secrets once respected;
Till thou alone, to pay the heauens their dutie
Within the Temple of thy sacred name,
With thine eyes kindling that Celestiall flame,
By those reflecting Sun-beames of thy beautie.
Here Chastity that Vestall most diuine,
Attends that Lampe with eye which neuer sleepeth;
The volumes of Religions lawes shee keepeth,
Making thy breast that sacred reliques shryne,
    Where blessed Angels, singing day and night,
    Praise him which made that fire, which lends that light.

Amour 6

In one whole world is but one Phoenix found,
A Phoenix thou, this Phoenix then alone:
By thy rare plume thy kind is easly knowne,
With heauenly colours dide, with natures wonder cround.
Heape thine own vertues, seasoned by their sunne,
On heauenly top of thy diuine desire;
Then with thy beautie set the same on fire,
So by thy death thy life shall be begunne.
Thy selfe, thus burned in this sacred flame,
With thine owne sweetnes al the heauens perfuming,
And stil increasing as thou art consuming,
Shalt spring againe from th' ashes of thy fame;
    And mounting vp shall to the heauens ascend:
    So maist thou liue, past world, past fame, past end.

Amour 7

Stay, stay, sweet Time; behold, or ere thou passe
From world to world, thou long hast sought to see,
That wonder now wherein all wonders be,

Where heauen beholds her in a mortall glasse.
Nay, looke thee, Time, in this Celesteall glasse,
And thy youth past in this faire mirror see:
Behold worlds Beautie in her infancie,
What shee was then, and thou, or ere shee was.
Now passe on, Time: to after-worlds tell this,
Tell truelie, Time, what in thy time hath beene,
That they may tel more worlds what Time hath seene,
And heauen may ioy to think on past worlds blisse.
    Heere make a Period, Time, and saie for mee,
    She was the like that neuer was, nor neuer more shalbe.

Amour 8

Vnto the World, to Learning, and to Heauen,
Three nines there are, to euerie one a nine;
One number of the earth, the other both diuine,
One wonder woman now makes three od numbers euen.
Nine orders, first, of Angels be in heauen;
Nine Muses doe with learning still frequent:
These with the Gods are euer resident.
Nine worthy men vnto the world were giuen.
My Worthie one to these nine Worthies addeth,
And my faire Muse one Muse vnto the nine;
And my good Angell, in my soule diuine,
With one more order these nine orders gladdeth.
    My Muse, my Worthy, and my Angell, then,
    Makes euery one of these three nines a ten.

Amour 9

Beauty sometime, in all her glory crowned,
Passing by that cleere fountain of thine eye,
Her sun-shine face there chaunsing to espy,
Forgot herselfe, and thought she had been drowned.
And thus, whilst Beautie on her beauty gazed,
Who then, yet liuing, deemd she had been dying,
And yet in death some hope of life espying,
At her owne rare perfections so amazed;
Twixt ioy and griefe, yet with a smyling frowning,
The glorious sun-beames of her eyes bright shining,
And shee, in her owne destiny diuining,
Threw in herselfe, to saue herselfe by drowning;
    The Well of Nectar, pau'd with pearle and gold,
    Where shee remaines for all eyes to behold.

Amour 10

Oft taking pen in hand, with words to cast my woes,
Beginning to account the sum of all my cares,
I well perceiue my griefe innumerable growes,
And still in reckonings rise more millions of dispayres.
And thus, deuiding of my fatall howres,
The payments of my loue I read, and reading crosse,
And in substracting set my sweets vnto my sowres;
Th' average of my ioyes directs me to my losse.
And thus mine eyes, a debtor to thine eye,
Who by extortion gaineth all theyr lookes,
My hart hath payd such grieuous vsury,
That all her wealth lyes in thy Beauties bookes;
    And all is thine which hath been due to mee,
    And I a Banckrupt, quite vndone by thee.

Amour 11

Thine eyes taught mee the Alphabet of loue,
To con my Cros-rowe ere I learn'd to spell;
For I was apt, a scholler like to proue,
Gaue mee sweet lookes when as I learned well.
Vowes were my vowels, when I then begun
At my first Lesson in thy sacred name:
My consonants the next when I had done,
Words consonant, and sounding to thy fame.
My liquids then were liquid christall teares,
My cares my mutes, so mute to craue reliefe;
My dolefull Dypthongs were my liues dispaires,
Redoubling sighes the accents of my griefe:
    My loues Schoole-mistris now hath taught me so,
    That I can read a story of my woe.

Amour 12

Some Atheist or vile Infidell in loue,
When I doe speake of thy diuinitie,
May blaspheme thus, and say I flatter thee,
And onely write my skill in verse to proue.
See myracles, ye vnbeleeuing! see
A dumbe-born Muse made to expresse the mind,
A cripple hand to write, yet lame by kind,
One by thy name, the other touching thee.

Blind were mine eyes, till they were seene of thine,
And mine eares deafe by thy fame healed be;
My vices cur'd by vertues sprung from thee,
My hopes reuiu'd, which long in graue had lyne:
    All vncleane thoughts, foule spirits, cast out in mee
    By thy great power, and by strong fayth in thee.

Amour 13

Cleere Ankor, on whose siluer-sanded shore
My soule-shrinde Saint, my faire Idea, lyes;
O blessed Brooke! whose milk-white Swans adore
The christall streame refined by her eyes:
Where sweet Myrh-breathing Zephyre in the spring
Gently distils his Nectar-dropping showers;
Where Nightingales in Arden sit and sing
Amongst those dainty dew-empearled flowers.
Say thus, fayre Brooke, when thou shall see thy Queene:
Loe! heere thy Shepheard spent his wandring yeeres,
And in these shades (deer Nimphe) he oft hath been,
And heere to thee he sacrifiz'd his teares.
    Fayre Arden, thou my Tempe art alone,
    And thou, sweet Ankor, art my Helicon.

Amour 14

Looking into the glasse of my youths miseries,
I see the ugly face of my deformed cares,
With withered browes, all wrinckled with dispaires,
That for my mis-spent youth the tears fel from my eyes.
Then, in these teares, the mirror of these eyes,
Thy fayrest youth and Beautie doe I see
Imprinted in my teares by looking still on thee:
Thus midst a thousand woes ten thousand joyes arise.
Yet in those joyes, the shadowes of my good,
In this fayre limned ground as white as snow,
Paynted the blackest Image of my woe,
With murthering hands imbru'd in mine own blood:
    And in this Image his darke clowdy eyes,
    My life, my youth, my loue, I heere Anotamize.

Amour 15

Now, Loue, if thou wilt proue a Conqueror,
Subdue thys Tyrant euer martyring mee;

And but appoint me for her Tormentor,
Then for a Monarch will I honour thee.
My hart shall be the prison for my fayre;
Ile fetter her in chaines of purest loue,
My sighs shall stop the passage of the ayre:
This punishment the pittilesse may moue.
With teares out of the Channels of mine eyes
She'st quench her thirst as duly as they fall:
Kinde words vnkindest meate I can deuise,
My sweet, my faire, my good, my best of all.
Ile binde her then with my torne-tressed haire,
And racke her with a thousand holy wishes;
Then, on a place prepared for her there,
Ile execute her with a thousand kisses.
    Thus will I crucifie, my cruell shee;
    Thus Ile plague her which hath so plagued mee.

Amour 16

Vertues Idea in virginitie,
By inspiration, came conceau'd with thought:
The time is come deliuered she must be,
Where first my loue into the world was brought.
Vnhappy borne, of all vnhappy day!
So luckles was my Babes nativity,
Saturne chiefe Lord of the Ascendant lay,
The wandring Moone in earths triplicitie.
Now, or by chaunce or heauens hie prouidence,
His Mother died, and by her Legacie
(Fearing the stars presaging influence)
Bequeath'd his wardship to my soueraignes eye;
Where hunger-staruen, wanting lookes to liue,
Still empty gorg'd, with cares consumption pynde,
Salt luke-warm teares shee for his drink did giue,
And euer-more with sighes he supt and dynde:
    And thus (poore Orphan) lying in distresse
    Cryes in his pangs, God helpe the motherlesse.

Amour 17

If euer wonder could report a wonder,
Or tongue of wonder worth could tell a wonder thought,
Or euer ioy expresse what perfect ioy hath taught,
Then wonder, tongue, then ioy, might wel report a wonder.
Could all conceite conclude, which past conceit admireth,

Or could mine eye but ayme her obiects past perfection,
My words might imitate my deerest thoughts direction,
And my soule then obtaine which so my soule desireth.
Were not Inuention stauld, treading Inuentions maze,
Or my swift-winged Muse tyred by too hie flying;
Did not perfection still on her perfection gaze,
Whilst Loue (my Phoenix bird) in her owne flame is dying,
    Inuention and my Muse, perfection and her loue,
    Should teach the world to know the wonder that I proue.

Amour 18

Some, when in ryme they of their Loues doe tell,
With flames and lightning their exordiums paynt:
Some inuocate the Gods, some spirits of Hell,
And heauen, and earth doe with their woes acquaint.
Elizia is too hie a seate for mee:
I wyll not come in Stixe or Phlegiton;
The Muses nice, the Furies cruell be,
I lyke not Limbo, nor blacke Acheron,
Spightful Erinnis frights mee with her lookes,
My manhood dares not with foule Ate mell:
I quake to looke on Hecats charming bookes,
I styll feare bugbeares in Apollos cell.
    I passe not for Minerua nor Astræa.
    But euer call vpon diuine Idea.

Amour 19

If those ten Regions, registred by Fame,
By theyr ten Sibils haue the world controld,
Who prophecied of Christ or ere he came,
And of his blessed birth before fore-told;
That man-god now, of whom they did diuine,
This earth of those sweet Prophets hath bereft,
And since the world to iudgement doth declyne,
Instead of ten, one Sibil to vs left.
Thys pure Idea, vertues right Idea,
Shee of whom Merlin long tyme did fore-tell,
Excelling her of Delphos or Cumæa,
Whose lyfe doth saue a thousand soules from hell:
    That life (I meane) which doth Religion teach,
    And by example true repentance preach.

Amour 20

Reading sometyme, my sorrowes to beguile,
I find old Poets hylls and floods admire:
One, he doth wonder monster-breeding Nyle,
Another meruailes Sulphure Aetnas fire.
Now broad-brymd Indus, then of Pindus height,
Pelion and Ossa, frosty Caucase old,
The Delian Cynthus, then Olympus weight,
Slow Arrer, franticke Gallus, Cydnus cold.
Some Ganges, Ister, and of Tagus tell,
Some whir-poole Po, and slyding Hypasis;
Some old Pernassus where the Muses dwell,
Some Helycon, and some faire Simois:
    A, fooles! thinke I, had you Idea seene,
    Poore Brookes and Banks had no such wonders beene.

Amour 21

Letters and lynes, we see, are soone defaced,
Mettles doe waste and fret with cankers rust;
The Diamond shall once consume to dust,
And freshest colours with foule staines disgraced.
Paper and yncke can paynt but naked words,
To write with blood of force offends the sight,
And if with teares, I find them all too light;
And sighes and signes a silly hope affoords.
O, sweetest shadow! how thou seru'st my turne,
Which still shalt be as long as there is Sunne,
Nor whilst the world is neuer shall be done,
Whilst Moone shall shyne by night, or any fire shall burne:
    That euery thing whence shadow doth proceede,
    May in his shadow my Loues story reade.

Amour 22

My hart, imprisoned in a hopeless Ile,
Peopled with Armies of pale iealous eyes,
The shores beset with thousand secret spyes,
Must passe by ayre, or else dye in exile.
He framd him wings with feathers of his thought,
Which by theyr nature learn'd to mount the skye;
And with the same he practised to flye,
Till he himself thys Eagles art had taught.
Thus soring still, not looking once below,

So neere thyne eyes celesteall sunne aspyred,
That with the rayes his wafting pyneons fired:
Thus was the wanton cause of his owne woe.
    Downe fell he, in thy Beauties Ocean drenched,
    Yet there he burnes in fire thats neuer quenched.

Amour 23

Wonder of Heauen, glasse of diuinitie,
Rare beautie, Natures joy, perfections Mother,
The worke of that vnited Trinitie,
Wherein each fayrest part excelleth other!
Loues Mithridate, the purest of perfection,
Celestiall Image, Load-stone of desire,
The soules delight, the sences true direction,
Sunne of the world, thou hart reuyuing fire!
Why should'st thou place thy Trophies in those eyes,
Which scorne the honor that is done to thee,
Or make my pen her name immortalize,
Who in her pride sdaynes once to look on me?
    It is thy heauen within her face to dwell,
    And in thy heauen, there onely, is my hell.

Amour 24

Our floods-Queene, Thames, for shyps and Swans is crowned,
And stately Seuerne for her shores is praised,
The christall Trent for Foords and fishe renowned,
And Auons fame to Albyons Cliues is raysed.
Carlegion Chester vaunts her holy Dee,
Yorke many wonders of her Ouse can tell,
The Peake her Doue, whose bancks so fertill bee,
And Kent will say her Medway doth excell.
Cotswoold commends her Isis and her Tame,
Our Northern borders boast of Tweeds faire flood;
Our Westerne parts extoll theyr Wilys fame,
And old Legea brags of Danish blood:
    Ardens sweet Ankor, let thy glory be
    That fayre Idea shee doth liue by thee.

Amour 25

The glorious sunne went blushing to his bed,
When my soules sunne, from her fayre Cabynet,
Her golden beames had now discouered,

Lightning the world, eclipsed by his set.
Some muz'd to see the earth enuy the ayre,
Which from her lyps exhald refined sweet,
A world to see, yet how he ioyd to heare
The dainty grasse make musicke with her feete.
But my most meruaile was when from the skyes,
So Comet-like, each starre aduanc'd her lyght,
As though the heauen had now awak'd her eyes,
And summond Angels to this blessed sight.
    No clowde was seene, but christalline the ayre,
    Laughing for ioy upon my louely fayre.

Amour 26

Cupid, dumbe-Idoll, peeuish Saint of loue,
No more shalt thou nor Saint nor Idoll be;
No God art thou, a Goddesse shee doth proue,
Of all thine honour shee hath robbed thee.
Thy Bowe, halfe broke, is peec'd with old desire;
Her Bowe is beauty with ten thousand strings
Of purest gold, tempred with vertues fire,
The least able to kyll an hoste of Kings.
Thy shafts be spent, and shee (to warre appointed)
Hydes in those christall quiuers of her eyes
More Arrowes, with hart-piercing mettel poynted,
Then there be starres at midnight in the skyes.
    With these she steales mens harts for her reliefe,
    Yet happy he thats robd of such a thiefe!

Amour 27

My Loue makes hote the fire whose heat is spent,
The water moisture from my teares deriueth,
And my strong sighes the ayres weake force reuiueth:
Thus loue, tears, sighes, maintaine each one his element.
The fire, vnto my loue, compare a painted fire,
The water, to my teares as drops to Oceans be,
The ayre, vnto my sighes as Eagle to the flie,
The passions of dispaire but ioyes to my desire.
Onely my loue is in the fire ingraued,
Onely my teares by Oceans may be gessed,
Onely my sighes are by the ayre expressed;
Yet fire, water, ayre, of nature not depriued.
    Whilst fire, water, ayre, twixt heauen and earth shal be,
    My loue, my teares, my sighes, extinguisht cannot be.

Amour 28

Some wits there be which lyke my method well,
And say my verse runnes in a lofty vayne;
Some say, I haue a passing pleasing straine,
Some say that in my humour I excell.
Some who reach not the height of my conceite,
They say, (as Poets doe) I vse to fayne,
And in bare words paynt out my passions payne:
Thus sundry men their sundry minds repeate.
I passe not I how men affected be,
Nor who commend, or discommend my verse;
It pleaseth me if I my plaints rehearse,
And in my lynes if shee my loue may see.
    I proue my verse autentique still in thys,
    Who writes my Mistres praise can neuer write amisse.

Amour 29

O eyes! behold your happy Hesperus,
That luckie Load-starre of eternall light,
Left as that sunne alone to comfort vs,
When our worlds sunne is vanisht out of sight.
O starre of starres! fayre Planet mildly moouing,
O Lampe of vertue! sun-bright, euer shyning,
O mine eyes Comet! so admyr'd by louing,
O cleerest day-starre! neuer more declyning.
O our worlds wonder! crowne of heauen aboue,
Thrice happy be those eyes which may behold thee!
Lou'd more then life, yet onely art his loue
Whose glorious hand immortal hath enrold thee!
    O blessed fayre! now vaile those heauenly eyes,
    That I may blesse mee at thy sweet arise.

Amour 30

Three sorts of serpents doe resemble thee;
That daungerous eye-killing Cockatrice,
Th' inchaunting Syren, which doth so entice,
The weeping Crocodile; these vile pernicious three.
The Basiliske his nature takes from thee,
Who for my life in secret wait do'st lye,
And to my heart send'st poyson from thine eye:
Thus do I feele the paine, the cause yet cannot see.
Faire-mayd no more, but Mayr-maid be thy name,

Who with thy sweet aluring harmony
Hast playd the thiefe, and stolne my hart from me,
And, like a Tyrant, mak'st my griefe thy game.
    The Crocodile, who, when thou hast me slaine,
    Lament'st my death with teares of thy disdaine.

Amour 31

Sitting alone, loue bids me goe and write;
Reason plucks backe, commaunding me to stay,
Boasting that shee doth still direct the way,
Els senceles loue could neuer once indite.
Loue, growing angry, vexed at the spleene,
And scorning Reasons maymed Argument,
Straight taxeth Reason, wanting to invent
Where shee with Loue conuersing hath not beene.
Reason, reproched with this coy disdaine,
Dispighteth Loue, and laugheth at her folly,
And Loue, contemning Reasons reason wholy,
Thought her in weight too light by many a graine.
    Reason, put back, doth out of sight remoue,
    And Loue alone finds reason in my loue.

Amour 32

Those teares, which quench my hope, still kindle my desire,
Those sighes, which coole my hart, are coles vnto my loue,
Disdayne, Ice to my life, is to my soule a fire:
With teares, sighes, and disdaine, this contrary I proue.
Quenchles desire makes hope burne, dryes my teares,
Loue heats my hart, my hart-heat my sighes warmeth;
With my soules fire my life disdaine out-weares,
Desire, my loue, my soule, my hope, hart, and life charmeth.
My hope becomes a friend to my desire,
My hart imbraceth Loue, Loue doth imbrace my hart;
My life a Phoenix is in my soules fire,
From thence (they vow) they neuer will depart.
    Desire, my loue, my soule, my hope, my hart, my life,
    With teares, sighes, and disdaine, shall haue immortal strife.

Amour 33

Whilst thus mine eyes doe surfet with delight,
My wofull hart, imprisond in my breast,
Wishing to be trans-formd into my sight,

To looke on her by whom mine eyes are blest;
But whilst mine eyes thus greedily doe gaze,
Behold! their obiects ouer-soone depart,
And treading in this neuer-ending maze,
Wish now to be trans-formd into my hart:
My hart, surcharg'd with thoughts, sighes in abundance raise,
My eyes, made dim with lookes, poure down a flood of tears;
And whilst my hart and eye enuy each others praise,
My dying lookes and thoughts are peiz'd in equall feares:
    And thus, whilst sighes and teares together doe contende,
    Each one of these doth ayde vnto the other lende.

Amour 34

My fayre, looke from those turrets of thine eyes,
Into the Ocean of a troubled minde,
Where my poor soule, the Barke of sorrow, lyes,
Left to the mercy of the waues and winde.
See where she flotes, laden with purest loue,
Which those fayre Ilands of thy lookes affoord,
Desiring yet a thousand deaths to proue,
Then so to cast her Ballase ouerboard.
See how her sayles be rent, her tacklings worne,
Her Cable broke, her surest Anchor lost:
Her Marryners doe leaue her all forlorne,
Yet how shee bends towards that blessed Coast!
    Loe! where she drownes in stormes of thy displeasure,
    Whose worthy prize should haue enricht thy treasure.

Amour 35

See, chaste Diana, where my harmles hart,
Rouz'd from my breast, his sure and safest layre,
Nor chaste by hound, nor forc'd by Hunters arte,
Yet see how right he comes vnto my fayre.
See how my Deere comes to thy Beauties stand,
And there stands gazing on those darting eyes,
Whilst from theyr rayes, by Cupids skilfull hand,
Into his hart the piercing Arrow flyes.
See how he lookes vpon his bleeding wound,
Whilst thus he panteth for his latest breath,
And, looking on thee, falls vpon the ground,
Smyling, as though he gloried in his death.
    And wallowing in his blood, some lyfe yet laft;
    His stone-cold lips doth kisse the blessed shaft.

Amour 36

Sweete, sleepe so arm'd with Beauties arrowes darting,
Sleepe in thy Beauty, Beauty in sleepe appeareth;
Sleepe lightning Beauty, Beauty sleepes, darknes cleereth,
Sleepes wonder Beauty, wonders to worlds imparting.
Sleep watching Beauty, Beauty waking, sleepe guarding
Beauty in sleepe, sleepe in Beauty charmed,
Sleepes aged coldnes with Beauties fire warmed,
Sleepe with delight, Beauty with loue rewarding.
Sleepe and Beauty, with equall forces stryuing,
Beauty her strength vnto sleepes weaknes lending,
Sleepe with Beauty, Beauty with sleepe contending,
Yet others force the others force reuiuing,
    And others foe the others foe imbrace.
    Myne eyes beheld thys conflict in thy face.

Amour 37

I euer loue where neuer hope appeares,
Yet hope drawes on my neuer-hoping care,
And my liues hope would die but for dyspaire;
My neuer certaine ioy breeds euer-certaine feares.
Vncertaine dread gyues wings vnto my hope,
Yet my hopes wings are loden so with feare,
As they cannot ascend to my hopes spheare,
Yet feare gyues them more then a heauenly scope.
Yet this large roome is bounded with dyspaire,
So my loue is still fettered with vaine hope,
And lyberty depriues him of hys scope,
And thus am I imprisond in the ayre:
    Then, sweet Dispaire, awhile hold vp thy head,
    Or all my hope for sorrow will be dead.

Amour 38

If chaste and pure deuotion of my youth,
Or glorie of my Aprill-springing yeeres,
Vnfained loue in naked simple truth,
A thousand vowes, a thousand sighes and teares;
Or if a world of faithful seruice done,
Words, thoughts, and deeds deuoted to her honor,
Or eyes that haue beheld her as theyr sunne,
With admiration euer looking on her:
A lyfe that neuer ioyd but in her loue,

A soule that euer hath ador'd her name,
A fayth that time nor fortune could not moue,
A Muse that vnto heauen hath raised her fame.
   Though these, nor these deserue to be imbraced,
   Yet, faire vnkinde, too good to be disgraced.

Amour 39

Die, die, my soule, and neuer taste of ioy,
If sighes, nor teares, nor vowes, nor prayers can moue;
If fayth and zeale be but esteemd a toy,
And kindnes be vnkindnes in my loue.
Then, with vnkindnes, Loue, reuenge thy wrong:
O sweet'st reuenge that ere the heauens gaue!
And with the swan record thy dying song,
And praise her still to thy vntimely graue.
So in loues death shall loues perfection proue
That loue diuine which I haue borne to you,
By doome concealed to the heauens aboue,
That yet the world vnworthy neuer knew;
      Whose pure Idea neuer tongue exprest:
      I feele, you know, the heauens can tell the rest.

Amour 40

O thou vnkindest fayre! most fayrest shee,
In thine eyes tryumph murthering my poore hart,
Now doe I sweare by heauens, before we part,
My halfe-slaine hart shall take reuenge on thee.
Thy mother dyd her lyfe to death resigne,
And thou an Angell art, and from aboue;
Thy father was a man, that will I proue,
Yet thou a Goddesse art, and so diuine.
And thus, if thou be not of humaine kinde,
A Bastard on both sides needes must thou be;
Our Lawes allow no land to basterdy:
By natures Lawes we thee a bastard finde.
   Then hence to heauen, vnkind, for thy childs part:
   Goe bastard goe, for sure of thence thou art.

Amour 41

Rare of-spring of my thoughts, my dearest Loue,
Begot by fancy on sweet hope exhortiue,
In whom all purenes with perfection stroue,

Hurt in the Embryon makes my ioyes abhortiue.
And you, my sighes, Symtomas of my woe,
The dolefull Anthems of my endelesse care,
Lyke idle Ecchoes euer answering; so,
The mournfull accents of my loues dispayre.
And thou, Conceite, the shadow of my blisse,
Declyning with the setting of my sunne,
Springing with that, and fading straight with this,
Now hast thou end, and now thou wast begun:
    Now was thy pryme, and loe! is now thy waine;
    Now wast thou borne, now in thy cradle slayne.

Amour 42

Plac'd in the forlorne hope of all dispayre
Against the Forte where Beauties Army lies,
Assayld with death, yet armed with gastly feare,
Loe! thus my loue, my lyfe, my fortune tryes.
Wounded with Arrowes from thy lightning eyes,
My tongue in payne my harts counsels bewraying,
My rebell thought for me in Ambushe lyes,
To my lyues foe her Chieftaine still betraying.
Record my loue in Ocean waues (vnkind)
Cast my desarts into the open ayre,
Commit my words vnto the fleeting wind,
Cancell my name, and blot it with dispayre;
    So shall I bee as I had neuer beene,
    Nor my disgraces to the world be seene.

Amour 43

Why doe I speake of ioy, or write of loue,
When my hart is the very Den of horror,
And in my soule the paynes of hell I proue,
With all his torments and infernall terror?
Myne eyes want teares thus to bewayle my woe,
My brayne is dry with weeping all too long;
My sighes be spent with griefe and sighing so,
And I want words for to expresse my wrong.
But still, distracted in loues lunacy,
And Bedlam like thus rauing in my griefe,
Now rayle vpon her hayre, now on her eye,
Now call her Goddesse, then I call her thiefe;
    Now I deny her, then I doe confesse her,
    Now I doe curse her, then againe I blesse her.

Amour 44

My hart the Anuile where my thoughts doe beate,
My words the hammers fashioning my desire,
My breast the forge, including all the heate,
Loue is the fuell which maintaines the fire:
My sighes the bellowes which the flame increaseth,
Filling mine eares with noise and nightly groning,
Toyling with paine my labour neuer ceaseth,
In greeuous passions my woes styll bemoning.
Myne eyes with teares against the fire stryuing,
With scorching gleed my hart to cynders turneth;
But with those drops the coles againe reuyuing,
Still more and more vnto my torment burneth.
    With Sisiphus thus doe I role the stone,
    And turne the wheele with damned Ixion.

Amour 45

Blacke pytchy Night, companyon of my woe,
The Inne of care, the Nurse of drery sorrow,
Why lengthnest thou thy darkest howres so,
Still to prolong my long tyme lookt-for morrow?
Thou Sable shadow, Image of dispayre,
Portraite of hell, the ayres black mourning weed,
Recorder of reuenge, remembrancer of care,
The shadow and the vaile of euery sinfull deed.
Death like to thee, so lyue thou still in death,
The graue of ioy, prison of dayes delight.
Let heauens withdraw their sweet Ambrozian breath,
Nor Moone nor stars lend thee their shining light;
    For thou alone renew'st that olde desire,
    Which still torments me in dayes burning fire.

Amour 46

Sweete secrecie, what tongue can tell thy worth?
What mortall pen sufficiently can prayse thee?
What curious Pensill serues to lim thee forth?
What Muse hath power aboue thy height to raise thee?
Strong locke of kindnesse, Closet of loues store,
Harts Methridate, the soules preseruatiue;
O vertue! which all vertues doe adore,
Cheefe good, from whom all good things wee deriue.

O rare effect! true bond of friendships measure,
Conceite of Angels, which all wisdom teachest;
O, richest Casket of all heauenly treasure,
In secret silence which such wonders preachest.
    O purest mirror! wherein men may see
    The liuely Image of Diuinitie.

Amour 47

The golden Sunne vpon his fiery wheeles
The horned Ram doth in his course awake,
And of iust length our night and day doth make,
Flinging the Fishes backward with his heeles:
Then to the Tropicke takes his full Careere,
Trotting his sun-steeds till the Palfrays sweat,
Bayting the Lyon in his furious heat,
Till Virgins smyles doe sound his sweet reteere.
But my faire Planet, who directs me still,
Vnkindly such distemperature doth bring,
Makes Summer Winter, Autumne in the Spring,
Crossing sweet nature by vnruly will.
    Such is the sunne who guides my youthfull season,
    Whose thwarting course depriues the world of reason.

Amour 48

Who list to praise the dayes delicious lyght,
Let him compare it to her heauenly eye,
The sun-beames to the lustre of her sight;
So may the learned like the similie.
The mornings Crimson to her lyps alike,
The sweet of Eden to her breathes perfume,
The fayre Elizia to her fayrer cheeke,
Vnto her veynes the onely Phoenix plume.
The Angels tresses to her tressed hayre,
The Galixia to her more then white.
Praysing the fayrest, compare it to my faire,
Still naming her in naming all delight.
    So may he grace all these in her alone,
    Superlatiue in all comparison.

Amour 49

Define my loue, and tell the ioyes of heauen,
Expresse my woes, and shew the paynes of hell;

Declare what fate vnlucky starres haue giuen,
And aske a world vpon my life to dwell.
Make knowne that fayth vnkindnes could not moue;
Compare my worth with others base desert:
Let vertue be the tuch-stone of my loue,
So may the heauens reade wonders in my hart.
Behold the Clowdes which haue eclips'd my sunne,
And view the crosses which my course doth let;
Tell mee, if euer since the world begunne,
So faire a Morning had so foule a set?
    And, by all meanes, let black vnkindnes proue
    The patience of so rare, diuine a loue.

Amour 50

When I first ended, then I first began;
The more I trauell, further from my rest;
Where most I lost, there most of all I wan;
Pyned with hunger, rysing from a feast.
Mee thinks I flee, yet want I legs to goe,
Wise in conceite, in acte a very sot;
Rauisht with ioy amidst a hell of woe,
What most I seeme, that surest I am not.
I build my hopes a world aboue the skye,
Yet with a Mole I creepe into the earth:
In plenty am I staru'd with penury,
And yet I serfet in the greatest dearth.
    I haue, I want, dispayre, and yet desire,
    Burn'd in a Sea of Ice, and drown'd amidst a fire.

Amour 51

Goe you, my lynes, Embassadours of loue,
With my harts tribute to her conquering eyes,
From whence, if you one tear of pitty moue
For all my woes, that onely shall suffise.
When you Minerua in the sunne behold,
At her perfections stand you then and gaze,
Where in the compasse of a Marygold,
Meridianis sits within a maze.
And let Inuention of her beauty vaunt
When Dorus sings his sweet Pamelas loue,
And tell the Gods, Mars is predominant,
Seated with Sol, and weares Mineruas gloue:
    And tell the world, that in the world there is

A heauen on earth, on earth no heauen but this.

FINIS.

[from the Edition of 1599]

Sonet 1

The worlds faire Rose, and Henries frosty fire,
Iohns tyrannie; and chast Matilda's wrong,
Th'inraged Queene, and furious Mortimer,
The scourge of Fraunce, and his chast loue I song;
Deposed Richard, Isabell exil'd,
The gallant Tudor, and fayre Katherine,
Duke Humfrey, and old Cobhams haplesse child,
Couragious Pole, and that braue spiritfull Queene;
Edward, and that delicious London Dame,
Brandon, and that rich dowager of Fraunce,
Surrey, with his fayre paragon of fame,
Dudleys mishap, and vertuous Grays mischance;
    Their seuerall loues since I before haue showne,
    Now giue me leaue at last to sing mine owne.

Sonet 2

To the Reader of his Poems

Into these loues who but for passion lookes,
At this first sight, here let him lay them by,
And seeke elsewhere in turning other bookes,
Which better may his labour satisfie.
No far-fetch'd sigh shall euer wound my brest,
Loue from mine eye, a teare shall neuer wring,
Nor in ah-mees my whyning Sonets drest,
(A Libertine) fantasticklie I sing;
My verse is the true image of my mind,
Euer in motion, still desiring change,
To choyce of all varietie inclin'd,
And in all humors sportiuely I range;
    My actiue Muse is of the worlds right straine,
    That cannot long one fashion entertaine.

Sonet 3

Many there be excelling in this kind,
Whose well trick'd rimes with all inuention swell,
Let each commend as best shall like his minde,
Some Sidney, Constable, some Daniell.
That thus theyr names familiarly I sing,

Let none think them disparaged to be,
Poore men with reuerence may speake of a King,
And so may these be spoken of by mee;
My wanton verse nere keepes one certaine stay,
But now, at hand; then, seekes inuention far,
And with each little motion runnes astray,
Wilde, madding, iocond, and irreguler;
    Like me that lust, my honest merry rimes,
    Nor care for Criticke, nor regard the times.

Sonet 5

My hart was slaine, and none but you and I,
Who should I thinke the murder should commit?
Since but your selfe, there was no creature by
But onely I, guiltlesse of murth'ring it.
It slew it selfe; the verdict on the view
Doe quit the dead and me not accessarie;
Well, well, I feare it will be prou'd by you,
The euidence so great a proofe doth carry.
But O, see, see, we need enquire no further,
Vpon your lips the scarlet drops are found,
And in your eye, the boy that did the murther,
Your cheekes yet pale since first they gaue the wound.
    By this, I see, how euer things be past,
    Yet heauen will still haue murther out at last.

Sonet 8

Nothing but no and I, and I and no,
How falls it out so strangely you reply?
I tell yee (Faire) Ile not be aunswered so,
With this affirming no, denying I,
I say I loue, you slightly aunswer I?
I say you loue, you pule me out a no;
I say I die, you eccho me with I,
Saue me I cry, you sigh me out a no:
Must woe and I, haue naught but no and I?
No, I am I, If I no more can haue,
Aunswer no more, with silence make reply,
And let me take my selfe what I doe craue;
    Let no and I, with I and you be so,
    Then aunswer no, and I, and I, and no.

Sonet 9

Loue once would daunce within my Mistres eye,
And wanting musique fitting for the place,
Swore that I should the Instrument supply,
And sodainly presents me with her face:
Straightwayes my pulse playes liuely in my vaines,
My panting breath doth keepe a meaner time,
My quau'ring artiers be the Tenours Straynes,
My trembling sinewes serue the Counterchime,
My hollow sighs the deepest base doe beare,
True diapazon in distincted sound:
My panting hart the treble makes the ayre,
And descants finely on the musiques ground;
    Thus like a Lute or Violl did I lye,
     Whilst the proud slaue daunc'd galliards in her eye.

Sonet 10

Loue in an humor played the prodigall,
And bids my sences to a solemne feast,
Yet more to grace the company withall,
Inuites my heart to be the chiefest guest;
No other drinke would serue this gluttons turne,
But precious teares distilling from mine eyne,
Which with my sighs this Epicure doth burne,
Quaffing carouses in this costly wine,
Where, in his cups or'come with foule excesse,
Begins to play a swaggering Ruffins part,
And at the banquet, in his drunkennes,
Slew my deare friend, his kind and truest hart;
    A gentle warning, friends, thus may you see
     What 'tis to keepe a drunkard company.

Sonet 11

To the Moone

Phœbe looke downe, and here behold in mee,
The elements within thy sphere inclosed,
How kindly Nature plac'd them vnder thee,
And in my world, see how they are disposed;
My hope is earth, the lowest, cold and dry,
The grosser mother of deepe melancholie,
Water my teares, coold with humidity,

Wan, flegmatick, inclind by nature wholie;
My sighs, the ayre, hote, moyst, ascending hier,
Subtile of sanguine, dy'de in my harts dolor,
My thoughts, they be the element of fire,
Hote, dry, and piercing, still inclind to choller,
    Thine eye the Orbe vnto all these, from whence,
    Proceeds th' effects of powerfull influence.

Sonet 12

To nothing fitter can I thee compare,
Then to the sonne of some rich penyfather,
Who hauing now brought on his end with care,
Leaues to his son all he had heap'd together;
This newe rich nouice, lauish of his chest,
To one man giues, and on another spends,
Then here he ryots, yet amongst the rest,
Haps to lend some to one true honest friend.
Thy gifts thou in obscuritie doost wast,
False friends thy kindnes, borne but to deceiue thee,
Thy loue, that is on the unworthy plac'd,
Time hath thy beauty, which with age will leaue thee;
    Onely that little which to me was lent,
    I giue thee back, when all the rest is spent.

Sonet 13

You not alone, when you are still alone,
O God from you that I could priuate be,
Since you one were, I neuer since was one,
Since you in me, my selfe since out of me
Transported from my selfe into your beeing
Though either distant, present yet to eyther,
Senceles with too much ioy, each other seeing,
And onely absent when we are together.
Giue me my selfe, and take your selfe againe,
Deuise some means but how I may forsake you,
So much is mine that doth with you remaine,
That taking what is mine, with me I take you,
    You doe bewitch me, O that I could flie
    From my selfe you, or from your owne selfe I.

Sonet 14

To the Soule

That learned Father which so firmly proues
The soule of man immortall and diuine,
And doth the seuerall offices define,
Anima. Giues her that name as shee the body moues,
Amor. Then is she loue imbracing Charitie,
Animus. Mouing a will in vs, it is the mind,
Mens. Retayning knowledge, still the same in kind;
Memoria. As intelectuall it is the memorie,
Ratio. In judging, Reason onely is her name,
Sensus. In speedy apprehension it is sence,
Conscientia. In right or wrong, they call her conscience.
Spiritus. The spirit, when it to Godward doth inflame.
 These of the soule the seuerall functions bee,
 Which my hart lightned by thy loue doth see.

Sonet 21

You cannot loue my pretty hart, and why?
There was a time, you told me that you would,
But now againe you will the same deny,
If it might please you, would to God you could;
What will you hate? nay, that you will not neither,
Nor loue, nor hate, how then? what will you do,
What will you keepe a meane then betwixt eyther?
Or will you loue me, and yet hate me to?
Yet serues not this, what next, what other shift?
You will, and will not, what a coyle is heere,
I see your craft, now I perceaue your drift,
And all this while, I was mistaken there.
 Your loue and hate is this, I now doe proue you,
 You loue in hate, by hate to make me loue you.

Sonet 22

An euill spirit your beauty haunts me still,
Where-with (alas) I haue been long possest,
Which ceaseth not to tempt me vnto ill,
Nor giues me once but one pore minutes rest.
In me it speakes, whether I sleepe or wake,
And when by meanes to driue it out I try,
With greater torments then it me doth take,

And tortures me in most extreamity.
Before my face, it layes all my dispaires,
And hasts me on vnto a suddaine death;
Now tempting me, to drown my selfe in teares,
And then in sighing to giue vp my breath:
    Thus am I still prouok'd to euery euill,
    By this good wicked spirit, sweet Angel deuill.

Sonet 23

To the Spheares

Thou which do'st guide this little world of loue,
Thy planets mansions heere thou mayst behold,
My brow the spheare where Saturne still doth moue,
Wrinkled with cares: and withered, dry, and cold;
Mine eyes the Orbe where Iupiter doth trace,
Which gently smile because they looke on thee,
Mars in my swarty visage takes his place,
Made leane with loue, where furious conflicts bee.
Sol in my breast with his hote scorching flame,
And in my hart alone doth Venus raigne:
Mercury my hands the Organs of thy fame,
And Luna glides in my fantastick braine;
    The starry heauen thy prayse by me exprest,
    Thou the first moouer, guiding all the rest.

Sonet 24

Love banish'd heauen, in earth was held in scorne,
Wandring abroad in neede and beggery,
And wanting friends though of a Goddesse borne,
Yet crau'd the almes of such as passed by.
I like a man, deuout and charitable;
Clothed the naked, lodg'd this wandring guest,
With sighs and teares still furnishing his table,
With what might make the miserable blest;
But this vngratefull for my good desart,
Entic'd my thoughts against me to conspire,
Who gaue consent to steale away my hart,
And set my breast his lodging on a fire:
    Well, well, my friends, when beggers grow thus bold,
    No meruaile then though charity grow cold.

Sonet 25

O why should nature nigardly restraine,
The Sotherne Nations relish not our tongue,
Else should my lines glide on the waues of Rhene,
And crowne the Pirens with my liuing song;
But bounded thus to Scotland get you forth:
Thence take you wing vnto the Orcades,
There let my verse get glory in the North,
Making my sighs to thawe the frozen seas,
And let the Bards within the Irish Ile,
To whom my Muse with fiery wings shall passe,
Call backe the stifneckd rebels from exile,
And molifie the slaughtering Galliglasse:
    And when my flowing numbers they rehearse,
    Let Wolues and Bears be charmed with my verse.

Sonet 27

I gaue my faith to Loue, Loue his to mee,
That hee and I, sworne brothers should remaine,
Thus fayth receiu'd, fayth giuen back againe,
Who would imagine bond more sure could be?
Loue flies to her, yet holds he my fayth taken,
Thus from my vertue raiseth my offence,
Making me guilty by mine innocence;
And surer bond by beeing so forsaken,
He makes her aske what I before had vow'd,
Giuing her that, which he had giuen me,
I bound by him, and he by her made free,
Who euer so hard breach of fayth alow'd?
    Speake you that should of right and wrong discusse,
    Was right ere wrong'd, or wrong ere righted thus?

Sonet 29

To the Sences

When conquering loue did first my hart assaile,
Vnto mine ayde I summond euery sence,
Doubting if that proude tyrant should preuaile,
My hart should suffer for mine eyes offence;
But he with beauty, first corrupted sight,
My hearing bryb'd with her tongues harmony,
My taste, by her sweet lips drawne with delight,

My smelling wonne with her breaths spicerie;
But when my touching came to play his part,
(The King of sences, greater than the rest)
That yeelds loue up the keyes vnto my hart,
And tells the other how they should be blest;
    And thus by those of whom I hop'd for ayde,
    To cruell Loue my soule was first betrayd.

Sonet 30

To the Vestalls

Those Priests, which first the Vestall fire begun,
Which might be borrowed from no earthly flame,
Deuisd a vessell to receiue the sunne,
Beeing stedfastly opposed to the same;
Where with sweet wood laid curiously by Art,
Whereon the sunne might by reflection beate,
Receiuing strength from euery secret part,
The fuell kindled with celestiall heate.
Thy blessed eyes, the sunne which lights this fire,
My holy thoughts, they be the Vestall flame,
The precious odors be my chast desire,
My breast the fuell which includes the same;
    Thou art my Vesta, thou my Goddesse art,
    Thy hollowed Temple, onely is my hart.

Sonet 31

Me thinks I see some crooked Mimick ieere
And taxe my Muse with this fantastick grace,
Turning my papers, asks what haue we heere?
Making withall, some filthy anticke face;
I feare no censure, nor what thou canst say,
Nor shall my spirit one iote of vigor lose,
Think'st thou my wit shall keepe the pack-horse way,
That euery dudgen low inuention goes?
Since Sonnets thus in bundles are imprest,
And euery drudge doth dull our satiate eare,
Think'st thou my loue, shall in those rags be drest
That euery dowdie, euery trull doth weare?
    Vnto my pitch no common iudgement flies,
    I scorne all earthlie dung-bred scarabies.

Sonet 34

To Admiration

Maruaile not Loue, though I thy power admire,
Rauish'd a world beyond the farthest thought,
That knowing more then euer hath beene taught,
That I am onely staru'd in my desire;
Maruaile not Loue, though I thy power admire,
Ayming at things exceeding all perfection,
To wisedoms selfe, to minister direction,
That I am onely staru'd in my desire;
Maruaile not Loue, though I thy power admire,
Though my conceite I farther seeme to bend,
Then possibly inuention can extend,
And yet am onely staru'd in my desire;
    If thou wilt wonder, heers the wonder loue,
    That this to mee doth yet no wonder proue.

Sonet 43

Whilst thus my pen striues to eternize thee,
Age rules my lines with wrincles in my face,
Where in the Map of all my misery,
Is modeld out the world of my disgrace,
Whilst in despight of tyrannizing times,
Medea like I make thee young againe,
Proudly thou scorn'st my world-outwearing rimes,
And murther'st vertue with thy coy disdaine;
And though in youth, my youth vntimely perrish,
To keepe thee from obliuion and the graue,
Ensuing ages yet my rimes shall cherrish,
Where I entomb'd, my better part shall saue;
    And though this earthly body fade and die
    My name shall mount vpon eternitie.

Sonet 44

Muses which sadly sit about my chayre,
Drownd in the teares extorted by my lines,
With heauy sighs whilst thus I breake the ayre,
Paynting my passions in these sad dissignes,
Since she disdaines to blesse my happy verse,
The strong built Trophies to her liuing fame,
Euer hence-forth my bosome be your hearse,

Wherein the world shal now entombe her name,
Enclose my musick you poor sencelesse walls,
Sith she is deafe and will not heare my mones,
Soften your selues with euery teare that falls,
Whilst I like Orpheus sing to trees and stones:
    Which with my plaints seeme yet with pitty moued,
    Kinder then she who I so long haue loued.

Sonet 45

Thou leaden braine, which censur'st what I write,
And say'st my lines be dull and doe not moue,
I meruaile not thou feelst not my delight,
Which neuer felt my fiery tuch of loue.
But thou whose pen hath like a Pack-horse seru'd,
Whose stomack vnto gaule hath turn'd thy foode,
Whose sences like poore prisoners hunger-staru'd,
Whose griefe hath parch'd thy body, dry'd thy blood.
Thou which hast scorned life, and hated death,
And in a moment mad, sober, glad, and sorry,
Thou which hast band thy thoughts and curst thy breath,
With thousand plagues more then in purgatory.
    Thou thus whose spirit Loue in his fire refines,
    Come thou and reade, admire, applaud my lines.

Sonet 55

Truce gentle loue, a parly now I craue,
Me thinks, 'tis long since first these wars begun,
Nor thou nor I, the better yet can haue:
Bad is the match where neither party wone.
I offer free conditions of faire peace,
My hart for hostage, that it shall remaine,
Discharge our forces heere, let malice cease,
So for my pledge, thou giue me pledge againe.
Or if nothing but death will serue thy turne,
Still thirsting for subuersion of my state;
Doe what thou canst, raze, massacre, and burne,
Let the world see the vtmost of thy hate:
    I send defiance, since if ouerthrowne,
    Thou vanquishing, the conquest is mine owne.

Sonet 56

A Consonet

Eyes with your teares, blind if you bee,
Why haue these teares such eyes to see,
Poore eyes, if yours teares cannot moue,
My teares, eyes, then must mone my loue,
    Then eyes, since you haue lost your sight,
    Weepe still, and teares shall lend you light,
    Till both desolu'd, and both want might.
No, no, cleere eyes, you are not blind,
But in my teares discerne my mind:
Teares be the language which you speake,
Which my hart wanting, yet must breake;
    My tongue must cease to tell my wrongs,
    And make my sighs to get them tongs,
    Yet more then this to her belongs.

Sonet 57

To Lucie Countesse of Bedford

Great Lady, essence of my chiefest good,
Of the most pure and finest tempred spirit,
Adorn'd with gifts, enobled by thy blood,
Which by discent true vertue do'st inherit:
That vertue which no fortune can depriue,
Which thou by birth tak'st from thy gracious mother,
Whose royall minds with equall motion striue,
Which most in honour shall excell the other;
Vnto thy fame my Muse herself shall taske,
Which rain'st vpon me thy sweet golden showers,
And but thy selfe, no subject will I aske,
Vpon whose praise my soule shall spend her powers.
    Sweet Lady yet, grace this poore Muse of mine,
    Whose faith, whose zeale, whose life, whose all is thine.

Sonet 58

To the Lady Anne Harington

Madam, my words cannot expresse my mind,
My zealous kindnes to make knowne to you,
When your desarts all seuerally I find;

In this attempt of me doe claim their due,
Your gracious kindnes that doth claime my hart;
Your bounty bids my hand to make it knowne,
Of me your vertues each doe claime a part,
And leaue me thus the least part of mine owne.
What should commend your modesty and wit,
Is by your wit and modesty commended
And standeth dumbe, in much admiring it,
And where it should begin, it there is ended;
   Returning this your prayses onely due,
   And to your selfe say you are onely you.

[from the Edition of 1602]

Sonnet 12

To Lunacie

As other men, so I my selfe doe muse,
Why in this sort I wrest Inuention so,
And why these giddy metaphors I vse,
Leauing the path the greater part doe goe;
I will resolue you; I am lunaticke,
And euer this in mad men you shall finde,
What they last thought on when the braine grew sick,
In most distraction keepe that still in minde.
Thus talking idely in this bedlam fit,
Reason and I, (you must conceiue) are twaine,
'Tis nine yeeres, now, since first I lost my wit
Beare with me, then, though troubled be my braine;
 With diet and correction, men distraught,
 (Not too farre past) may to their wits be brought.

Sonnet 17

If hee from heauen that filch'd that liuing fire,
Condemn'd by Ioue to endlesse torment be,
I greatly meruaile how you still goe free,
That farre beyond Promethius did aspire?
The fire he stole, although of heauenly kinde,
Which from aboue he craftily did take,
Of liueles clods vs liuing men to make,
Againe bestow'd in temper of the mind.
But you broke in to heauens immortall store,
Where vertue, honour, wit, and beautie lay,
Which taking thence, you haue escap'd away,
Yet stand as free as ere you did before.
 But old Promethius punish'd for his rape,
 Thus poore theeues suffer, when the greater scape.

Sonnet 25

To Folly

With fooles and children good discretion beares,
Then honest people beare with Loue and me,
Nor older yet, nor wiser made by yeeres,

Amongst the rest of fooles and children be;
Loues still a Baby, playes with gaudes and toyes,
And like a wanton sports with euery feather,
And Idiots still are running after boyes,
Then fooles and children fitt'st to goe together;
He still as young as when he first was borne,
No wiser I, then when as young as he,
You that behold vs, laugh vs not to scorne,
Giue Nature thanks, you are not such as we;
    Yet fooles and children sometimes tell in play,
    Some wise in showe, more fooles in deede, then they.

Sonnet 27

I heare some say, this man is not in loue,
Who, can he loue? a likely thing they say:
Reade but his verse, and it will easily proue;
O iudge not rashly (gentle Sir) I pray,
Because I loosely tryfle in this sort,
As one that faine his sorrowes would beguile:
You now suppose me, all this time in sport,
And please your selfe with this conceit the while.
You shallow censures; sometime see you not
In greatest perills some men pleasant be,
Where fame by death is onely to be got,
They resolute, so stands the case with me;
    Where other men, in depth of passion cry,
    I laugh at fortune, as in iest to die.

Sonnet 31

To such as say thy loue I ouer-prize,
And doe not sticke to terme my praises folly,
Against these folkes that think them selues so wise,
I thus appose my force of reason wholly,
Though I giue more, then well affords my state,
In which expense the most suppose me vaine,
Would yeeld them nothing at the easiest rate,
Yet at this price, returnes me treble gaine,
They value not, vnskilfull how to vse,
And I giue much, because I gaine thereby,
I that thus take, or they that thus refuse,
Whether are these deccaued then, or I?
    In euery thing I hold this maxim still,
    The circumstance doth make it good or ill.

Sonnet 41

Deare, why should you commaund me to my rest
When now the night doth summon all to sleepe?
Me thinks this time becommeth louers best,
Night was ordained together friends to keepe.
How happy are all other liuing things,
Which though the day disioyne by seuerall flight,
The quiet euening yet together brings,
And each returnes vnto his loue at night.
O thou that art so curteous vnto all,
Why shouldst thou Night abuse me onely thus,
That euery creature to his kinde doost call,
And yet tis thou doost onely seuer vs.
    Well could I wish it would be euer day,
    If when night comes you bid me goe away.

Sonnet 58

To Prouerbe

As Loue and I, late harbour'd in one Inne,
With Prouerbs thus each other intertaine;
In loue there is no lacke, thus I beginne?
Faire words makes fooles, replieth he againe?
That spares to speake, doth spare to speed (quoth I)
As well (saith he) too forward as too slow.
Fortune assists the boldest, I replie?
A hasty man (quoth he) nere wanted woe.
Labour is light, where loue (quoth I) doth pay,
(Saith he) light burthens heauy, if farre borne?
(Quoth I) the maine lost, cast the by away:
You haue spunne a faire thred, he replies in scorne.
    And hauing thus a while each other thwarted,
    Fooles as we met, so fooles againe we parted.

Sonnet 63

To the high and mighty Prince, James, King of Scots

Not thy graue Counsells, nor thy Subiects loue,
Nor all that famous Scottish royaltie,
Or what thy soueraigne greatnes may approue,
Others in vaine doe but historifie,

When thine owne glorie from thy selfe doth spring,
As though thou did'st, all meaner prayses scorne:
Of Kings a Poet, and the Poets King,
They Princes, but thou Prophets do'st adorne;
Whilst others by their Empires are renown'd,
Thou do'st enrich thy Scotland with renowne,
And Kings can but with Diadems be crown'd,
But with thy Laurell, thou doo'st crowne thy Crowne;
    That they whose pens, euen life to Kings doe giue,
    In thee a King, shall seeke them selues to liue.

Sonnet 66

To the Lady L.S.

Bright starre of Beauty, on whose eyelids sit,
A thousand Nimph-like and enamoured Graces,
The Goddesses of memory and wit,
Which in due order take their seuerall places,
In whose deare bosome, sweet delicious loue,
Layes downe his quiuer, that he once did beare,
Since he that blessed Paradice did proue,
Forsooke his mothers lap to sport him there.
Let others striue to entertaine with words,
My soule is of another temper made;
I hold it vile that vulgar wit affords,
Deuouring time my faith, shall not inuade:
    Still let my praise be honoured thus by you,
    Be you most worthy, whilst I be most true.

[from the Edition of 1605]

Sonnet 43

Why should your faire eyes with such soueraine grace,
Dispearse their raies on euery vulgar spirit,
Whilst I in darknes in the selfesame place,
Get not one glance to recompence my merit:
So doth the plow-man gaze the wandring starre,
And onely rests contented with the light,
That neuer learnd what constellations are,
Beyond the bent of his vnknowing sight.
O why should beautie (custome to obey)
To their grosse sence applie her selfe so ill?
Would God I were as ignorant as they
When I am made vnhappy by my skill;
    Onely compeld on this poore good to boast,
    Heauens are not kind to them that know them most.

Sonnet 46

Plain-path'd Experience the vnlearneds guide,
Her simple followers euidently shewes,
Sometime what schoolemen scarcely can decide,
Nor yet wise Reason absolutely knowes:
In making triall of a murther wrought,
If the vile actor of the heinous deede,
Neere the dead bodie happily be brought,
Oft hath been prou'd the breathlesse coarse will bleed;
She comming neere that my poore hart hath slaine,
Long since departed, (to the world no more)
The auncient wounds no longer can containe,
But fall to bleeding as they did before:
    But what of this? should she to death be led,
    It furthers iustice, but helpes not the dead.

Sonnet 47

In pride of wit, when high desire of fame
Gaue life and courage to my labouring pen,
And first the sound and vertue of my name,
Won grace and credit in the eares of men:
With those the thronged Theaters that presse,
I in the circuite for the Lawrell stroue,

Where the full praise I freely must confesse,
In heate of blood a modest minde might moue:
With showts and claps at euerie little pawse,
When the prowd round on euerie side hath rung,
Sadly I sit vnmou'd with the applawse,
As though to me it nothing did belong:
    No publique glorie vainely I pursue,
    The praise I striue, is to eternize you.

Sonnet 50

As in some Countries far remote from hence,
The wretched creature destined to die,
Hauing the iudgement due to his offence,
By Surgeons begg'd, their Art on him to trie:
Which on the liuing worke without remorce,
First make incision on each maistring vaine,
Then stanch the bleeding, then transperce the coarse,
And with their balmes recure the wounds againe,
Then poison and with Phisicke him restore,
Not that they feare the hopelesse man to kill,
But their experience to encrease the more;
Euen so my Mistresse works vpon my ill,
    By curing me, and killing me each howre,
    Onely to shew her beauties soueraigne powre.

Sonnet 51

Calling to minde since first my loue begunne,
Th' incertaine times oft varying in their course,
How things still vnexpectedly haue runne,
As please the fates, by their resistlesse force:
Lastly, mine eyes amazedly haue scene,
Essex great fall, Tyrone his peace to gaine,
The quiet end of that long-liuing Queene,
This Kings faire entrance, and our peace with Spaine,
We and the Dutch at length our selues to seuer.
Thus the world doth, and euermore shall reele,
Yet to my goddesse am I constant euer;
How ere blind fortune turne her giddy wheele:
    Though heauen and earth proue both to mee vntrue,
    Yet am I still inuiolate to you.

Sonnet 57

You best discern'd of my interior eies,
And yet your graces outwardly diuine,
Whose deare remembrance in my bosome lies,
Too riche a relique for so poore a shrine:
You in whome Nature chose herselfe to view,
When she her owne perfection would admire,
Bestowing all her excellence on you;
At whose pure eies Loue lights his halowed fire,
Euen as a man that in some traunce hath scene,
More than his wondring vttrance can vnfolde,
That rapt in spirite in better worlds hath beene,
So must your praise distractedly be tolde;
    Most of all short, when I should shew you most,
    In your perfections altogether lost.

Sonnet 58

In former times, such as had store of coyne,
In warres at home, or when for conquests bound,
For feare that some their treasures should purloyne,
Gaue it to keepe to spirites within the ground;
And to attend it, them so strongly tide,
Till they return'd, home when they neuer came,
Such as by art to get the same haue tride,
From the strong spirits by no means get the same,
Neerer you come, that further flies away,
Striuing to holde it strongly in the deepe:
Euen as this spirit, so she alone doth play,
With those rich Beauties heauen giues her to keepe:
    Pitty so left, to coldenes of her blood,
    Not to auaile her, nor do others good.

To Sir Walter Aston, Knight of the honourable order of the Bath, and my most worthy Patron

I will not striue m' inuention to inforce,
With needlesse words your eyes to entertaine,
T' obserue the formall ordinarie course
That euerie one so vulgarly doth faine:
Our interchanged and deliberate choise,
Is with more firme and true election sorted,
Then stands in censure of the common voice.

That with light humor fondly is transported:
Nor take I patterne of another's praise,
Then what my pen may constantly avow.
Nor walke more publique nor obscurer waies
Then vertue bids, and iudgement will allow;
    So shall my tone, and best endeuours serue you,
    And still shall studie, still so to deserue you.
Michaell Drayton.

[from the Edition of 1619]

1

Like an aduenturous Sea-farer am I,
Who hath some long and dang'rous Voyage beene,
And call'd to tell of his Discouerie,
How farre he sayl'd, what Countries he had seene,
Proceeding from the Port whence he put forth,
Shewes by his Compasse, how his Course he steer'd,
When East, when West, when South, and when by North,
As how the Pole to eu'ry place was rear'd,
What Capes he doubled, of what Continent,
The Gulphes and Straits, that strangely he had past,
Where most becalm'd, wherewith foule Weather spent,
And on what Rocks in perill to be cast?
Thus in my Loue, Time calls me to relate
My tedious Trauels, and oft-varying Fate.

6

How many paltry, foolish, painted things,
That now in Coaches trouble eu'ry Street,
Shall be forgotten, whom no Poet sings,
Ere they be well wrap'd in their winding Sheet?
Where I to thee Eternitie shall giue,
When nothing else remayneth of these dayes,
And Queenes hereafter shall be glad to liue
Vpon the Almes of thy superfluous prayse;
Virgins and Matrons reading these my Rimes,
Shall be so much delighted with thy story,
That they shall grieue, they liu'd not in these Times,
To haue seene thee, their Sexes onely glory:
    So shalt thou flye aboue the vulgar Throng,
    Still to suruiue in my immortall Song.

8

There's nothing grieues me, but that Age should haste,
That in my dayes I may not see thee old,
That where those two deare sparkling Eyes are plac'd,
Onely two Loope-holes, then I might behold.
That louely, arched, yuorie, pollish'd Brow,
Defac'd with Wrinkles, that I might but see,
Thy daintie Hayre, so curl'd, and crisped now,

Like grizzled Mosse vpon some aged Tree;
Thy Cheeke, now flush with Roses, sunke, and leane,
Thy Lips, with age, as any Wafer thinne,
Thy Pearly teeth out of thy head so cleane,
That when thou feed'st, thy Nose shall touch thy Chinne:
    These Lines that now thou scorn'st, which should delight thee,
    Then would I make thee read, but to despight thee.

15

His Remedie for Loue

Since to obtaine thee, nothing me will sted,
I haue a Med'cine that shall cure my Loue,
The powder of her Heart dry'd, when she is dead,
That Gold nor Honour ne'r had power to moue;
Mix'd with her Teares, that ne'r her true-Loue crost,
Nor at Fifteene ne'r long'd to be a Bride,
Boyl'd with her Sighes, in giuing vp the Ghost,
That for her late deceased Husband dy'd;
Into the same then let a Woman breathe,
That being chid, did neuer word replie,
With one thrice-marry'd's Pray'rs, that did bequeath
A Legacie to stale Virginitie.
    If this Receit haue not the pow'r to winne me,
    Little Ile say, but thinke the Deuill's in me.

21

A witlesse Gallant, a young Wench that woo'd,
(Yet his dull Spirit her not one iot could moue)
Intreated me, as e'r I wish'd his good,
To write him but one Sonnet to his Loue:
When I, as fast as e'r my Penne could trot,
Powr'd out what first from quicke Inuention came;
Nor neuer stood one word thereof to blot,
Much like his Wit, that was to vse the same:
But with my Verses he his Mistres wonne,
Who doted on the Dolt beyond all measure.
But soe, for you to Heau'n for Phraze I runne,
And ransacke all APOLLO'S golden Treasure;
    Yet by my Troth, this Foole his Loue obtaines,
    And I lose you, for all my Wit and Paines.

27

Is not Loue here, as 'tis in other Clymes,
And diff'reth it, as doe the seu'rall Nations?
Or hath it lost the Vertue, with the Times,
Or in this land alt'reth with the Fashions?
Or haue our Passions lesser pow'r then theirs,
Who had lesse Art them liuely to expresse?
Is Nature growne lesse pow'rfull in their Heires,
Or in our Fathers did the more transgresse?
I am sure my Sighes come from a Heart as true,
As any Mans, that Memory can boast,
And my Respects and Seruices to you
Equall with his, that loues his Mistris most:
    Or Nature must be partiall in my Cause,
    Or onely you doe violate her Lawes.

36

Cupid coniured

Thou purblind Boy, since thou hast been so slacke
To wound her Heart, whose Eyes haue wounded me,
And suff'red her to glory in my Wracke,
Thus to my aid, I lastly coniure thee;
By Hellish Styx (by which the THUND'RER sweares)
By thy faire Mothers vnauoided Power,
By HECAT'S Names, by PROSERPINE'S sad Teares,
When she was rapt to the infernall Bower,
By thine own loued PSYCHES, by the Fires
Spent on thine Altars, flaming vp to Heau'n;
By all the Louers Sighes, Vowes, and Desires,
By all the Wounds that euer thou hast giu'n;
    I coniure thee by all that I haue nam'd,
    To make her loue, or CUPID be thou damn'd.

48

Cupid, I hate thee, which I'de haue thee know,
A naked Starueling euer may'st thou be,
Poore Rogue, goe pawne thy Fascia and thy Bow,
For some few Ragges, wherewith to couer thee;
Or if thou'lt not, thy Archerie forbeare,
To some base Rustick doe thy selfe preferre,
And when Corne's sowne, or growne into the Eare,

Practise thy Quiuer, and turne Crow-keeper;
Or being Blind (as fittest for the Trade)
Goe hyre thy selfe some bungling Harpers Boy;
They that are blind, are Minstrels often made,
So may'st thou liue, to thy faire Mothers Ioy:
    That whilst with MARS she holdeth her old way,
    Thou, her Blind Sonne, may'st sit by them, and play.

52

What dost thou meane to Cheate me of my Heart,
To take all Mine, and giue me none againe?
Or haue thine Eyes such Magike, or that Art,
That what They get, They euer doe retaine?
Play not the Tyrant, but take some Remorse,
Rebate thy Spleene, if but for Pitties sake;
Or Cruell, if thou can'st not; let vs scorse,
And for one Piece of Thine, my whole heart take.
But what of Pitty doe I speake to Thee,
Whose Brest is proofe against Complaint or Prayer?
Or can I thinke what my Reward shall be
From that proud Beauty, which was my betrayer?
    What talke I of a Heart, when thou hast none?
    Or if thou hast, it is a flinty one.

61

Since there 's no helpe, Come let vs kisse and part,
Nay, I haue done: You get no more of Me,
And I am glad, yea glad withall my heart,
That thus so cleanly, I my Selfe can free,
Shake hands for euer, Cancell all our Vowes,
And when we meet at any time againe,
Be it not scene in either of our Browes,
That We one iot of former Loue reteyne;
Now at the last gaspe of Loues latest Breath,
When his Pulse fayling, Passion speechlesse lies,
When Faith is kneeling by his bed of Death,
And Innocence is closing vp his Eyes,
    Now if thou would'st, when all haue giuen him ouer,
    From Death to Life, thou might'st him yet recouer.

ODES

[from the Edition of 1619]

TO HIMSELFE AND THE HARPE

And why not I, as hee
That's greatest, if as free,
    (In sundry strains that striue,
Since there so many be)
    Th' old Lyrick kind reuiue?

I will, yea, and I may;
Who shall oppose my way?
    For what is he alone,
That of himselfe can say,
    Hee's Heire of Helicon? 10

APOLLO, and the Nine,
Forbid no Man their Shrine,
    That commeth with hands pure;
Else be they so diuine,
    They will not him indure.

For they be such coy Things,
That they care not for Kings,
    And dare let them know it;
Nor may he touch their Springs,
    That is not borne a Poet. 20

[1]The Phocean it did proue,
Whom when foule Lust did moue,
    Those Mayds vnchast to make,
Fell, as with them he stroue,
    His Neck and iustly brake.

That instrument ne'r heard,
Strooke by the skilfull Bard,
    It strongly to awake;
But it th' infernalls skard,
    And made Olympus quake. 30

---

[1] Pyreneus, King of Phocis, attempting to rauish the Muses.

[2]As those Prophetike strings
Whose sounds with fiery Wings,
   Draue Fiends from their abode,
Touch'd by the best of Kings,
   That sang the holy Ode.

[3]So his, which Women slue,
And it int' Hebrus threw,
   Such sounds yet forth it sent,
The Bankes to weepe that drue,
   As downe the streame it went.   40

[4]That by the Tortoyse shell,
To MAYAS Sonne it fell,
   The most thereof not doubt
But sure some Power did dwell,
   In Him who found it out.

[5]The Wildest of the field,
   And Ayre, with Riuers t' yeeld,
      Which mou'd; that sturdy Glebes,
And massie Oakes could weeld,
   To rayse the pyles of Thebes.   50

   And diuersly though Strung,
So anciently We sung,
   To it, that Now scarce knowne,
If first it did belong
   To Greece, or if our Owne.

[6]The Druydes imbrew'd,
With Gore, on Altars rude
   With Sacrifices crown'd,
In hollow Woods bedew'd,
   Ador'd the Trembling sound. 60

---

[2] Sam. lib. 1. cap. 16.
[3] Orpheus the Thracian Poet. Caput, Hebre, lyramque Excipis. &c. Ouid. lib. 11.
Metam.
[4] Mercury inuentor of the Harpe, as Horace Ode 10. lib. 1. curuaq; lyra parente.
[5] Thebes fayned to haue beene raysed by Musicke.
[6] The ancient British Priests so called of their abode in woods.

[7]Though wee be All to seeke,
Of PINDAR that Great Greeke,
   To Finger it aright,
   The Soule with power to strike,
     His hand retayn'd such Might.

[8]Or him that Rome did grace
Whose Ayres we all imbrace,
   That scarcely found his Peere,
   Nor giueth PHOEBVS place,
     For Strokes diuinely cleere.   70

[9]The Irish I admire,
Harpe.And still cleaue to that Lyre,
   As our Musike's Mother,
   And thinke, till I expire,
     APOLLO'S such another.

As Britons, that so long
Haue held this Antike Song,
   And let all our Carpers
   Forbeare their fame to wrong,
     Th' are right skilfull Harpers.   80

[10]Southerne, I long thee spare,
Yet wish thee well to fare,
   Who me pleased'st greatly,
   As first, therefore more rare,
     Handling thy Harpe neatly.

To those that with despight
Shall terme these Numbers slight,
   Tell them their Iudgement's blind,
   Much erring from the right,
     It is a Noble kind.   90

[11]Nor is 't the Verse doth make,
That giueth, or doth take,

---

[7] Pindar Prince of the Greeke lyricks, of whom Horace: Pindarum quisquis studet, &c.
Ode 2. lib. 4.
[8] Horace first of the Romans in that kind.
[9] The Irish
[10] Southerne, an English Lyrick.
[11] An old English Rymer.

    'Tis possible to clyme,
  To kindle, or to slake,
      Although in SKELTON'S Ryme.

TO THE NEW YEERE

Rich Statue, double-faced,
With Marble Temples graced,
    To rayse thy God-head hyer,
In flames where Altars shining,
Before thy Priests diuining,
    Doe od'rous Fumes expire.

Great IANVS, I thy pleasure,
With all the Thespian treasure,
    Doe seriously pursue;
To th' passed yeere returning,
As though the old adiourning,
    Yet bringing in the new.

Thy ancient Vigils yeerely,
I haue obserued cleerely,
    Thy Feasts yet smoaking bee;
Since all thy store abroad is,
Giue something to my Goddesse,
    As hath been vs'd by thee.

Giue her th' Eoan brightnesse,
Wing'd with that subtill lightnesse,
    That doth trans-pierce the Ayre;
The Roses of the Morning
The rising Heau'n adorning,
    To mesh with flames of Hayre.

Those ceaselesse Sounds, aboue all,
Made by those Orbes that moue all,
    And euer swelling there,
Wrap'd vp in Numbers flowing,
Them actually bestowing,
    For Iewels at her Eare.

O Rapture great and holy,
Doe thou transport me wholly,
    So well her forme to vary,
That I aloft may beare her,

10

20

30

Whereas I will insphere her,
    In Regions high and starry.

And in my choise Composures,
The soft and easie Closures,
    So amorously shall meet;
That euery liuely Ceasure   40
Shall tread a perfect Measure
    Set on so equall feet.

That Spray to fame so fertle,
The Louer-crowning Mirtle,
    In Wreaths of mixed Bowes,
Within whose shades are dwelling
Those Beauties most excelling,
    Inthron'd vpon her Browes.

Those Paralels so euen,
Drawne on the face of Heauen,   50
    That curious Art supposes,
Direct those Gems, whose cleerenesse
Farre off amaze by neerenesse,
    Each Globe such fire incloses.

Her Bosome full of Blisses,
By Nature made for Kisses,
    So pure and wond'rous cleere,
Whereas a thousand Graces
Behold their louely Faces,
    As they are bathing there.   60

O, thou selfe-little blindnesse,
The kindnesse of vnkindnesse,
    Yet one of those diuine;
Thy Brands to me were leuer,
Thy Fascia, and thy Quiuer,
    And thou this Quill of mine.

This Heart so freshly bleeding,
Vpon it owne selfe feeding,
    Whose woundes still dropping be;
O Loue, thy selfe confounding,   70
Her coldnesse so abounding,
    And yet such heat in me.

Yet if I be inspired,
Ile leaue thee so admired,
   To all that shall succeed,
That were they more then many,
'Mongst all, there is not any,
   That Time so oft shall read.

Nor Adamant ingraued,
That hath been choisely 'st saued,   80
   IDEA'S Name out-weares;
So large a Dower as this is,
The greatest often misses,
   The Diadem that beares.

TO HIS VALENTINE

Muse, bid the Morne awake,
   Sad Winter now declines,
Each Bird doth chuse a Make,
   This day 's Saint VALENTINE'S;
For that good Bishop's sake
Get vp, and let vs see,
What Beautie it shall bee,
   That Fortune vs assignes.

But lo, in happy How'r,
   The place wherein she lyes,   10
In yonder climbing Tow'r,
   Gilt by the glitt'ring Rise;
O IOVE! that in a Show'r,
As once that Thund'rer did,
When he in drops lay hid,
   That I could her surprize.

Her Canopie Ile draw,
   With spangled Plumes bedight,
No Mortall euer saw
   So rauishing a sight;   20
That it the Gods might awe,
And pow'rfully trans-pierce
The Globie Vniuerse,
   Out-shooting eu'ry Light.

My Lips Ile softly lay
   Vpon her heau'nly Cheeke,

Dy'd like the dawning Day,
    As polish'd Iuorie sleeke:
And in her Eare Ile say;
O, thou bright Morning-Starre,   30
'Tis I that come so farre,
    My Valentine to seeke.

Each little Bird, this Tyde,
    Doth chuse her loued Pheere,
Which constantly abide
    In Wedlock all the yeere,
As Nature is their Guide:
So may we two be true,
This yeere, nor change for new,
    As Turtles coupled were.   40

The Sparrow, Swan, the Doue,
    Though VENVS Birds they be,
Yet are they not for Loue
    So absolute as we:
For Reason vs doth moue;
They but by billing woo:
Then try what we can doo,
    To whom each sense is free.

Which we haue more then they,
    By liuelyer Organs sway'd,   50
Our Appetite each way
    More by our Sense obay'd:
Our Passions to display,
This Season vs doth fit;
Then let vs follow it,
    As Nature vs doth lead.

One Kisse in two let's breake,
    Confounded with the touch,
But halfe words let vs speake,
    Our Lip's imploy'd so much,   60
Vntill we both grow weake,
With sweetnesse of thy breath;
O smother me to death:
    Long let our Ioyes be such.

Let's laugh at them that chuse
    Their Valentines by lot,

To weare their Names that vse,
    Whom idly they haue got:
Such poore choise we refuse,
Saint VALENTINE befriend; 70
We thus this Morne may spend,
    Else Muse, awake her not.

THE HEART

If thus we needs must goe,
What shall our one Heart doe,
This One made of our Two?

Madame, two Hearts we brake,
And from them both did take
The best, one Heart to make.

Halfe this is of your Heart,
Mine in the other part,
Ioyn'd by our equall Art.

Were it cymented, or sowne,   10
By Shreds or Pieces knowne,
We each might find our owne.

But 'tis dissolu'd, and fix'd,
And with such cunning mix'd,
No diffrence that betwixt.

But how shall we agree,
By whom it kept shall be,
Whether by you, or me?

It cannot two Brests fill,
One must be heartlesse still,   20
Vntill the other will.

It came to me one day,
When I will'd it to say,
With whether it would stay?

It told me, in your Brest,
Where it might hope to rest:
For if it were my Ghest,

For certainety it knew,
That I would still anew
Be sending it to you.   30

Neuer, I thinke, had two
Such worke, so much to doo,
A Vnitie to woo.

Yours was so cold and chaste,
Whilst mine with zeale did waste,
Like Fire with Water plac'd.

How did my Heart intreat,
How pant, how did it beat,
Till it could giue yours heat!

Till to that temper brought,   40
Through our perfection wrought,
That blessing eythers Thought.

In such a Height it lyes,
From this base Worlds dull Eyes,
That Heauen it not enuyes.

All that this Earth can show,
Our Heart shall not once know,
For it too vile and low.

THE SACRIFICE TO APOLLO

Priests of APOLLO, sacred be the Roome,
For this learn'd Meeting: Let no barbarous Groome,
        How braue soe'r he bee,
        Attempt to enter;
        But of the Muses free,
        None here may venter;
This for the Delphian Prophets is prepar'd:
The prophane Vulgar are from hence debar'd.

And since the Feast so happily begins,
Call vp those faire Nine, with their Violins;   10
        They are begot by IOVE,
        Then let vs place them,
        Where no Clowne in may shoue,
        That may disgrace them:

But let them neere to young APOLLO sit;
So shall his Foot-pace ouer-flow with Wit.

Where be the Graces, where be those fayre Three?
In any hand they may not absent bee:
      They to the Gods are deare,
      And they can humbly   20
      Teach vs, our Selues to beare,
      And doe things comely:
They, and the Muses, rise both from one Stem,
They grace the Muses, and the Muses them.

Bring forth your Flaggons (fill'd with sparkling Wine)
Whereon swolne BACCHVS, crowned with a Vine,
      Is grauen, and fill out,
      It well bestowing,
      To eu'ry Man about,
      In Goblets flowing: 30
Let not a Man drinke, but in Draughts profound;
To our God PHOEBVS let the Health goe Round.

Let your Iests flye at large; yet therewithall
See they be Salt, but yet not mix'd with Gall:
      Not tending to disgrace,
      But fayrely giuen,
      Becomming well the place,
      Modest, and euen;
That they with tickling Pleasure may prouoke
Laughter in him, on whom the Iest is broke.   40

Or if the deeds of HEROES ye rehearse,
Let them be sung in so well-ord'red Verse,
      That each word haue his weight,
      Yet runne with pleasure;
      Holding one stately height,
      In so braue measure,
That they may make the stiffest Storme seeme weake,
And dampe IOVES Thunder, when it lowd'st doth speake.

And if yee list to exercise your Vayne,
Or in the Sock, or in the Buskin'd Strayne,   50
      Let Art and Nature goe
      One with the other;
      Yet so, that Art may show
      Nature her Mother;

The thick-brayn'd Audience liuely to awake,
Till with shrill Claps the Theater doe shake.

Sing Hymnes to BACCHVS then, with hands vprear'd,
Offer to IOVE, who most is to be fear'd;
    From him the Muse we haue,
    From him proceedeth   60
    More then we dare to craue;
    'Tis he that feedeth
Them, whom the World would starue; then let the Lyre
Sound, whilst his Altars endlesse flames expire.

TO CVPID

Maydens, why spare ye?
Or whether not dare ye
    Correct the blind Shooter?
Because wanton VENVS,
So oft that doth paine vs,
    Is her Sonnes Tutor.

Now in the Spring,
He proueth his Wing,
    The Field is his Bower,
And as the small Bee,   10
About flyeth hee,
    From Flower to Flower.

And wantonly roues,
Abroad in the Groues,
    And in the Ayre houers,
Which when it him deweth,
His Fethers he meweth,
    In sighes of true Louers.

And since doom'd by Fate,
(That well knew his Hate)   20
    That Hee should be blinde;
For very despite,
Our Eyes be his White,
    So wayward his kinde.

If his Shafts loosing,
(Ill his Mark choosing)
    Or his Bow broken;

The Moane VENVS maketh,
And care that she taketh,
   Cannot be spoken.   30

To VULCAN commending
Her loue, and straight sending
   Her Doues and her Sparrowes,
With Kisses vnto him,
And all but to woo him,
   To make her Sonne Arrowes.

Telling what he hath done,
(Sayth she, Right mine owne Sonne)
   In her Armes she him closes,
Sweetes on him fans,   40
Layd in Downe of her Swans,
   His Sheets, Leaues of Roses.

And feeds him with Kisses;
Which oft when he misses,
   He euer is froward:
The Mothers o'r-ioying,
Makes by much coying,
   The Child so vntoward.

Yet in a fine Net,
That a Spider set,   50
   The Maydens had caught him;
Had she not beene neere him,
And chanced to heare him,
   More good they had taught him.

AN AMOVRET ANACREONTICK

Most good, most faire,
Or Thing as rare,
To call you's lost;
For all the cost
Words can bestow,
So poorely show
Vpon your prayse,
That all the wayes
Sense hath, come short:
Whereby Report   10
Falls them vnder;

That when Wonder
More hath seyzed,
Yet not pleased,
That it in kinde
Nothing can finde,
You to expresse:
Neuerthelesse,
As by Globes small,
This Mightie ALL   20
Is shew'd, though farre
From Life, each Starre
A World being:
So wee seeing
You, like as that,
Onely trust what
Art doth vs teach;
And when I reach
At Morall Things,
And that my Strings   30
Grauely should strike,
Straight some mislike
Blotteth mine ODE.
As with the Loade,
The Steele we touch,
Forced ne'r so much,
Yet still remoues
To that it loues,
Till there it stayes;
So to your prayse   40
I turne euer,
And though neuer
From you mouing,
Happie so louing.

LOVES CONQVEST

Wer't granted me to choose,
How I would end my dayes;
Since I this life must loose,
It should be in Your praise;
For there is no Bayes
Can be set aboue you.

S' impossibly I loue You,
And for you sit so hie,

Whence none may remoue You
In my cleere Poesie,   10
That I oft deny
    You so ample Merit.

    The freedome of my Spirit
Maintayning (still) my Cause,
    Your Sex not to inherit,
Vrging the Salique Lawes;
But your Vertue drawes
    From me euery due.

    Thus still You me pursue,
That no where I can dwell,   20
    By Feare made iust to You,
Who naturally rebell,
Of You that excell
    That should I still Endyte,

    Yet will You want some Ryte.
That lost in your high praise
    I wander to and fro,
As seeing sundry Waies:
Yet which the right not know
    To get out of this Maze.   30

TO THE VIRIGINIAN VOYAGE

You braue Heroique minds,
Worthy your Countries Name;
    That Honour still pursue,
    Goe, and subdue,
Whilst loyt'ring Hinds
Lurke here at home, with shame.

Britans, you stay too long,
Quickly aboard bestow you,
    And with a merry Gale
    Swell your stretch'd Sayle,   10
With Vowes as strong,
As the Winds that blow you.

Your Course securely steere,
West and by South forth keepe,
    Rocks, Lee-shores, nor Sholes,

When EOLVS scowles,
You need not feare,
So absolute the Deepe.

And cheerefully at Sea,
Successe you still intice,   20
    To get the Pearle and Gold,
    And ours to hold,
VIRGINIA,
Earth's onely Paradise.

Where Nature hath in store
Fowle, Venison, and Fish,
    And the Fruitfull'st Soyle,
    Without your Toyle,
Three Haruests more,
All greater then your Wish.   30

And the ambitious Vine
Crownes with his purple Masse,
    The cedar reaching hie
    To kisse the Sky
The Cypresse, Pine
And vse-full Sassafras.

To whome, the golden Age
Still Natures lawes doth giue,
    No other Cares that tend,
    But Them to defend   40
From Winters rage,
That long there doth not liue.

When as the Lushious smell
Of that delicious Land,
    Aboue the Seas that flowes,
    The cleere Wind throwes,
Your Hearts to swell
Approaching the deare Strande.

In kenning of the Shore
(Thanks to God first giuen,)   50
    O you the happy'st men,
    Be Frolike then,
Let Cannons roare,
Frighting the wide Heauen.

And in Regions farre
Such Heroes bring yee foorth,
 As those from whom We came,
 And plant Our name,
Vnder that Starre
Not knowne vnto our North.   60

And as there Plenty growes
Of Lawrell euery where,
 APOLLO'S Sacred tree,
 You may it see,
A Poets Browes
To crowne, that may sing there.

Thy Voyages attend,
Industrious HACKLVIT,
 Whose Reading shall inflame
 Men to seeke Fame,   70
And much commend
To after-Times thy Wit.

AN ODE WRITTEN IN THE PEAKE

This while we are abroad,
 Shall we not touch our Lyre?
Shall we not sing an ODE?
 Shall that holy Fire,
In vs that strongly glow'd,
 In this cold Ayre expire?

Long since the Summer layd
 Her lustie Brau'rie downe,
The Autumne halfe is way'd,
 And BOREAS 'gins to frowne,   10
Since now I did behold
 Great BRVTES first builded Towne.

Though in the vtmost Peake,
 A while we doe remaine,
Amongst the Mountaines bleake
 Expos'd to Sleet and Raine,
No Sport our Houres shall breake,
 To exercise our Vaine.

What though bright PHOEBVS Beames
   Refresh the Southerne Ground,   20
And though the Princely Thames
   With beautious Nymphs abound,
And by old Camber's Streames
   Be many Wonders found;

Yet many Riuers cleare
   Here glide in Siluer Swathes,
And what of all most deare,
   Buckston's delicious Bathes,
Strong Ale and Noble Cheare,
   T' asswage breeme Winters scathes.   30

Those grim and horrid Caues,
   Whose Lookes affright the day,
Wherein nice Nature saues,
   What she would not bewray,
Our better leasure craues,
   And doth inuite our Lay.

In places farre or neere,
   Or famous, or obscure,
Where wholesome is the Ayre,
   Or where the most impure,   40
All times, and euery-where,
   The Muse is still in vre.

HIS DEFENCE AGAINST THE IDLE CRITICK

The Ryme nor marres, nor makes,
Nor addeth it, nor takes,
   From that which we propose;
Things imaginarie
Doe so strangely varie,
   That quickly we them lose.

And what 's quickly begot,
As soone againe is not,
   This doe I truely know:
Yea, and what 's borne with paine,   10
That Sense doth long'st retaine,
   Gone with a greater Flow.

Yet this Critick so sterne,
But whom, none must discerne,
   Nor perfectly haue seeing,
Strangely layes about him,
As nothing without him
   Were worthy of being.

That I my selfe betray
To that most publique way,   20
   Where the Worlds old Bawd,
Custome, that doth humor,
And by idle rumor,
   Her Dotages applaud.

That whilst he still prefers
Those that be wholly hers,
   Madnesse and Ignorance,
I creepe behind the Time,
From spertling with their Crime,
   And glad too with my Chance.   30

O wretched World the while,
When the euill most vile,
   Beareth the fayrest face,
And inconstant lightnesse,
With a scornefull slightnesse,
   The best Things doth disgrace.

Whilst this strange knowing Beast,
Man, of himselfe the least,
   His Enuie declaring,
Makes Vertue to descend,   40
Her title to defend,
   Against him, much preparing.

Yet these me not delude,
Nor from my place extrude,
   By their resolued Hate;
Their vilenesse that doe know;
Which to my selfe I show,
   To keepe aboue my Fate.

TO HIS RIVALL

Her lou'd I most,
  By thee that 's lost,
Though she were wonne with leasure;
  She was my gaine,
  But to my paine,
Thou spoyl'st me of my Treasure.

  The Ship full fraught
  With Gold, farre sought,
Though ne'r so wisely helmed,
  May suffer wracke   10
  In sayling backe,
By Tempest ouer-whelmed.

  But shee, good Sir,
  Did not preferre
You, for that I was ranging;
  But for that shee
  Found faith in mee,
And she lou'd to be changing.

  Therefore boast not
  Your happy Lot,   20
Be silent now you haue her;
  The time I knew
  She slighted you,
When I was in her fauour.

  None stands so fast,
  But may be cast
By Fortune, and disgraced:
  Once did I weare
  Her Garter there,
Where you her Gloue haue placed.   30

  I had the Vow
  That thou hast now,
And Glances to discouer
  Her Loue to mee,
  And she to thee
Reades but old Lessons ouer.

She hath no Smile
That can beguile,
But as my Thought I know it;
   Yea, to a Hayre,   40
Both when and where,
And how she will bestow it.

What now is thine,
Was onely mine,
And first to me was giuen;
   Thou laugh'st at mee,
I laugh at thee,
And thus we two are euen.

But Ile not mourne,
But stay my Turne,   50
The Wind may come about, Sir,
   And once againe
May bring me in,
And help to beare you out, Sir.

A SKELTONIAD

The Muse should be sprightly,
Yet not handling lightly
Things graue; as much loath,
Things that be slight, to cloath
Curiously: To retayne
The Comelinesse in meane,
Is true Knowledge and Wit.
Not me forc'd Rage doth fit,
That I thereto should lacke
Tabacco, or need Sacke,   10
Which to the colder Braine
Is the true Hyppocrene;
Nor did I euer care
For great Fooles, nor them spare.
Vertue, though neglected,
Is not so deiected,
As vilely to descend
To low Basenesse their end;
Neyther each ryming Slaue
Deserues the Name to haue   20
Of Poet: so the Rabble
Of Fooles, for the Table,

That haue their Iests by Heart,
As an Actor his Part,
Might assume them Chayres
Amongst the Muses Heyres.
Parnassus is not clome
By euery such Mome;
Vp whose steep side who swerues,
It behoues t' haue strong Nerues: 30
My Resolution such,
How well, and not how much
To write, thus doe I fare,
Like some few good that care
(The euill sort among)
How well to liue, and not how long.

THE CRYER

Good Folke, for Gold or Hyre,
  But helpe me to a Cryer;
For my poore Heart is runne astray
After two Eyes, that pass'd this way.
    O yes, O yes, O yes,
      If there be any Man,
      In Towne or Countrey, can
      Bring me my Heart againe,
      Ile please him for his paine;
And by these Marks I will you show,   10
That onely I this Heart doe owe.
      It is a wounded Heart,
        Wherein yet sticks the Dart,
    Eu'ry piece sore hurt throughout it,
    Faith, and Troth, writ round about it:
It was a tame Heart, and a deare,
      And neuer vs'd to roame;
But hauing got this Haunt, I feare
      'Twill hardly stay at home.
For Gods sake, walking by the way,   20
      If you my Heart doe see,
Either impound it for a Stray,
      Or send it backe to me.

TO HIS COY LOVE

A CANZONET

I pray thee leaue, loue me no more,
    Call home the Heart you gaue me,
I but in vaine that Saint adore,
    That can, but will not saue me:
These poore halfe Kisses kill me quite;
    Was euer man thus serued?
Amidst an Ocean of Delight,
    For Pleasure to be sterued.

Shew me no more those Snowie Brests,
    With Azure Riuerets branched,   10
Where whilst mine Eye with Plentie feasts,
    Yet is my Thirst not stanched.
O TANTALVS, thy Paines n'er tell,
    By me thou art preuented;
'Tis nothing to be plagu'd in Hell,
    But thus in Heauen tormented.

Clip me no more in those deare Armes,
    Nor thy Life's Comfort call me;
O, these are but too pow'rfull Charmes,
    And doe but more inthrall me.   20
But see, how patient I am growne,
    In all this coyle about thee;
Come nice thing, let my Heart alone,
    I cannot liue without thee.

A HYMNE TO HIS LADIES BIRTH-PLACE

    Couentry, that do'st adorne
  The Countrey wherein I was borne,
  Yet therein lyes not thy prayse
  Why I should crowne thy Tow'rs with Bayes:
  [1]'Tis not thy Wall, me to thee weds
Thy Ports, nor thy proud Pyrameds,
Nor thy Trophies of the Bore,
    But that Shee which I adore,
Which scarce Goodnesse selfe can payre,
  First their breathing blest thy Ayre;   10

---

[1] Couentry finely' walled. The Shoulder-bone of a hare of mighty bignesse.

IDEA, in which Name I hide
Her, in my heart Deifi'd,
For what good, Man's mind can see,
Onely her IDEAS be;
She, in whom the Vertues came
In Womans shape, and tooke her Name,
She so farre past Imitation,
As but Nature our Creation
Could not alter, she had aymed,
More then Woman to haue framed: 20
She, whose truely written Story,
To thy poore Name shall adde more glory,
Then if it should haue beene thy Chance,
T' haue bred our Kings that Conquer'd France.
Had She beene borne the former Age,
[2]That house had beene a Pilgrimage,
And reputed more Diuine,
Then Walsingham or BECKETS Shrine.
That Princesse, to whom thou do'st owe
Thy Freedome, whose Cleere blushing snow,   30
[3]The enuious Sunne saw, when as she
Naked rode to make Thee free,
Was but her Type, as to foretell,
Thou should'st bring forth one, should excell
Her Bounty, by whom thou should'st haue
More Honour, then she Freedome gaue;
And that great Queene, which but of late
[4]Rul'd this Land in Peace and State,
Had not beene, but Heauen had sworne,
A Maide should raigne, when she was borne.   40
[5]Of thy Streets, which thou hold'st best,
And most frequent of the rest,
Happy Mich-Parke eu'ry yeere,
[6]On the fourth of August there,
Let thy Maides from FLORA'S bowers,
With their Choyce and daintiest flowers
Decke Thee vp, and from their store,
With braue Garlands crowne that dore.

---

[2] Two famous Pilgrimages, the one in Norfolk, the other in Kent.
[3] Godiua, Duke Leofricks wife, who obtained the Freedome of the city, of her husband, by riding thorow it naked.
[4] Queene Elizabeth.
[5] A noted Streete in Couentry.
[6] His Mistresse birth-day.

The old Man passing by that way,
To his Sonne in time shall say, 50
There was that Lady borne, which long
To after-Ages shall be sung;
Who vnawares being passed by,
Back to that House shall cast his Eye,
Speaking my Verses as he goes,
And with a Sigh shut eu'ry Close.
    Deare Citie, trauelling by thee,
When thy rising Spyres I see,
Destined her place of Birth;
Yet me thinkes the very Earth 60
Hallowed is, so farre as I
Can thee possibly descry:
Then thou dwelling in this place,
Hearing some rude Hinde disgrace
Thy Citie with some scuruy thing,
Which some Iester forth did bring,
Speake these Lines where thou do'st come,
And strike the Slaue for euer dumbe.

TO THE CAMBRO-BRITANS and their Harpe, his Ballad of AGINCOVRT

Faire stood the Wind for France,
When we our Sayles aduance,
Nor now to proue our chance,
    Longer will tarry;
But putting to the Mayne,
At Kaux, the Mouth of Sene,
With all his Martiall Trayne,
    Landed King HARRY.

And taking many a Fort,
Furnish'd in Warlike sort, 10
Marcheth tow'rds Agincourt,
    In happy howre;
Skirmishing day by day,
With those that stop'd his way,
Where the French Gen'rall lay,
    With all his Power.

Which in his Hight of Pride,
King HENRY to deride,
His Ransome to prouide

      To the King sending.   20
Which he neglects the while,
As from a Nation vile,
Yet with an angry smile,
      Their fall portending.

And turning to his Men,
Quoth our braue HENRY then,
Though they to one be ten,
      Be not amazed.
Yet haue we well begunne,
Battels so brauely wonne,   30
Haue euer to the Sonne,
      By Fame beene raysed.

And, for my Selfe (quoth he),
This my full rest shall be,
England ne'r mourne for Me,
      Nor more esteeme me.
Victor I will remaine,
Or on this Earth lie slaine,
Neuer shall Shee sustaine,
      Losse to redeeme me.   40

Poiters and Cressy tell,
When most their Pride did swell,
Vnder our Swords they fell,
      No lesse our skill is,
Than when our Grandsire Great,
Clayming the Regall Seate,
By many a Warlike feate,
      Lop'd the French Lillies.

The Duke of Yorke so dread,
The eager Vaward led;   50
With the maine, HENRY sped,
      Among'st his Hench-men.
EXCESTER had the Rere,
A Brauer man not there,
O Lord, how hot they were,
      On the false French-men!

They now to fight are gone,
Armour on Armour shone,
Drumme now to Drumme did grone,

To heare, was wonder; 60
That with the Cryes they make,
The very Earth did shake,
Trumpet to Trumpet spake,
    Thunder to Thunder.

Well it thine Age became,
O Noble ERPINGHAM,
Which didst the Signall ayme,
    To our hid Forces;
When from a Medow by,
Like a Storme suddenly, 70
The English Archery
    Stuck the French Horses,

With Spanish Ewgh so strong,
Arrowes a Cloth-yard long,
That like to Serpents stung,
    Piercing the Weather;
None from his fellow starts,
But playing Manly parts,
And like true English hearts,
    Stuck close together. 80

When downe their Bowes they threw,
And forth their Bilbowes drew,
And on the French they flew,
    Not one was tardie;
Armes were from shoulders sent,
Scalpes to the Teeth were rent,
Downe the French Pesants went,
    Our Men were hardie.

This while our Noble King,
His broad Sword brandishing, 90
Downe the French Hoast did ding,
    As to o'r-whelme it;
And many a deepe Wound lent,
His Armes with Bloud besprent,
And many a cruell Dent
    Bruised his Helmet.

GLOSTER, that Duke so good,
Next of the Royall Blood,
For famous England stood,

With his braue Brother;   100
CLARENCE, in Steele so bright,
Though but a Maiden Knight,
Yet in that furious Fight,
    Scarce such another,

WARWICK in Bloud did wade,
OXFORD the Foe inuade,
And cruell slaughter made,
    Still as they ran vp;
SVFFOLKE his Axe did ply,
BEAVMONT and WILLOVGHBY   110
Bare them right doughtily,
    FERRERS and FANHOPE.

Vpon Saint CRISPIN'S day
Fought was this Noble Fray,
Which Fame did not delay,
    To England to carry;
O, when shall English Men
With such Acts fill a Pen,
Or England breed againe,
    Such a King HARRY?   120

[from the Edition of 1606]

Ode 4

To my worthy frend, Master John Sauage of the Inner Temple

Vppon this sinfull earth
If man can happy be,
And higher then his birth,
(Frend) take him thus from me.

Whome promise not deceiues
That he the breach should rue,
Nor constant reason leaues
Opinion to pursue.

To rayse his mean estate
That sooths no wanton's sinne,   10
Doth that preferment hate
That virtue doth not winne.

Nor brauery doth admire,
Nor doth more loue professe
To that he doth desire,
Then that he doth possesse.

Loose humor nor to please,
That neither spares nor spends,
But by discretion weyes
What is to needfull ends.   20

To him deseruing not
Not yeelding, nor doth hould
What is not his, doing what
He ought not what he could.

Whome the base tyrants will
Soe much could neuer awe
As him for good or ill
From honesty to drawe.

Whose constancy doth rise
'Boue vndeserued spight   30
Whose valewr's to despise
That most doth him delight.

That earely leaue doth take
Of th' world though to his payne
For virtues onely sake
And not till need constrayne.

Noe man can be so free
Though in imperiall seate
Nor Eminent as he
That deemeth nothing greate.   40

Ode 8

Singe wee the Rose
Then which no flower there growes
    Is sweeter:
And aptly her compare
With what in that is rare
    A parallel none meeter.

Or made poses,
Of this that incloses
    Suche blisses,
That naturally flusheth   10
As she blusheth
    When she is robd of kisses.

Or if strew'd
When with the morning dew'd
    Or stilling,
Or howe to sense expos'd
All which in her inclos'd,
    Ech place with sweetnes filling.

That most renown'd
By Nature richly crownd   20
    With yellow,
Of that delitious layre
And as pure, her hayre
    Vnto the same the fellowe,

Fearing of harme
Nature that flower doth arme
    From danger,
The touch giues her offence

But with reuerence
   Vnto her selfe a stranger.   30

That redde, or white,
Or mixt, the sence delyte
   Behoulding,
In her complexion
All which perfection
   Such harmony infouldinge.

That deuyded
Ere it was descided
   Which most pure,
Began the greeuous war   40
Of York and Lancaster,
   That did many yeeres indure.

Conflicts as greate
As were in all that heate
   I sustaine:
By her, as many harts
As men on either parts
   That with her eies hath slaine.

The Primrose flower
The first of Flora's bower   50
   Is placed,
Soo is shee first as best
Though excellent the rest,
   All gracing, by none graced.

ELEGIES VPON SVNDRY OCCASIONS

[from the Edition of 1627]

Of his Ladies not Comming to London

That ten-yeares-trauell'd Greeke return'd from Sea
Ne'r ioyd so much to see his Ithaca,
As I should you, who are alone to me,
More then wide Greece could to that wanderer be.
The winter windes still Easterly doe keepe,
And with keene Frosts haue chained vp the deepe,
The Sunne's to vs a niggard of his Rayes,
But reuelleth with our Antipodes;
And seldome to vs when he shewes his head,
Muffled in vapours, he straight hies to bed.　　　　10
In those bleake mountaines can you liue where snowe
Maketh the vales vp to the hilles to growe;
Whereas mens breathes doe instantly congeale,
And attom'd mists turne instantly to hayle;
Belike you thinke, from this more temperate cost,
My sighes may haue the power to thawe the frost,
Which I from hence should swiftly send you thither,
Yet not so swift, as you come slowly hither.
How many a time, hath Phebe from her wayne,
With Phoebus fires fill'd vp her hornes againe;　　　　20
Shee through her Orbe, still on her course doth range,
But you keep yours still, nor for me will change.
The Sunne that mounted the sterne Lions back,
Shall with the Fishes shortly diue the Brack,
But still you keepe your station, which confines
You, nor regard him trauelling the signes.
Those ships which when you went, put out to Sea,
Both to our Groenland, and Virginia,
Are now return'd, and Custom'd haue their fraught,
Yet you arriue not, nor returne me ought.　　　　30
　　The Thames was not so frozen yet this yeare,
As is my bosome, with the chilly feare
Of your not comming, which on me doth light,
As on those Climes, where halfe the world is night.
　　Of euery tedious houre you haue made two,
All this long Winter here, by missing you:
Minutes are months, and when the houre is past,
A yeare is ended since the Clocke strooke last,
When your Remembrance puts me on the Racke,

And I should Swound to see an Almanacke,   40
To reade what silent weekes away are slid,
Since the dire Fates you from my sight haue hid.
    I hate him who the first Deuisor was
Of this same foolish thing, the Hower-glasse,
And of the Watch, whose dribbling sands and Wheele,
With their slow stroakes, make mee too much to feele
Your slackenesse hither, O how I doe ban,
Him that these Dialls against walles began,
Whose Snayly motion of the moouing hand,
(Although it goe) yet seeme to me to stand;   50
As though at Adam it had first set out
And had been stealing all this while about,
And when it backe to the first point should come,
It shall be then iust at the generall Doome.
    The Seas into themselues retract their flowes.
The changing Winde from euery quarter blowes,
Declining Winter in the Spring doth call,
The Starrs rise to vs, as from vs they fall;
Those Birdes we see, that leaue vs in the Prime,
Againe in Autumne re-salute our Clime.   60
Sure, either Nature you from kinde hath made,
Or you delight else to be Retrograde.
    But I perceiue by your attractiue powers,
Like an Inchantresse you haue charm'd the bowers
Into short minutes, and haue drawne them back,
So that of vs at London, you doe lack
Almost a yeare, the Spring is scarce begonne
There where you liue, and Autumne almost done.
With vs more Eastward, surely you deuise,
By your strong Magicke, that the Sunne shall rise   70
Where now it setts, and that in some few yeares
You'l alter quite the Motion of the Spheares.
    Yes, and you meane, I shall complaine my loue
To grauell'd Walkes, or to a stupid Groue,
Now your companions; and that you the while
(As you are cruell) will sit by and smile,
To make me write to these, while Passers by,
Sleightly looke in your louely face, where I
See Beauties heauen, whilst silly blockheads, they
Like laden Asses, plod vpon their way,   80
And wonder not, as you should point a Clowne
Vp to the Guards, or Ariadnes Crowne;
Of Constellations, and his dulnesse tell.
Hee'd thinke your words were certainly a Spell;

Or him some piece from Creet, or Marcus show,
In all his life which till that time ne'r saw
Painting: except in Alehouse or old Hall
Done by some Druzzler, of the Prodigall.
    Nay doe, stay still, whilst time away shall steale
Your youth, and beautie, and your selfe conceale   90
From me I pray you, you haue now inur'd
Me to your absence, and I haue endur'd
Your want this long, whilst I haue starued bine
For your short Letters, as you helde it sinne
To write to me, that to appease my woe,
I reade ore those, you writ a yeare agoe,
Which are to me, as though they had bin made,
Long time before the first Olympiad.
    For thankes and curt'sies sell your presence then
To tatling Women, and to things like men,   100
And be more foolish then the Indians are
For Bells, for Kniues, for Glasses, and such ware,
That sell their Pearle and Gold, but here I stay,
So I would not haue you but come away.

To Master GEORGE SANDYS

Treasurer for the English Colony in VIRGINIA

    Friend, if you thinke my Papers may supplie
You, with some strange omitted Noueltie,
Which others Letters yet haue left vntould,
You take me off, before I can take hould
Of you at all; I put not thus to Sea,
For two monthes Voyage to Virginia,
With newes which now, a little something here,
But will be nothing ere it can come there.
I feare, as I doe Stabbing; this word, State,
I dare not speake of the Palatinate,   10
Although some men make it their hourely theame,
And talke what's done in Austria, and in Beame,
I may not so; what Spinola intends,
Nor with his Dutch, which way Prince Maurice bends;
To other men, although these things be free,
Yet (GEORGE) they must be misteries to mee.
    I scarce dare praise a vertuous friend that's dead,
Lest for my lines he should be censured;
It was my hap before all other men
To suffer shipwrack by my forward pen: 20

When King IAMES entred; at which ioyfull time
I taught his title to this Ile in rime:
And to my part did all the Muses win,
With high-pitch Pæans to applaud him in:
When cowardise had tyed vp euery tongue,
And all stood silent, yet for him I sung;
And when before by danger I was dar'd,
I kick'd her from me, nor a iot I spar'd.
Yet had not my cleere spirit in Fortunes scorne,
Me aboue earth and her afflictions borne;   30
He next my God on whom I built my trust,
Had left me troden lower then the dust:
But let this passe; in the extreamest ill,
Apollo's brood must be couragious still,
Let Pies, and Dawes, sit dumb before their death,
Onely the Swan sings at the parting breath.
And (worthy GEORGE) by industry and vse,
Let's see what lines Virginia will produce;
Goe on with OVID, as you haue begunne,
With the first fiue Bookes; let your numbers run   40
Glib as the former, so shall it liue long,
And doe much honour to the English tongue:
Intice the Muses thither to repaire,
Intreat them gently, trayne them to that ayre,
For they from hence may thither hap to fly,
T'wards the sad time which but to fast doth hie,
For Poesie is follow'd with such spight,
By groueling drones that neuer raught her height,
That she must hence, she may no longer staye:
The driery fates prefixed haue the day,   50
Of her departure, which is now come on,
And they command her straight wayes to be gon;
That bestiall heard so hotly her pursue,
And to her succour, there be very few,
Nay none at all, her wrongs that will redresse,
But she must wander in the wildernesse,
Like to the woman, which that holy IOHN
Beheld in Pathmos in his vision.
     As th' English now, so did the stiff-neckt Iewes,
Their noble Prophets vtterly refuse,   60
And of these men such poore opinions had;
They counted Esay and Ezechiel mad;
When Ieremy his Lamentations writ,
They thought the Wizard quite out of his wit,
Such sots they were, as worthily to ly,

Lock't in the chaines of their captiuity,
Knowledge hath still her Eddy in her Flow,
So it hath beene, and it will still be so.
    That famous Greece where learning flourisht most,
Hath of her muses long since left to boast,   70
Th' vnlettered Turke, and rude Barbarian trades,
Where HOMER sang his lofty Iliads;
And this vaste volume of the world hath taught,
Much may to passe in little time be brought.
    As if to Symptoms we may credit giue,
This very time, wherein we two now liue,
Shall in the compasse, wound the Muses more,
Then all the old English ignorance before;
Base Balatry is so belou'd and sought,
And those braue numbers are put by for naught,   80
Which rarely read, were able to awake,
Bodyes from graues, and to the ground to shake
The wandring clouds, and to our men at armes,
'Gainst pikes and muskets were most powerfull charmes.
That, but I know, insuing ages shall,
Raise her againe, who now is in her fall;
And out of dust reduce our scattered rimes,
Th' reiected iewels of these slothfull times,
Who with the Muses would misspend an hower,
But let blind Gothish Barbarisme deuoure   90
These feuerous Dogdays, blest by no record,
But to be euerlastingly abhord.
    If you vouchsafe rescription, stuffe your quill
With naturall bountyes, and impart your skill,
In the description of the place, that I,
May become learned in the soyle thereby;
Of noble Wyats health, and let me heare,
The Gouernour; and how our people there,
Increase and labour, what supplyes are sent,
Which I confesse shall giue me much content;   100
But you may saue your labour if you please,
To write to me ought of your Sauages.
As sauage slaues be in great Britaine here,
As any one that you can shew me there
And though for this, Ile say I doe not thirst,
Yet I should like it well to be the first,
Whose numbers hence into Virginia flew,
So (noble Sandis) for this time adue.

To my noble friend Master WILLIAM BROWNE, of the euill time

Deare friend, be silent and with patience see,
What this mad times Catastrophe will be;
The worlds first Wisemen certainly mistooke
Themselues, and spoke things quite beside the booke,
And that which they haue of said of God, vntrue,
Or else expect strange iudgement to insue.
    This Isle is a meere Bedlam, and therein,
We all lye rauing, mad in euery sinne,
And him the wisest most men use to call,
Who doth (alone) the maddest thing of all;   10
He whom the master of all wisedome found,
For a marckt foole, and so did him propound,
The time we liue in, to that passe is brought,
That only he a Censor now is thought;
And that base villaine, (not an age yet gone,)
Which a good man would not haue look'd vpon;
Now like a God, with diuine worship follow'd,
And all his actions are accounted hollow'd.
    This world of ours, thus runneth vpon wheeles,
Set on the head, bolt vpright with her heeles;   20
Which makes me thinke of what the Ethnicks told
Th' opinion, the Pythagorists vphold,
Wander That the immortall soule doth transmigrate;
From body Then I suppose by the strong power of fate,
to body.And since that time now many a lingering yeare,
Through fools, and beasts, and lunatiques haue past,
Are heere imbodyed in this age at last,
And though so long we from that time be gone,
Yet taste we still of that confusion.
For certainely there's scarse one found that now,   30
Knowes what t' approoue, or what to disallow,
All arsey varsey, nothing is it's owne,
But to our prouerbe, all turnd vpside downe;
To doe in time, is to doe out of season,
And that speeds best, thats done the farth'st from reason,
Hee 's high'st that 's low'st, hee 's surest in that 's out,
He hits the next way that goes farth'st about,
He getteth vp vnlike to rise at all,
He slips to ground as much vnlike to fall;
Which doth inforce me partly to prefer,   40
Zeno. The opinion of that mad Philosopher,
Who taught, that those all-framing powers aboue,
(As 'tis suppos'd) made man not out of loue

To him at all, but only as a thing,
To make them sport with, which they vse to bring
As men doe munkeys, puppets, and such tooles
Of laughter: so men are but the Gods fooles.
Such are by titles lifted to the sky,
As wherefore no man knowes, God scarcely why;
The vertuous man depressed like a stone,   50
For that dull Sot to raise himselfe vpon;
He who ne're thing yet worthy man durst doe,
Neuer durst looke vpon his countrey's foe,
Nor durst attempt that action which might get
Him fame with men: or higher might him set
Then the base begger (rightly if compar'd;)
This Drone yet neuer braue attempt that dar'd,
Yet dares be knighted, and from thence dares grow
To any title Empire can bestow;
For this beleeue, that Impudence is now   60
A Cardinall vertue, and men it allow
Reuerence, nay more, men study and inuent
New wayes, nay, glory to be impudent.
    Into the clouds the Deuill lately got,
And by the moisture doubting much the rot,
A medicine tooke to make him purge and cast;
Which in short time began to worke so fast,
That he fell too 't, and from his backeside flew,
A rout of rascall a rude ribauld crew
Of base Plebeians, which no sooner light,   70
Vpon the earth, but with a suddaine flight,
They spread this Ile, and as Deucalion once
Ouer his shoulder backe, by throwing stones
They became men, euen so these beasts became,
Owners of titles from an obscure name.
    He that by riot, of a mighty rent,
Hath his late goodly Patrimony spent,
And into base and wilfull beggery run
This man as he some glorious acte had done,
With some great pension, or rich guift releeu'd,   80
When he that hath by industry atchieu'd
Some noble thing, contemned and disgrac'd,
In the forlorne hope of the times is plac'd,
As though that God had carelessely left all
That being hath on this terrestriall ball,
To fortunes guiding, nor would haue to doe
With man, nor aught that doth belong him to,
Or at the least God hauing giuen more

Power to the Deuill, then he did of yore,
Ouer this world: the feind as he doth hate90
The vertuous man; maligning his estate,
All noble things, and would haue by his will,
To be damn'd with him, vsing all his skill,
By his blacke hellish ministers to vexe
All worthy men, and strangely to perplexe
Their constancie, there by them so to fright,
That they should yeeld them wholely to his might.
But of these things I vainely doe but tell,
Where hell is heauen, and heau'n is now turn'd hell;
Where that which lately blasphemy hath bin,   100
Now godlinesse, much lesse accounted sin;
And a long while I greatly meruail'd why
Buffoons and Bawdes should hourely multiply,
Till that of late I construed it that they
To present thrift had got the perfect way,
When I concluded by their odious crimes,
It was for vs no thriuing in these times.
      As men oft laugh at little Babes, when they
Hap to behold some strange thing in their play,
To see them on the suddaine strucken sad,   110
As in their fancie some strange formes they had,
Which they by pointing with their fingers showe,
Angry at our capacities so slowe,
That by their countenance we no sooner learne
To see the wonder which they so discerne:
So the celestiall powers doe sit and smile
At innocent and vertuous men the while,
They stand amazed at the world ore-gone,
So farre beyond imagination,
With slauish basenesse, that the silent sit   120
Pointing like children in describing it.
      Then noble friend the next way to controule
These worldly crosses, is to arme thy soule
With constant patience: and with thoughts as high
As these be lowe, and poore, winged to flye
To that exalted stand, whether yet they
Are got with paine, that sit out of the way
Of this ignoble age, which raiseth none
But such as thinke their black damnation
To be a trifle; such, so ill, that when   130
They are aduanc'd, those few poore honest men
That yet are liuing, into search doe runne
To finde what mischiefe they haue lately done,

Which so preferres them; say thou he doth rise,
That maketh vertue his chiefe exercise.
And in this base world come what euer shall,
Hees worth lamenting, that for her doth fall.

Vpon the three Sonnes of the Lord SHEFFIELD, drowned in HVMBER

    Light Sonnets hence, and to loose Louers flie,
And mournfull Maydens sing an Elegie
On those three SHEFFIELDS, ouer-whelm'd with waues,
Whose losse the teares of all the Muses craues;
A thing so full of pitty as this was,
Me thinkes for nothing should not slightly passe.
Treble this losse was, why should it not borrowe,
Through this Iles treble parts, a treble sorrowe:
But Fate did this, to let the world to knowe,
That sorrowes which from common causes growe,   10
Are not worth mourning for, the losse to beare,
But of one onely sonne, 's not worth one teare.
Some tender-hearted man, as I, may spend
Some drops (perhaps) for a deceased friend.
Some men (perhaps) their Wifes late death may rue;
Or Wifes their Husbands, but such be but fewe.
Cares that haue vs'd the hearts of men to tuch
So oft, and deepely, will not now be such;
Who'll care for loss of maintenance, or place,
Fame, liberty, or of the Princes grace;   20
Or sutes in law, by base corruption crost,
When he shall finde, that this which he hath lost,
Alas, is nothing to his, which did lose,
Three sonnes at once so excellent as those:
Nay, it is feard that this in time may breed
Hard hearts in men to their owne naturall seed;
That in respect of this great losse of theirs,
Men will scarce mourne the death of their owne heires.
    Through all this Ile their losse so publique is,
That euery man doth take them to be his,   30
And as a plague which had beginning there,
So catching is, and raigning euery where,
That those the farthest off as much doe rue them,
As those the most familiarly that knew them;
Children with this disaster are wext sage,
And like to men that strucken are in age;
Talke what it is, three children at one time
Thus to haue drown'd, and in their very prime;

Yea, and doe learne to act the same so well,
That then olde folke, they better can it tell.   40
Inuention, oft that Passion vs'd to faine,
In sorrowes of themselves but slight, and meane,
To make them seeme great, here it shall not need,
For that this Subiect doth so farre exceed
All forc'd Expression, that what Poesie shall
Happily thinke to grace it selfe withall,
Falls so belowe it, that it rather borrowes
Grace from their griefe, then addeth to their sorrowes,
For sad mischance thus in the losse of three,
To shewe it selfe the vtmost it could bee: 50
Exacting also by the selfe same lawe,
The vtmost teares that sorrowe had to drawe
All future times hath vtterly preuented
Of a more losse, or more to be lamented.
    Whilst in faire youth they liuely flourish'd here,
To their kinde Parents they were onely deere:
But being dead, now euery one doth take
Them for their owne, and doe like sorrowe make:
As for their owne begot, as they pretended
Hope in the issue, which should haue discended   60
From them againe; nor here doth end our sorrow,
But those of vs, that shall be borne to morrowe
Still shall lament them, and when time shall count,
To what vast number passed yeares shall mount,
They from their death shall duly reckon so,
As from the Deluge, former vs'd to doe.
    O cruell Humber guilty of their gore,
I now beleeue more then I did before
The Brittish Story, whence thy name begun
Of Kingly Humber, an inuading Hun,   70
By thee deuoured, for't is likely thou
With blood wert Christned, bloud-thirsty till now.
The Ouse, the Done, and thou farre clearer Trent,
To drowne the SHEFFIELDS as you gaue consent,
Shall curse the time, that ere you were infus'd,
Which haue your waters basely thus abus'd.
The groueling Boore yee hinder not to goe,
And at his pleasure Ferry to and fro.
The very best part of whose soule, and bloud,
Compared with theirs, is viler then your mud.   80
But wherefore paper, doe I idely spend,
On those deafe waters to so little end,
And vp to starry heauen doe I not looke,

In which, as in an euerlasting booke,
Our ends are written; O let times rehearse
Their fatall losse, in their sad Aniuerse.

To the noble Lady, the Lady I.S. of worldly crosses

 Madame, to shew the smoothnesse of my vaine,
Neither that I would haue you entertaine
The time in reading me, which you would spend
In faire discourse with some knowne honest friend,
I write not to you. Nay, and which is more,
My powerfull verses striue not to restore,
What time and sicknesse haue in you impair'd,
To other ends my Elegie is squar'd.
 Your beauty, sweetnesse, and your gracefull parts
That haue drawne many eyes, wonne many hearts,   10
Of me get little, I am so much man,
That let them doe their vtmost that they can,
I will resist their forces: and they be
Though great to others, yet not so to me.
The first time I beheld you, I then sawe
That (in it selfe) which had the power to drawe
My stayd affection, and thought to allowe
You some deale of my heart; but you have now
Got farre into it, and you haue the skill
(For ought I see) to winne vpon me still.   20
 When I doe thinke how brauely you haue borne
Your many crosses, as in Fortunes scorne,
And how neglectfull you have seem'd to be,
Of that which hath seem'd terrible to me,
I thought you stupid, nor that you had felt
Those griefes which (often) I haue scene to melt
Another woman into sighes and teares,
A thing but seldome in your sexe and yeares,
But when in you I haue perceiu'd agen,
(Noted by me, more then by other men)   30
How feeling and how sensible you are
Of your friends sorrowes, and with how much care
You seeke to cure them, then my selfe I blame,
That I your patience should so much misname,
Which to my vnderstanding maketh knowne
Who feeles anothers griefe, can feele their owne.
When straight me thinkes, I heare your patience say,
Are you the man that studied Seneca:
Plinies most learned letters; and must I

Read you a Lecture in Philosophie, 40
T'auoid the afflictions that haue vs'd to reach you;
I'le learne you more, Sir, then your bookes can teach you.
    Of all your sex, yet neuer did I knowe,
Any that yet so actually could showe
Such rules for patience, such an easie way,
That who so sees it, shall be forc'd to say,
Loe what before seem'd hard to be discern'd,
Is of this Lady, in an instant learn'd.
It is heauens will that you should wronged be
By the malicious, that the world might see 50
Your Doue-like meekenesse; for had the base scumme,
The spawne of Fiends, beene in your slander dumbe,
Your vertue then had perish'd, neuer priz'd,
For that the same you had not exercised;
And you had lost the Crowne you haue, and glory,
Nor had you beene the subiect of my Story.
Whilst they feele Hell, being damned in their hate,
Their thoughts like Deuils them excruciate,
Which by your noble suffrings doe torment
Them with new paines, and giues you this content 60
To see your soule an Innocent, hath suffred,
And vp to heauen before your eyes be offred:
Your like we in a burning Glasse may see,
When the Sunnes rayes therein contracted be
Bent on some obiect, which is purely white,
We finde that colour doth dispierce the light,
And stands vntainted: but if it hath got
Some little sully; or the least small spot,
Then it soon fiers it; so you still remaine
Free, because in you they can finde no staine. 70
    God doth not loue them least, on whom he layes
The great'st afflictions; but that he will praise
Himselfe most in them, and will make them fit,
Near'st to himselfe who is the Lambe to sit:
For by that touch, like perfect gold he tries them,
Who are not his, vntill the world denies them.
And your example may work such effect,
That it may be the beginning of a Sect
Of patient women; and that many a day
All Husbands may for you their Founder pray. 80
    Nor is to me your Innocence the lesse,
In that I see you striue not to suppresse
Their barbarous malice; but your noble heart
Prepar'd to act so difficult a part,

With vnremoued constancie is still
The same it was, that of your proper ill,
The effect proceeds from your owne selfe the cause,
Like some iust Prince, who to establish lawes,
Suffers the breach at his best lou'd to strike,
To learne the vulgar to endure the like.   90
You are a Martir thus, nor can you be
Lesse to the world so valued by me:
If as you haue begun, you still perseuer
Be euer good, that I may loue you euer.

An Elegie vpon the death of the Lady PENELOPE CLIFTON

    Must I needes write, who's hee that can refuse,
He wants a minde, for her that hath no Muse,
The thought of her doth heau'nly rage inspire,
Next powerfull, to those clouen tongues of fire.
    Since I knew ought time neuer did allowe
Me stuffe fit for an Elegie, till now;
When France and England's HENRIES dy'd, my quill,
Why, I know not, but it that time lay still.
'Tis more then greatnesse that my spirit must raise,
To obserue custome I vse not to praise;   10
Nor the least thought of mine yet ere depended,
On any one from whom she was descended;
That for their fauour I this way should wooe,
As some poor wretched things (perhaps) may doe;
I gaine the end, whereat I onely ayme,
If by my freedome, I may giue her fame.
    Walking then forth being newly vp from bed,
O Sir (quoth one) the Lady CLIFTON'S dead.
When, but that reason my sterne rage withstood,
My hand had sure beene guilty of his blood.   20
If shee be so, must thy rude tongue confesse it
(Quoth I) and com'st so coldly to expresse it.
Thou shouldst haue giuen a shreeke, to make me feare thee;
That might haue slaine what euer had beene neere thee.
Thou shouldst haue com'n like Time with thy scalpe bare,
And in thy hands thou shouldst haue brought thy haire,
Casting vpon me such a dreadfull looke,
As seene a spirit, or th'adst beene thunder-strooke,
And gazing on me so a little space,
Thou shouldst haue shot thine eye balls in my face,   30
Then falling at my feet, thou shouldst haue said,
O she is gone, and Nature with her dead.

With this ill newes amaz'd by chance I past,
By that neere Groue, whereas both first and last,
I saw her, not three moneths before shee di'd.
When (though full Summer gan to vaile her pride,
And that I sawe men leade home ripened Corne,
Besides aduis'd me well,) I durst haue sworne
The lingring yeare, the Autumne had adiourn'd,
And the fresh Spring had beene againe return'd,   40
Her delicacie, louelinesse, and grace,
With such a Summer brauery deckt the place:
But now alas, it lookt forlorne and dead;
And where she stood, the fading leaues were shed,
Presenting onely sorrowe to my sight,
O God (thought I) this is her Embleme right.
And sure I thinke it cannot but be thought,
That I to her by prouidence was brought.
For that the Fates fore-dooming, shee should die,
Shewed me this wondrous Master peece, that I   50
Should sing her Funerall, that the world should know it,
That heauen did thinke her worthy of a Poet;
My hand is fatall, nor doth fortune doubt,
For what it writes, not fire shall ere race out.
A thousand silken Puppets should haue died,
And in their fulsome Coffins putrified,
Ere in my lines, you of their names should heare
To tell the world that such there euer were,
Whose memory shall from the earth decay,
Before those Rags be worne they gaue away: 60
Had I her god-like features neuer seene,
Poore slight Report had tolde me she had beene
A hansome Lady, comely, very well,
And so might I haue died an Infidell,
As many doe which neuer did her see,
Or cannot credit, what she was, by mee.
    Nature, her selfe, that before Art prefers
To goe beyond all our Cosmographers,
By Charts and Maps exactly that haue showne,
All of this earth that euer can be knowne,   70
For that she would beyond them all descrie
What Art could not by any mortall eye;
A Map of heauen in her rare features drue,
And that she did so liuely and so true,
That any soule but seeing it might sweare
That all was perfect heauenly that was there.
If euer any Painter were so blest,

To drawe that face, which so much heau'n exprest,
If in his best of skill he did her right,
I wish it neuer may come in my sight, 80
I greatly doubt my faith (weake man) lest I
Should to that face commit Idolatry.
    Death might haue tyth'd her sex, but for this one,
Nay, haue ta'n halfe to haue let her alone;
Such as their wrinkled temples to supply,
Cyment them vp with sluttish Mercury,
Such as vndrest were able to affright,
A valiant man approching him by night;
Death might haue taken such, her end deferd,
Vntill the time she had beene climaterd; 90
When she would haue bin at threescore yeares and three,
Such as our best at three and twenty be,
With enuie then, he might haue ouerthrowne her,
When age nor time had power to ceaze vpon her.
    But when the vnpittying Fates her end decreed,
They to the same did instantly proceed,
For well they knew (if she had languish'd so)
As those which hence by naturall causes goe,
So many prayers, and teares for her had spoken,
As certainly their Iron lawes had broken, 100
And had wak'd heau'n, who clearely would haue show'd
That change of Kingdomes to her death it ow'd;
And that the world still of her end might thinke,
It would haue let some Neighbouring mountaine sinke.
Or the vast Sea it in on vs to cast,
As Seuerne did about some fiue yeares past:
Or some sterne Comet his curld top to reare,
Whose length should measure halfe our Hemisphere.
Holding this height, to say some will not sticke,
That now I raue, and am growne lunatique: 110
You of what sexe so ere you be, you lye,
'Tis thou thy selfe is lunatique, not I.
I charge you in her name that now is gone,
That may coniure you, if you be not stone,
That you no harsh, nor shallow rimes decline,
Vpon that day wherein you shall read mine.
Such as indeed are falsely termed verse,
And will but sit like mothes vpon her herse;
Nor that no child, nor chambermaide, nor page,
Disturbe the Rome, the whilst my sacred rage, 120
In reading is; but whilst you heare it read,
Suppose, before you, that you see her dead,

The walls about you hung with mournfull blacke,
And nothing of her funerall to lacke,
And when this period giues you leaue to pause,
Cast vp your eyes, and sigh for my applause.

Vpon the noble Lady ASTONS departure for Spaine

I many a time haue greatly marueil'd, why
Men say, their friends depart when as they die,
How well that word, a dying, doth expresse,
I did not know (I freely must confesse,)
Till her departure: for whose missed sight,
I am enforc'd this Elegy to write:
But since resistlesse fate will haue it so,
That she from hence must to Iberia goe,
And my weak wishes can her not detaine,
I will of heauen in policy complaine,   10
That it so long her trauell should adiourne,
Hoping thereby to hasten her returne.
    [1]Can those of Norway for their wage procure,
By their blacke spells a winde that shall endure
Northerly Till from aboard the wished land men see,
And fetch the harbour, where they long to be,
Can they by charmes doe this and cannot I
 Who am the Priest of Phoebus, and so hie,
Sit in his fauour, winne the Poets god,
To send swift Hermes with his snaky rod,   20
To Æolus Caue, commanding him with care,
His prosperous winds, that he for her prepare,
And from that howre, wherein shee takes the seas,
Nature bring on the quiet Halcion dayes,
And in that hower that bird begin her nest,
Nay at that very instant, that long rest
May seize on Neptune, who may still repose,
And let that bird nere till that hower disclose,
Wherein she landeth, and for all that space
Be not a wrinkle seene on Thetis face,   30
Onely so much breath with a gentle gale,
As by the easy swelling of her saile,
May at [2]Sebastians safely set her downe
Where, with her goodnes she may blesse the towne.
If heauen in iustice would haue plagu'd by thee

---

[1] The witches of the legions sell windes to passengers.
[2] The nearest Harbour of Spaine.

Some Pirate, and grimme Neptune thou should'st be
His Executioner, or what is his worse,
The gripple Merchant, borne to be the curse
Of this braue Iland; let them for her sake,
Who to thy safeguard doth her selfe betake,   40
Escape vndrown'd, vnwrackt, nay rather let
Them be at ease in some safe harbour set,
Where with much profit they may vent their wealth
That they haue got by villany and stealth,
Rather great Neptune, then when thou dost raue,
Thou once shouldst wet her saile but with a waue.
    Or if some proling Rouer shall but dare,
To seize the ship wherein she is to fare,
Let the fell fishes of the Maine appeare,
And tell those Sea-thiefes, that once such they were   50
As they are now, till they assaid to rape
Grape-crowned Bacchus in a striplings shape,
That came aboard them, and would faine haue saild,
To vine-spread [3]Naxus but that him they faild,
Which he perceiuing, them so monstrous made,
And warnd them how they passengers inuade.
    Ye South and Westerne winds now cease to blow
Autumne is come, there be no flowers to grow,
Yea from that place respire, to which she goes,
And to her sailes should show your selfe but foes,   60
But Boreas and yee Esterne windes arise,
To send her soon to Spaine, but be precise,
That in your aide you seeme not still so sterne,
As we a summer should no more discerne,
For till that here againe, I may her see,
It will be winter all the yeare with mee.
    [4]Ye swanne-begotten lonely brother-stars,
So oft auspicious to poore Mariners,
Ye twin-bred lights of louely Leda's brood,
Ioues egge-borne issue smile vpon the flood,   70
And in your mild'st aspect doe ye appeare
To be her warrant from all future feare.
And if thou ship that bear'st her, doe proue good,
May neuer time by wormes, consume thy wood
Nor rust thy iron, may thy tacklings last,
Till they for reliques be in temples plac't;

---

[3] An Ile for the abundance of wine supposed to be the habitation of Bachus.
[4] Castor and Polox begot by Ioue on Leda in the forme of a Swanne. A constellation ominous to Mariners.

Maist thou be ranged with that mighty Arke,
Wherein iust Noah did all the world imbarque,
With that which after Troyes so famous wracke,
From ten yeares trauell brought Vlisses backe,   80
That Argo which to Colchos went from Greece,
And in her botome brought the goulden fleece
Vnder braue Iason; or that same of Drake,
Wherein he did his famous voyage make
About the world; or Candishes that went
As far as his, about the Continent.
 And yee milde winds that now I doe implore,
Not once to raise the least sand on the shore,
Nor once on forfait of your selues respire:
When once the time is come of her retire,   90
If then it please you, but to doe your due,
What for these windes I did, Ile doe for you;
Ile wooe you then, and if that not suffice,
My pen shall prooue you to haue dietyes,
Ile sing your loues in verses that shall flow,
And tell the storyes of your weale and woe,
Ile prooue what profit to the earth you bring,
And how t'is you that welcome in the spring;
Ile raise vp altars to you, as to show,
The time shall be kept holy, when you blow.   100
O blessed winds! your will that it may be,
To send health to her, and her home to me.

To my most dearely-loued friend HENERY REYNOLDS Esquire, of Poets & Poesie

My dearely loued friend how oft haue we,
In winter evenings (meaning to be free,)
To some well-chosen place vs'd to retire;
And there with moderate meate, and wine, and fire,
Haue past the howres contentedly with chat,
Now talk of this, and then discours'd of that,
Spoke our owne verses 'twixt our selves, if not
Other mens lines, which we by chance had got,
Or some Stage pieces famous long before,
Of which your happy memory had store;   10
And I remember you much pleased were,
Of those who liued long agoe to heare,
As well as of those, of these latter times,
Who have inricht our language with their rimes,
And in succession, how still vp they grew,

Which is the subiect, that I now pursue;
For from my cradle, (you must know that) I,
Was still inclin'd to noble Poesie,
And when that once Pueriles I had read,
And newly had my Cato construed,   20
In my small selfe I greatly marueil'd then,
Amonst all other, what strange kinde of men
These Poets were; And pleased with the name,
To my milde Tutor merrily I came,
(For I was then a proper goodly page,
Much like a Pigmy, scarse ten yeares of age)
Clasping my slender armes about his thigh.
O my deare master! cannot you (quoth I)
Make me a Poet, doe it if you can,
And you shall see, Ile quickly bee a man,   30
Who me thus answered smiling, boy quoth he,
If you'le not play the wag, but I may see
You ply your learning, I will shortly read
Some Poets to you; Phoebus be my speed,
Too't hard went I, when shortly he began,
And first read to me honest Mantuan,
Then Virgils Eglogues, being entred thus,
Me thought I straight had mounted Pegasus,
And in his full Careere could make him stop,
And bound vpon Parnassus' by-clift top.   40
I scornd your ballet then though it were done
And had for Finis, William Elderton.
But soft, in sporting with this childish iest,
I from my subiect haue too long digrest,
Then to the matter that we tooke in hand,
Ioue and Apollo for the Muses stand.
      Then noble Chaucer, in those former times,
The first inrich'd our English with his rimes,
And was the first of ours, that euer brake,
Into the Muses treasure, and first spake   50
In weighty numbers, deluing in the Mine
Of perfect knowledge, which he could refine,
And coyne for currant, and as much as then
The English language could expresse to men,
He made it doe; and by his wondrous skill,
Gaue vs much light from his abundant quill.
      And honest Gower, who in respect of him,
Had only sipt at Aganippas brimme,
And though in yeares this last was him before,
Yet fell he far short of the others store.   60

When after those, foure ages very neare,
They with the Muses which conuersed, were
That Princely Surrey, early in the time
Of the Eight Henry, who was then the prime
Of Englands noble youth; with him there came
Wyat; with reuerence whom we still doe name
Amongst our Poets, Brian had a share
With the two former, which accompted are
That times best makers, and the authors were
Of those small poems, which the title beare,   70
Of songs and sonnets, wherein oft they hit
On many dainty passages of wit.
    Gascoine and Churchyard after them againe
In the beginning of Eliza's raine,
Accoumpted were great Meterers many a day,
But not inspired with braue fier, had they
Liu'd but a little longer, they had seene,
Their works before them to have buried beene.
    Graue morrall Spencer after these came on
Then whom I am perswaded there was none   80
Since the blind Bard his Iliads vp did make,
Fitter a taske like that to vndertake,
To set downe boldly, brauely to inuent,
In all high knowledge, surely excellent.
    The noble Sidney with this last arose,
That Heroe for numbers, and for Prose.
That throughly pac'd our language as to show,
The plenteous English hand in hand might goe
With Greek or Latine, and did first reduce
Our tongue from Lillies writing then in vse;   90
Talking of Stones, Stars, Plants, of fishes, Flyes,
Playing with words, and idle Similies,
As th' English, Apes and very Zanies be,
Of euery thing, that they doe heare and see,
So imitating his ridiculous tricks,
They spake and writ, all like meere lunatiques.
    Then Warner though his lines were not so trim'd,
Nor yet his Poem so exactly lim'd
And neatly ioynted, but the Criticke may
Easily reprooue him, yet thus let me say;   100
For my old friend, some passages there be
In him, which I protest haue taken me,
With almost wonder, so fine, cleere, and new
As yet they haue bin equalled by few.
    Neat Marlow bathed in the Thespian springs

Had in him those braue translunary things,
That the first Poets had, his raptures were,
All ayre, and fire, which made his verses cleere,
For that fine madnes still he did retaine,
Which rightly should possesse a Poets braine.   110
    And surely Nashe, though he a Proser were
A branch of Lawrell yet deserues to beare,
Sharply Satirick was he, and that way
He went, since that his being, to this day
Few haue attempted, and I surely thinke
Those wordes shall hardly be set downe with inke;
Shall scorch and blast, so as his could, where he,
Would inflict vengeance, and be it said of thee,
Shakespeare, thou hadst as smooth a Comicke vaine,
Fitting the socke, and in thy naturall braine,   120
As strong conception, and as Cleere a rage,
As any one that trafiqu'd with the stage.
    Amongst these Samuel Daniel, whom if I
May spake of, but to sensure doe denie,
Onely haue heard some wisemen him rehearse,
To be too much Historian in verse;
His rimes were smooth, his meeters well did close
But yet his maner better fitted prose:
Next these, learn'd Johnson, in this List I bring,
Who had drunke deepe of the Pierian spring,   130
Whose knowledge did him worthily prefer,
And long was Lord here of the Theater,
Who in opinion made our learn'st to sticke,
Whether in Poems rightly dramatique,
Strong Seneca or Plautus, he or they,
Should beare the Buskin, or the Socke away.
Others againe here liued in my dayes,
That haue of vs deserued no lesse praise
For their translations, then the daintiest wit
That on Parnassus thinks, he highst doth sit,   140
And for a chaire may mongst the Muses call,
As the most curious maker of them all;
As reuerent Chapman, who hath brought to vs,
Musæus, Homer and Hesiodus
Out of the Greeke; and by his skill hath reard
Them to that height, and to our tongue endear'd,
That were those Poets at this day aliue,
To see their bookes thus with vs to suruiue,
They would think, hauing neglected them so long,
They had bin written in the English tongue.   150

And Siluester who from the French more weake,
Made Bartas of his sixe dayes labour speake
In naturall English, who, had he there stayd,
He had done well, and neuer had bewraid
His owne inuention, to haue bin so poore
Who still wrote lesse, in striuing to write more.
    Then dainty Sands that hath to English done,
Smooth sliding Ouid, and hath made him run
With so much sweetnesse and vnusuall grace,
As though the neatnesse of the English pace,   160
Should tell the Ietting Lattine that it came
But slowly after, as though stiff and lame.
    So Scotland sent vs hither, for our owne
That man, whose name I euer would haue knowne,
To stand by mine, that most ingenious knight,
My Alexander, to whom in his right,
I want extreamely, yet in speaking thus
I doe but shew the loue, that was twixt vs,
And not his numbers which were braue and hie,
So like his mind, was his clear Poesie,   170
And my deare Drummond to whom much I owe
For his much loue, and proud I was to know,
His poesie, for which two worthy men,
I Menstry still shall loue, and Hauthorne-den.
Then the two Beamounts and my Browne arose,
My deare companions whom I freely chose
My bosome friends; and in their seuerall wayes,
Rightly borne Poets, and in these last dayes,
Men of much note, and no lesse nobler parts,
Such as haue freely tould to me their hearts,   180
As I have mine to them; but if you shall
Say in your knowledge, that these be not all
Haue writ in numbers, be inform'd that I
Only my selfe, to these few men doe tye,
Whose works oft printed, set on euery post,
To publique censure subiect haue bin most;
For such whose poems, be they nere so rare,
In priuate chambers, that incloistered are,
And by transcription daintyly must goe;
As though the world vnworthy were to know,   190
Their rich composures, let those men that keepe
These wonderous reliques in their iudgement deepe;
And cry them vp so, let such Peeces bee
Spoke of by those that shall come after me,
I passe not for them: nor doe meane to run,

In quest of these, that them applause haue wonne,
Vpon our Stages in these latter dayes,
That are so many, let them haue their bayes
That doe deserue it; let those wits that haunt
Those publique circuits, let them freely chaunt   200
Their fine Composures, and their praise pursue
And so my deare friend, for this time adue.

Vpon the death of his incomparable friend Sir HENRY RAYNSFORD of CLIFFORD

Could there be words found to expresse my losse,
There were some hope, that this my heauy crosse
Might be sustained, and that wretched I
Might once finde comfort: but to haue him die
Past all degrees that was so deare to me;
As but comparing him with others, hee
Was such a thing, as if some Power should say
I'le take Man on me, to shew men the way
What a friend should be. But words come so short
Of him, that when I thus would him report,   10
I am vndone, and hauing nought to say,
Mad at my selfe, I throwe my penne away,
And beate my breast, that there should be a woe
So high, that words cannot attaine thereto.
T'is strange that I from my abundant breast,
Who others sorrowes haue so well exprest:
Yet I by this in little time am growne
So poore, that I want to expresse mine owne.
I thinke the Fates perceiuing me to beare
My worldly crosses without wit or feare: 20
Nay, with what scorne I euer haue derided,
Those plagues that for me they haue oft prouided,
Drew them to counsaile; nay, conspired rather,
And in this businesse laid their heads together
To finde some one plague, that might me subuert,
And at an instant breake my stubborne heart;
They did indeede, and onely to this end
They tooke from me this more then man, or friend.
Hard-hearted Fates, your worst thus haue you done,
Then let vs see what lastly you haue wonne   30
By this your rigour, in a course so strict,
Why see, I beare all that you can inflict:
And hee from heauen your poore reuenge to view,
Laments my losse of him, but laughes at you,

Whilst I against you execrations breath;
Thus are you scorn'd aboue, and curst beneath.
  Me thinks that man (vnhappy though he be)
Is now thrice happy in respect of me,
Who hath no friend; for that in hauing none
He is not stirr'd as I am, to bemone   40
My miserable losse, who but in vaine,
May euer looke to find the like againe.
This more then mine own selfe; that who had seene
His care of me where euer I had beene,
And had not knowne his actiue spirit before,
Vpon some braue thing working euermore:
He would haue sworne that to no other end
He had been borne: but onely for my friend.
I had been happy if nice Nature had
(Since now my lucke falls out to be so bad)   50
Made me vnperfect, either of so soft
And yeelding temper, that lamenting oft,
I into teares my mournefull selfe might melt;
Or else so dull, my losse not to haue felt.
I haue by my too deare experience bought,
That fooles and mad men, whom I euer thought
The most vnhappy, are in deede not so:
And therefore I lesse pittie can bestowe
(Since that my sence, my sorrowe so can sound)
On those in Bedlam that are bound,   60
And scarce feele scourging; and when as I meete
A foole by Children followed in the Streete,
Thinke I (poor wretch) thou from my griefe art free,
Nor couldst thou feele it, should it light on thee;
But that I am a Christian, and am taught
By him who with his precious bloud me bought,
Meekly like him my crosses to endure,
Else would they please me well, that for their cure,
When as they feele their conscience doth them brand,
Vpon themselues dare lay a violent hand;   70
Not suffering Fortune with her murdering knife,
Stand like a Surgeon working on the life,
Deserting this part, that ioynt off to cut,
Shewing that Artire, ripping then that gut,
Whilst the dull beastly World with her squint eye,
Is to behold the strange Anatomie.
  I am persuaded that those which we read
To be man-haters, were not so indeed,
The Athenian Timon, and beside him more

Of which the Latines, as the Greekes haue store;   80
Nor not did they all humane manners hate,
Nor yet maligne mans dignity and state.
But finding our fraile life how euery day,
It like a bubble vanisheth away:
For this condition did mankinde detest,
Farre more incertaine then that of the beast.
    Sure heauen doth hate this world and deadly too,
Else as it hath done it would neuer doe,
For if it did not, it would ne're permit
A man of so much vertue, knowledge, wit,   90
Of naturall goodnesse, supernaturall grace,
Whose courses when considerately I trace
Into their ends, and diligently looke,
They serue me for Oeconomike booke.
By which this rough world I not onely stemme,
In goodnesse but grow learn'd by reading them.
    O pardon me, it my much sorrow is,
Which makes me vse this long Parenthesis;
Had heauen this world not hated as I say,
In height of life it had not, tane away   100
A spirit so braue, so actiue, and so free,
That such a one who would not wish to bee,
Rather then weare a Crowne, by Armes though got,
So fast a friend, so true a Patriot.
In things concerning both the worlds so wise,
Besides so liberall of his faculties,
That where he would his industrie bestowe,
He would haue done, e're one could think to doe.
No more talke of the working of the Starres,
For plenty, scarcenesse, or for peace, or Warres: 110
They are impostures, therefore get you hence
With all your Planets, and their influence.
No more doe I care into them to looke,
Then in some idle Chiromantick booke,
Shewing the line of life, and Venus mount,
Nor yet no more would I of them account,
Then what that tells me, since what that so ere
Might promise man long life: of care and feare,
By nature freed, a conscience cleare, and quiet,
His health, his constitution, and his diet;   120
Counting a hundred, fourscore at the least,
Propt vp by prayers, yet more to be encreast,
All these should faile, and in his fiftieth yeare
He should expire, henceforth let none be deare,

To me at all, lest for my haplesse sake,
Before their time heauen from the world them take,
And leaue me wretched to lament their ends
As I doe his, who was a thousand friends.

Vpon the death of the Lady OLIVE STANHOPE

Canst thou depart and be forgotten so,
STANHOPE thou canst not, no deare STANHOPE, no:
But in despight of death the world shall see,
That Muse which so much graced was by thee
Can black Obliuion vtterly out-braue,
And set thee vp aboue thy silent Graue.
I meruail'd much the Derbian Nimphes were dumbe,
Or of those Muses, what should be become,
That of all those, the mountaines there among,
Not one this while thy Epicediumsung;   10
But so it is, when they of thee were reft,
They all those hills, and all those Riuers left,
And sullen growne, their former seates remoue,
Both from cleare Darwin, and from siluer Doue,
And for thy losse, they greeued are so sore,
That they haue vow'd they will come there no more;
But leaue thy losse to me, that I should rue thee,
Vnhappy man, and yet I neuer knew thee:
Me thou didst loue vnseene, so did I thee,
It was our spirits that lou'd then and not wee;   20
Therefore without profanenesse I may call
The loue betwixt vs, loue spirituall:
But that which thou affectedst was so true,
As that thereby thee perfectly I knew;
And now that spirit, which thou so lou'dst, still mine,
Shall offer this a Sacrifice to thine,
And reare this Trophe, which for thee shall last,
When this most beastly Iron age is past;
I am perswaded, whilst we two haue slept,
Our soules haue met, and to each other wept,   30
That destenie so strongly should forbid,
Our bodies to conuerse as oft they did:
For certainly refined spirits doe know,
As doe the Angels, and doe here belowe
Take the fruition of that endlesse blisse,
As those aboue doe, and what each one is.
They see diuinely, and as those there doe,
They know each others wills, so soules can too.

About that dismall time, thy spirit hence flew,
Mine much was troubled, but why, I not knew,   40
In dull and sleepy sounds, it often left me,
As of it selfe it ment to haue bereft me,
I asked it what the cause was, of such woe,
Or what it might be, that might vexe it so,
But it was deafe, nor my demand would here,
But when that ill newes came, to touch mine eare,
I straightwayes found this watchfull sperit of mine,
Troubled had bin to take it leaue of thine,
For when fate found, what nature late had done,
How much from heauen, she for the earth had won   50
By thy deare birth; said, that it could not be
In so yong yeares, what it perceiu'd in thee,
But nature sure, had fram'd thee long before;
And as Rich Misers of their mighty store,
Keepe the most precious longst, so from times past,
She onely had reserued thee till the last;
So did thy wisedome, not thy youth behold,
And tooke thee hence, in thinking thou wast old.
Thy shape and beauty often haue to me
Bin highly praysed, which I thought might be,   60
Truely reported, for a spirit so braue,
Which heauen to thee so bountifully gaue;
Nature could not in recompence againe,
In some rich lodging but to entertaine.
Let not the world report then, that the Peake,
Is but a rude place only vast and bleake;
And nothing hath to boast of but her Lead,
When she can say that happily she bred
Thee, and when she shall of her wonders tell
Wherein she doth all other Tracts excell,   70
Let her account thee greatst, and still to time
Of all the rest, accord thee for the prime.

To Master WILLIAM IEFFREYS, Chaplaine to the Lord Ambassadour in Spaine

My noble friend, you challenge me to write
To you in verse, and often you recite,
My promise to you, and to send you newes;
As 'tis a thing I very seldome vse,
And I must write of State, if to Madrid,
A thing our Proclamations here forbid,
And that word State such Latitude doth beare,
As it may make me very well to feare
To write, nay speake at all, these let you know
Your power on me, yet not that I will showe   10
The loue I beare you, in that lofty height,
So cleere expression, or such words of weight,
As into Spanish if they were translated,
Might make the Poets of that Realme amated;
Yet these my least were, but that you extort
These numbers from me, when I should report
In home-spunne prose, in good plaine honest words
The newes our wofull England vs affords.

The Muses here sit sad, and mute the while
A sort of swine vnseasonably defile   20
Those sacred springs, which from the by-clift hill
Dropt their pure Nectar into euery quill;
In this with State, I hope I doe not deale,
This onely tends the Muses common-weale.

What canst thou hope, or looke for from his pen,
Who liues with beasts, though in the shapes of men,
And what a poore few are we honest still,
And dare to be so, when all the world is ill.

I finde this age of our markt with this Fate,
That honest men are still precipitate   30
Vnder base villaines, which till th' earth can vent
This her last brood, and wholly hath them spent,
Shall be so, then in reuolution shall
Vertue againe arise by vices fall;
But that shall I not see, neither will I
Maintaine this, as one doth a Prophesie,
That our King Iames to Rome shall surely goe,
And from his chaire the Pope shall ouerthrow.
But O this world is so giuen vp to hell,
That as the old Giants, which did once rebell,   40
Against the Gods, so this now-liuing race
Dare sin, yet stand, and Ieere heauen in the face.

    But soft my Muse, and make a little stay,
Surely thou art not rightly in thy way,
To my good Ieffrayes was not I about
To write, and see, I suddainely am out,
This is pure Satire, that thou speak'st, and I
Was first in hand to write an Elegie.
To tell my countreys shame I not delight.
But doe bemoane 't I am no Democrite: 50
O God, though Vertue mightily doe grieue
For all this world, yet will I not beleeue
But that shees faire and louely, and that she
So to the period of the world shall be;
Else had she beene forsaken (sure) of all,
For that so many sundry mischiefes fall
Vpon her dayly, and so many take
Armes vp against her, as it well might make
Her to forsake her nature, and behind,
To leaue no step for future time to find,   60
As she had neuer beene, for he that now
Can doe her most disgrace, him they alow
The times chiefe Champion, and he is the man,
The prize, and Palme that absolutely wanne,
For where Kings Clossets her free seat hath bin
She neere the Lodge, not suffered is to Inne,
For ignorance against her stands in state,
Like some great porter at a Pallace gate;
So dull and barbarous lately are we growne,
And there are some this slauery that haue sowne,   70
That for mans knowledge it enough doth make,
If he can learne, to read an Almanacke;
By whom that trash of Amadis de Gaule,
Is held an author most authenticall,
And things we haue like Noblemen that be
In little time, which I haue hope to see
Vpon their foot-clothes, as the streets they ride
To haue their hornebookes at their girdles ti'd.
But all their superfluity of spite
On vertues hand-maid Poesy doth light,   80
And to extirpe her all their plots they lay,
But to her ruine they shall misse the way,
For his alone the Monuments of wit,
Aboue the rage of Tyrants that doe sit,
And from their strength, not one himselfe can saue,
But they shall tryumph o'r his hated graue.
    In my conceipt, friend, thou didst neuer see

A righter Madman then thou hast of me,
For now as Elegiack I bewaile
These poor base times; then suddainely I raile 90
And am Satirick, not that I inforce
My selfe to be so, but euen as remorse,
Or hate, in the proud fulnesse of their hight
Master my fancy, iust so doe I write.
    But gentle friend as soone shall I behold
That stone of which so many haue vs tould,
(Yet neuer any to this day could make)
The great Elixar or to vndertake
The Rose-crosse knowledge which is much like that
A Tarrying-iron for fooles to labour at, 100
As euer after I may hope to see,
(A plague vpon this beastly world for me,)
Wit so respected as it was of yore;
And if hereafter any it restore,
It must be those that yet for many a yeare,
Shall be vnborne that must inhabit here,
And such in vertue as shall be asham'd
Almost to heare their ignorant Grandsires nam'd,
With whom so many noble spirits then liu'd,
That were by them of all reward depriu'd. 110
    My noble friend, I would I might haue quit
This age of these, and that I might haue writ,
Before all other, how much the braue pen,
Had here bin honoured of the English men;
Goodnesse and knowledge, held by them in prise,
How hatefull to them Ignorance and vice;
But it falls out the contrary is true,
And so my Ieffreyes for this time adue.

Vpon the death of Mistris ELIANOR FALLOWFIELD

    Accursed Death, what neede was there at all
Of thee, or who to councell thee did call;
The subiect whereupon these lines I spend
For thee was most vnfit, her timelesse end
Too soone thou wroughtst, too neere her thou didst stand;
Thou shouldst haue lent thy leane and meager hand
To those who oft the help thereof beseech,
And can be cured by no other Leech.
    In this wide world how many thousands be,
That hauing past fourescore, doe call for thee. 10
The wretched debtor in the Iayle that lies,

Yet cannot this his Creditor suffice
Doth woe thee oft with many a sigh and teare,
Yet thou art coy, and him thou wilt not heare.
The Captiue slaue that tuggeth at the Oares,
And vnderneath the Bulls tough sinewes rores,
Begs at thy hand, in lieu of all his paines,
That thou wouldst but release him of his chaines;
Yet thou a niggard listenest not thereto,
With one short gaspe which thou mightst easily do,   20
But thou couldst come to her ere there was neede,
And euen at once destroy both flower and seede.
    But cruell Death if thou so barbarous be,
To those so goodly, and so young as shee;
That in their teeming thou wilt shew thy spight;
Either from marriage thou wilt Maides affright,
Or in their wedlock, Widowes liues to chuse
Their Husbands bed, and vtterly refuse,
Fearing conception; so shalt thou thereby
Extirpate mankinde by thy cruelty.   30
    If after direfull Tragedy thou thirst,
Extinguish Himens Torches at the first;
Build Funerall pyles, and the sad pauement strewe,
With mournfull Cypresse, and the pale-leau'd Yewe.
Away with Roses, Myrtle, and with Bayes;
Ensignes of mirth, and iollity, as these;
Neuer at Nuptials vsed be againe,
But from the Church the new Bride entertaine
With weeping Nenias, euer and among,
As at departings be sad Requiems song.   40
    Lucina by th' olde Poets that wert sayd,
Women in Childe-birth euermore to ayde,
Because thine Altars, long haue layne neglected:
Nor as they should, thy holy fiers reflected
Vpon thy Temples, therefore thou doest flye,
And wilt not helpe them in necessitie.
    Thinking vpon thee, I doe often muse,
Whether for thy deare sake I should accuse
Nature or Fortune, Fortune then I blame,
And doe impute it as her greatest shame,   50
To hast thy timelesse end, and soone agen
I vexe at Nature, nay I curse her then,
That at the time of need she was no stronger,
That we by her might haue enioy'd thee longer.
    But whilst of these I with my selfe debate,
I call to minde how flinty-hearted Fate

Seaseth the olde, the young, the faire, the foule,
No thing on earth can Destinie controule:
But yet that Fate which hath of life bereft thee,
Still to eternall memory hath left thee,   60
Which thou enioy'st by the deserued breath,
That many a great one hath not after death.

NIMPHIDIA

THE COVRT OF FAYRIE

Olde CHAVCER doth of Topas tell,
Mad RABLAIS of Pantagruell,
A latter third of Dowsabell,
    With such poore trifles playing:
Others the like haue laboured at
Some of this thing, and some of that,
And many of they know not what,
    But that they must be saying.

Another sort there bee, that will
Be talking of the Fayries still,   10
Nor neuer can they have their fill,
    As they were wedded to them;
No Tales of them their thirst can slake,
So much delight therein they take,
And some strange thing they fame would make,
    Knew they the way to doe them.

Then since no Muse hath bin so bold,
Or of the Later, or the ould,
Those Eluish secrets to vnfold,
    Which lye from others reading,   20
My actiue Muse to light shall bring,
The court of that proud Fayry King,
And tell there, of the Reuelling,
    Ioue prosper my proceeding.

And thou NIMPHIDIA gentle Fay,
Which meeting me vpon the way,
These secrets didst to me bewray,
    Which now I am in telling:
My pretty light fantastick mayde,
I here inuoke thee to my ayde,   30
That I may speake what thou hast sayd,
    In numbers smoothly swelling.

This Pallace standeth in the Ayre,
By Nigromancie placed there,
That it no Tempests needs to feare,
    Which way so ere it blow it.
And somewhat Southward tow'rd the Noone,

Whence lyes a way vp to the Moone,
And thence the Fayrie can as soone
 Passe to the earth below it.   40

The Walls of Spiders legs are made,
Well mortized and finely layd,
He was the master of his Trade
 It curiously that builded:
The Windowes of the eyes of Cats,
And for the Roofe, instead of Slats,
Is couer'd with the skinns of Batts,
 With Mooneshine that are guilded.

Hence Oberon him sport to make,
(Their rest when weary mortalls take)   50
And none but onely Fayries wake,
 Desendeth for his pleasure.
And Mab his meerry Queene by night
Bestrids young Folks that lye vpright,
(In elder Times the Mare that hight)
 Which plagues them out of measure.

Hence Shaddowes, seeming Idle shapes,
Of little frisking Elues and Apes,
To Earth doe make their wanton skapes,
 As hope of pastime hasts them: 60
Which maydes think on the Hearth they see,
When Fyers well nere consumed be,
Their daunsing Hayes by two and three,
 Iust as their Fancy casts them.

These make our Girles their sluttery rue,
By pinching them both blacke and blew,
And put a penny in their shue,
 The house for cleanely sweeping:
And in their courses make that Round,
In Meadowes, and in Marshes found,   70
Of them so call'd the Fayrie ground,
 Of which they haue the keeping.

Thus when a Childe haps to be gott,
Which after prooues an Ideott,
When Folke perceiue it thriueth not,
 The fault therein to smother:
Some silly doting brainlesse Calfe,

That vnderstands things by the halfe,
Say that the Fayrie left this Aulfe,
    And tooke away the other.   80

But listen and I shall you tell,
A chance in Fayrie that befell,
Which certainly may please some well;
    In Loue and Armes delighting:
Of Oberon that Iealous grewe,
Of one of his owne Fayrie crue,
Too well (he fear'd) his Queene that knew,
    His loue but ill requiting.

Pigwiggen was this Fayrie knight,
One wondrous gratious in the sight   90
Of faire Queene Mab, which day and night,
    He amorously obserued;
Which made king Oberon suspect,
His Seruice tooke too good effect,
His saucinesse, and often checkt,
    And could have wisht him starued.

Pigwiggen gladly would commend,
Some token to queene Mab to send,
If Sea, or Land, him ought could lend,
    Were worthy of her wearing: 100
At length this Louer doth deuise,
A Bracelett made of Emmotts eyes,
A thing he thought that shee would prize,
    No whitt her state impayring.

And to the Queene a Letter writes,
Which he most curiously endites,
Coniuring her by all the rites
    Of loue, she would be pleased,
To meete him her true Seruant, where
They might without suspect or feare,   110
Themselues to one another cleare,
    And haue their poore hearts eased.

At mid-night the appointed hower,
And for the Queene a fitting bower,
(Quoth he) is that faire Cowslip flower,
    On Hipcut hill that groweth,
In all your Trayne there's not a Fay,

That euer went to gather May,
But she hath made it in her way,
   The tallest there that growth

              120

When by Tom Thum a Fayrie Page,
He sent it, and doth him engage,
By promise of a mighty wage,
   It secretly to carrie:
Which done, the Queene her maydes doth call,
And bids them to be ready all,
She would goe see her Summer Hall,
   She could no longer tarrie.

Her Chariot ready straight is made,
Each thing therein is fitting layde,
That she by nothing might be stayde,
   For naught must be her letting,

              130

Foure nimble Gnats the Horses were,
Their Harnasses of Gossamere,
Flye Cranion her Chariottere,
   Vpon the Coach-box getting.

Her Chariot of a Snayles fine shell,
Which for the colours did excell:
The faire Queene Mab, becomming well,
   So liuely was the limming:

              140

The seate the soft wooll of the Bee;
The couer, (gallantly to see)
The wing of a pyde Butterflee,
   I trowe t'was simple trimming.

The wheeles compos'd of Crickets bones,
And daintily made for the nonce,
For feare of ratling on the stones,
   With Thistle-downe they shod it;
For all her Maydens much did feare,
If Oberon had chanc'd to heare,

              150

That Mab his Queene should haue bin there,
   He would not haue aboad it.

She mounts her Chariot with a trice,
Nor would she stay for no advice,
Vntill her Maydes that were so nice,
   To wayte on her were fitted,
But ranne her selfe away alone;

Which when they heard there was not one,
But hasted after to be gone,
   As she had beene diswitted.   160

Hop, and Mop, and Drop so cleare,
Pip, and Trip, and Skip that were,
To Mab their Soueraigne euer deare:
   Her speciall Maydes of Honour;
Fib, and Tib, and Pinck, and Pin,
Tick, and Quick, and Iill, and Iin,
Tit, and Nit, and Wap, and Win,
   The Trayne that wayte vpon her.

Vpon a Grashopper they got,
And what with Amble, and with Trot,   170
For hedge nor ditch they spared not,
   But after her they hie them.
A Cobweb ouer them they throw,
To shield the winde if it should blowe,
Themselues they wisely could bestowe,
   Lest any should espie them.

But let vs leaue Queene Mab a while,
Through many a gate, o'r many a stile,
That now had gotten by this wile,
   Her deare Pigwiggin kissing,   180
And tell how Oberon doth fare,
Who grew as mad as any Hare,
When he had sought each place with care,
   And found his Queene was missing.

By grisly Pluto he doth sweare,
He rent his cloths, and tore his haire,
And as he runneth, here and there,
   An Acorne cup he greeteth;
Which soone he taketh by the stalke
About his head he lets it walke,   190
Nor doth he any creature balke,
   But lays on all he meeteth.

The Thuskan Poet doth aduance,
The franticke Paladine of France,
And those more ancient doe inhaunce,
   Alcides in his fury.
And others Aiax Telamon,

But to this time there hath bin non,
So Bedlam as our Oberon,
    Of which I dare assure you.   200

And first encountring with a waspe,
He in his armes the Fly doth claspe
As though his breath he forth would graspe,
    Him for Pigwiggen taking:
Where is my wife thou Rogue, quoth he,
Pigwiggen, she is come to thee,
Restore her, or thou dy'st by me,
    Whereat the poore waspe quaking,

Cryes, Oberon, great Fayrie King,
Content thee I am no such thing,   210
I am a Waspe behold my sting,
    At which the Fayrie started:
When soone away the Waspe doth goe,
Poore wretch was neuer frighted so,
He thought his wings were much to slow,
    O'rioyd, they so were parted.

He next vpon a Glow-worme light,
(You must suppose it now was night),
Which for her hinder part was bright,
    He tooke to be a Deuill.   220
And furiously doth her assaile
For carrying fier in her taile
He thrasht her rough coat with his flayle,
    The mad King fear'd no euill.

O quoth the Gloworme hold thy hand,
Thou puisant King of Fayrie land,
Thy mighty stroaks who may withstand,
    Hould, or of life despaire I:
Together then her selfe doth roule,
And tumbling downe into a hole,   230
She seem'd as black as any Cole,
    Which vext away the Fayrie.

From thence he ran into a Hiue,
Amongst the Bees he letteth driue
And downe their Coombes begins to riue,
    All likely to haue spoyled:
Which with their Waxe his face besmeard,

And with their Honey daub'd his Beard
It would haue made a man afeard,
   To see how he was moyled.   240

A new Aduenture him betides,
He mett an Ant, which he bestrides,
And post thereon away he rides,
   Which with his haste doth stumble;
And came full ouer on her snowte,
Her heels so threw the dirt about,
For she by no meanes could get out,
   But ouer him doth tumble.

And being in this piteous case,
And all be-slurried head and face,   250
On runs he in this Wild-goose chase
   As here, and there, he rambles
Halfe blinde, against a molehill hit,
And for a Mountaine taking it,
For all he was out of his wit,
   Yet to the top he scrambles.

And being gotten to the top,
Yet there himselfe he could not stop,
But downe on th' other side doth chop,
   And to the foot came rumbling: 260
So that the Grubs therein that bred,
Hearing such turmoyle ouer head,
Thought surely they had all bin dead,
   So fearefull was the Iumbling.

And falling downe into a Lake,
Which him vp to the neck doth take,
His fury somewhat it doth slake,
   He calleth for a Ferry;
Where you may some recouery note,
What was his Club he made his Boate,   270
And in his Oaken Cup doth float,
   As safe as in a Wherry.

Men talke of the Aduentures strange,
Of Don Quishott, and of their change
Through which he Armed oft did range,
   Of Sancha Panchas trauell:
But should a man tell euery thing,

Done by this franticke Fayrie king.
And them in lofty numbers sing
   It well his wits might grauell.   280

Scarse set on shore, but therewithall,
He meeteth Pucke, which most men call
Hobgoblin, and on him doth fall,
   With words from frenzy spoken;
Hoh, hoh, quoth Hob, God saue thy grace,
Who drest thee in this pitteous case,
He thus that spoild my soueraignes face,
   I would his necke were broken.

This Puck seemes but a dreaming dolt,
Still walking like a ragged Colt,   290
And oft out of a Bush doth bolt,
   Of purpose to deceiue vs.
And leading vs makes vs to stray,
Long Winters nights out of the way,
And when we stick in mire and clay,
   Hob doth with laughter leaue vs.

Deare Puck (quoth he) my wife is gone
As ere thou lou'st King Oberon,
Let euery thing but this alone
   With vengeance, and pursue her;   300
Bring her to me aliue or dead,
Or that vilde thief, Pigwiggins head,
That villaine hath defil'd my bed
   He to this folly drew her.

Quoth Puck, My Liege Ile neuer lin,
But I will thorough thicke and thinne,
Vntill at length I bring her in,
   My dearest Lord nere doubt it:
Thorough Brake, thorough Brier,
Thorough Muck, thorough Mier,   310
Thorough Water, thorough Fier,
   And thus goes Puck about it.

This thing Nimphidia ouer hard
That on this mad King had a guard
Not doubting of a great reward,
   For first this businesse broching;
And through the ayre away doth goe

Swift as an Arrow from the Bowe,
To let her Soueraigne Mab to know,
   What perill was approaching.   320

The Queene bound with Loues powerfulst charme
Sate with Pigwiggen arme in arme,
Her Merry Maydes that thought no harme,
   About the roome were skipping:
A Humble-Bee their Minstrell, playde
Vpon his Hoboy; eu'ry Mayde
Fit for this Reuells was arayde,
   The Hornepype neatly tripping.

In comes Nimphidia, and doth crie,
My Soueraigne for your safety flie,   330
For there is danger but too nie,
   I posted to forewarne you:
The King hath sent Hobgoblin out,
To seeke you all the Fields about,
And of your safety you may doubt,
   If he but once discerne you.

When like an vprore in a Towne,
Before them euery thing went downe,
Some tore a Ruffe, and some a Gowne,
   Gainst one another iustling: 340
They flewe about like Chaffe i' th winde,
For hast some left their Maskes behinde;
Some could not stay their Gloues to finde,
   There neuer was such bustling.

Forth ranne they by a secret way,
Into a brake that neere them lay;
Yet much they doubted there to stay,
   Lest Hob should hap to find them:
He had a sharpe and piercing sight,
All one to him the day and night,   350
And therefore were resolu'd by flight,
   To leave this place behind them.

At length one chanc'd to find a Nut,
In th' end of which a hole was cut,
Which lay vpon a Hazell roote,
   There scatt'red by a Squirill:
Which out the kernell gotten had;

When quoth this Fay deare Queene be glad,
Let Oberon be ne'r so mad,
   Ile set you safe from perill.   360

Come all into this Nut (quoth she)
Come closely in be rul'd by me,
Each one may here a chuser be,
   For roome yee need not wrastle:
Nor neede yee be together heapt;
So one by one therein they crept,
And lying downe they soundly slept,
   And safe as in a Castle.

Nimphidia that this while doth watch,
Perceiu'd if Puck the Queene should catch   370
That he should be her ouer-match,
   Of which she well bethought her;
Found it must be some powerfull Charme,
The Queene against him that must arme,
Or surely he would doe her harme,
   For throughly he had sought her.

And listning if she ought could heare,
That her might hinder, or might feare:
But finding still the coast was cleare,
   Nor creature had discride her;   380
Each circumstance and hauing scand,
She came thereby to vnderstand,
Puck would be with them out of hand
   When to her Charmes she hide her:

And first her Ferne seede doth bestowe,
The kernell of the Missletowe:
And here and there as Puck should goe,
   With terrour to affright him:
She Night-shade strawes to work him ill,
Therewith her Veruayne and her Dill,   390
That hindreth Witches of their will,
   Of purpose to dispight him.

Then sprinkles she the iuice of Rue,
That groweth vnderneath the Yeu:
With nine drops of the midnight dewe,
   From Lunarie distilling:
The Molewarps braine mixt therewithall;

And with the same the Pismyres gall,
For she in nothing short would fall;
   The Fayrie was so willing.   400

Then thrice vnder a Bryer doth creepe,
Which at both ends was rooted deepe,
And ouer it three times shee leepe;
   Her Magicke much auayling:
Then on Proserpyna doth call,
And so vpon her spell doth fall,
Which here to you repeate I shall,
   Not in one tittle fayling.

By the croking of the Frogge;
By the howling of the Dogge;   410
By the crying of the Hogge,
   Against the storme arising;
By the Euening Curphewe bell;
By the dolefull dying knell,
O let this my direfull Spell,
   Hob, hinder thy surprising.

By the Mandrakes dreadfull groanes;
By the Lubricans sad moans;
By the noyse of dead mens bones,
   In Charnell houses ratling: 420
By the hissing of the Snake,
The rustling of the fire-Drake,
I charge thee thou this place forsake,
   Nor of Queene Mab be pratling.

By the Whirlwindes hollow sound,
By the Thunders dreadfull stound,
Yells of Spirits vnder ground,
   I chardge thee not to feare vs:
By the Shreech-owles dismall note,
By the Blacke Night-Rauens throate,   430
I charge thee Hob to teare thy Coate
   With thornes if thou come neere vs,

Her Spell thus spoke she stept aside,
And in a Chincke her selfe doth hide,
To see there of what would betyde,
   For shee doth onely minde him:
When presently shee Puck espies,

And well she markt his gloating eyes,
How vnder euery leafe he spies,
   In seeking still to finde them.   440

But once the Circle got within,
The Charmes to worke doe straight begin,
And he was caught as in a Gin;
   For as he thus was busie,
A paine he in his Head-peece feeles,
Against a stubbed Tree he reeles,
And vp went poore Hobgoblins heeles,
   Alas his braine was dizzie.

At length vpon his feete he gets,
Hobgoblin fumes, Hobgoblin frets,   450
And as againe he forward sets,
   And through the Bushes scrambles;
A Stump doth trip him in his pace,
Down comes poore Hob vpon his face,
And lamentably tore his case,
   Amongst the Bryers and Brambles.

A plague vpon Queene Mab, quoth hee,
And all her Maydes where ere they be,
I thinke the Deuill guided me,
   To seeke her so prouoked.   460
Where stumbling at a piece of Wood,
He fell into a dich of mudd,
Where to the very Chin he stood,
   In danger to be choked.

Now worse than e're he was before:
Poore Puck doth yell, poore Puck doth rore;
That wak'd Queene Mab who doubted sore
   Some Treason had been wrought her:
Vntill Nimphidia told the Queene
What she had done, what she had seene,   470
Who then had well-neere crack'd her spleene
   With very extreame laughter.

But leaue we Hob to clamber out:
Queene Mab and all her Fayrie rout,
And come againe to haue about
   With Oberon yet madding:
And with Pigwiggen now distrought,

Who much was troubled in his thought,
That he so long the Queene had sought,
   And through the Fields was gadding.   480

And as he runnes he still doth crie,
King Oberon I thee defie,
And dare thee here in Armes to trie,
   For my deare Ladies honour:
For that she is a Queene right good,
In whose defence Ile shed my blood,
And that thou in this iealous mood
   Hast lay'd this slander on her.

And quickly Armes him for the Field,
A little Cockle-shell his Shield,   490
Which he could very brauely wield:
   Yet could it not be pierced:
His Speare a Bent both stiffe and strong,
And well-neere of two Inches long;
The Pyle was of a Horse-flyes tongue,
   Whose sharpnesse nought reuersed.

And puts him on a coate of Male,
Which was of a Fishes scale,
That when his Foe should him assaile,
   No poynt should be preuayling: 500
His Rapier was a Hornets sting,
It was a very dangerous thing:
For if he chanc'd to hurt the King,
   It would be long in healing.

His Helmet was a Bettles head,
Most horrible and full of dread,
That able was to strike one dead,
   Yet did it well become him:
And for a plume, a horses hayre,
Which being tossed with the ayre,   510
Had force to strike his Foe with feare,
   And turne his weapon from him.

Himselfe he on an Earewig set,
Yet scarce he on his back could get,
So oft and high he did coruet,
   Ere he himselfe could settle:
He made him turne, and stop, and bound,

To gallop, and to trot the Round,
He scarce could stand on any ground,
 He was so full of mettle.   520

When soone he met with Tomalin,
One that a valiant Knight had bin,
And to King Oberon of kin;
 Quoth he thou manly Fayrie:
Tell Oberon I come prepar'd,
Then bid him stand vpon his Guard;
This hand his basenesse shall reward,
 Let him be ne'r so wary.

Say to him thus, that I defie,
His slanders, and his infamie,   530
And as a mortall enemie,
 Doe publickly proclaime him:
Withall, that if I had mine owne,
He should not weare the Fayrie Crowne,
But with a vengeance should come downe:
 Nor we a King should name him.

This Tomalin could not abide,
To heare his Soueraigne vilefide:
But to the Fayrie Court him hide;
 Full furiously he posted,   540
With eu'ry thing Pigwiggen sayd:
How title to the Crowne he layd,
And in what Armes he was aray'd,
 As how himselfe he boasted.

Twixt head and foot, from point to point,
He told th'arming of each ioint,
In every piece, how neate, and quaint,
 For Tomalin could doe it:
How fayre he sat, how sure he rid,
As of the courser he bestrid,   550
How Mannag'd, and how well he did;
 The King which listened to it,

Quoth he, goe Tomalin with speede,
Prouide me Armes, prouide my Steed,
And euery thing that I shall neede,
 By thee I will be guided;
To strait account, call thou thy witt,

See there be wanting not a whitt,
In euery thing see thou me fitt,
   Just as my foes prouided.   560

Soone flewe this newes through Fayrie land
Which gaue Queene Mab to vnderstand,
The combate that was then in hand,
   Betwixt those men so mighty:
Which greatly she began to rew,
Perceuing that all Fayrie knew,
The first occasion from her grew,
   Of these affaires so weighty.

Wherefore attended with her maides,
Through fogs, and mists, and dampes she wades,   570
To Proserpine the Queene of shades
   To treat, that it would please her,
The cause into her hands to take,
For ancient loue and friendships sake,
And soone therof an end to make,
   Which of much care would ease her.

A While, there let we Mab alone,
And come we to King Oberon,
Who arm'd to meete his foe is gone,
   For Proud Pigwiggen crying: 580
Who sought the Fayrie King as fast,
And had so well his iourneyes cast,
That he arriued at the last,
   His puisant foe espying:

Stout Tomalin came with the King,
Tom Thum doth on Pigwiggen bring,
That perfect were in euery thing,
   To single fights belonging:
And therefore they themselues ingage,
To see them exercise their rage,   590
With faire and comely equipage,
   Not one the other wronging.

So like in armes, these champions were,
As they had bin, a very paire,
So that a man would almost sweare,
   That either, had bin either;
Their furious steedes began to naye

That they were heard a mighty way,
Their staues vpon their rests they lay;
    Yet e'r they flew together,   600

Their Seconds minister an oath,
Which was indifferent to them both,
That on their Knightly faith, and troth,
    No magicke them supplyed;
And sought them that they had no charmes,
Wherewith to worke each others harmes,
But came with simple open armes,
    To haue their causes tryed.

Together furiously they ran,
That to the ground came horse and man,   610
The blood out of their Helmets span,
    So sharpe were their incounters;
And though they to the earth were throwne,
Yet quickly they regain'd their owne,
Such nimblenesse was neuer showne,
    They were two Gallant Mounters.

When in a second Course againe,
They forward came with might and mayne,
Yet which had better of the twaine,
    The Seconds could not iudge yet;   620
Their shields were into pieces cleft,
Their helmets from their heads were reft,
And to defend them nothing left,
    These Champions would not budge yet.

Away from them their Staues they threw,
Their cruell Swords they quickly drew,
And freshly they the fight renew;
    They euery stroke redoubled:
Which made Proserpina take heed,
And make to them the greater speed,   630
For fear lest they too much should bleed,
    Which wondrously her troubled.

When to th' infernall Stix she goes,
She takes the Fogs from thence that rose,
And in a Bagge doth them enclose;
    When well she had them blended:
She hyes her then to Lethe spring,

A Bottell and thereof doth bring,
Wherewith she meant to worke the thing,
    Which onely she intended.   640

Now Proserpine with Mab is gone
Vnto the place where Oberon
And proud Pigwiggen, one to one,
    Both to be slaine were likely:
And there themselues they closely hide,
Because they would not be espide;
For Proserpine meant to decide
    The matter very quickly.

And suddainly vntyes the Poke,
Which out of it sent such a smoke,   650
As ready was them all to choke,
    So greeuous was the pother;
So that the Knights each other lost,
And stood as still as any post,
Tom Thum, nor Tomalin could boast
    Themselues of any other.

But when the mist gan somewhat cease,
Proserpina commanded peace:
And that a while they should release,
    Each other of their perill: 660
Which here (quoth she) I doe proclaime
To all in dreadfull Plutos name,
That as yee will eschewe his blame,
    You let me heare the quarrell,

But here your selues you must engage,
Somewhat to coole your spleenish rage:
Your greeuous thirst and to asswage,
    That first you drinke this liquor:
Which shall your vnderstanding cleare,
As plainely shall to you appeare;   670
Those things from me that you shall heare,
    Conceiuing much the quicker.

This Lethe water you must knowe,
The memory destroyeth so,
That of our weale, or of our woe,
    It all remembrance blotted;
Of it nor can you euer thinke:

For they no sooner tooke this drinke,
But nought into their braines could sinke,
   Of what had them besotted.   680

King Oberon forgotten had,
That he for iealousie ranne mad:
But of his Queene was wondrous glad,
   And ask'd how they came thither:
Pigwiggen likewise doth forget,
That he Queene Mab had euer met;
Or that they were so hard beset,
   When they were found together.

Nor neither of them both had thought,
That e'r they had each other sought;   690
Much lesse that they a Combat fought,
   But such a dreame were lothing:
Tom Thum had got a little sup,
And Tomalin scarce kist the Cup,
Yet had their braines so sure lockt vp,
   That they remembred nothing.

Queene Mab and her light Maydes the while,
Amongst themselues doe closely smile,
To see the King caught with this wile,
   With one another testing: 700
And to the Fayrie Court they went,
With mickle ioy and merriment,
Which thing was done with good intent,
   And thus I left them feasting.

FINIS.

THE QVEST OF CYNTHIA

What time the groues were clad in greene,
    The Fields drest all in flowers,
And that the sleeke-hayred Nimphs were seene,
    To seeke them Summer Bowers.

Forth rou'd I by the sliding Rills,
    To finde where CYNTHIA sat,
Whose name so often from the hills,
    The Ecchos wondred at.

When me vpon my Quest to bring,
    That pleasure might excell,   10
The Birds stroue which should sweetliest sing,
    The Flowers which sweet'st should smell.

Long wand'ring in the Woods (said I)
    Oh whether's CYNTHIA gone?
When soone the Eccho doth reply,
    To my last word, goe on.

At length vpon a lofty Firre,
    It was my chance to finde,
Where that deare name most due to her,
    Was caru'd vpon the rynde.   20

Which whilst with wonder I beheld,
    The Bees their hony brought,
And vp the carued letters fild,
    As they with gould were wrought.

And neere that trees more spacious roote,
    Then looking on the ground,
The shape of her most dainty foot,
    Imprinted there I found.

Which stuck there like a curious seale,
    As though it should forbid   30
Vs, wretched mortalls, to reueale,
    What vnder it was hid.

Besides the flowers which it had pres'd,
    Apeared to my vew,
More fresh and louely than the rest,

That in the meadowes grew:

The cleere drops in the steps that stood,
    Of that dilicious Girle,
The Nimphes amongst their dainty food,
    Drunke for dissolued pearle.   40

The yeilding sand, where she had troad,
    Vntutcht yet with the winde,
By the faire posture plainely show'd,
    Where I might Cynthia finde.

When on vpon my waylesse walke,
    As my desires me draw,
I like a madman fell to talke,
    With euery thing I saw:

I ask'd some Lillyes why so white,
    They from their fellowes were;   50
Who answered me, that Cynthia's sight,
    Had made them looke so cleare:

I ask'd a nodding Violet why,
    It sadly hung the head,
It told me Cynthia late past by,
    Too soone from it that fled:

A bed of Roses saw I there,
    Bewitching with their grace:
Besides so wondrous sweete they were,
    That they perfum'd the place,   60

I of a Shrube of those enquir'd,
    From others of that kind,
Who with such virtue them enspir'd,
    It answer'd (to my minde).

As the base Hemblocke were we such,
    The poysned'st weed that growes,
Till Cynthia by her god-like tuch,
    Transform'd vs to the Rose:

Since when those Frosts that winter brings
    Which candy euery greene,   70
Renew vs like the Teeming Springs,

And we thus Fresh are scene.

At length I on a Fountaine light,
    Whose brim with Pincks was platted;
The Banck with Daffadillies dight,
    With grasse like Sleaue was matted,

When I demanded of that Well,
    What power frequented there;
Desiring, it would please to tell
    What name it vsde to beare.   80

It tolde me it was Cynthias owne,
    Within whose cheerefull brimmes,
That curious Nimph had oft beene knowne
    To bath her snowy Limmes.

Since when that Water had the power,
    Lost Mayden-heads to restore,
And make one Twenty in an howre,
    Of Esons age before.

And told me that the bottome cleere,
    Now layd with many a fett   90
Of seed-pearle, ere shee bath'd her there:
    Was knowne as blacke as Jet,

As when she from the water came,
    Where first she touch'd the molde,
In balls the people made the same
    For Pomander, and solde.

When chance me to an Arbour led,
    Whereas I might behold:
Two blest Elizeums in one sted,
    The lesse the great enfold.   100

The place which she had chosen out,
    Her selfe in to repose;
Had they com'n downe, the gods no doubt
    The very same had chose.

The wealthy Spring yet neuer bore
    That sweet, nor dainty flower
That damask'd not, the chequer'd flore

Of CYNTHIAS Summer Bower.

The Birch, the Mirtle, and the Bay,
    Like Friends did all embrace;   110
And their large branches did display,
    To Canapy the place.

Where she like VENVS doth appeare,
    Vpon a Rosie bed;
As Lillyes the soft pillowes weare,
    Whereon she layd her head.

Heau'n on her shape such cost bestow'd,
    And with such bounties blest:
No lim of hers but might haue made
    A Goddesse at the least.   120

The Flyes by chance mesht in her hayre,
    By the bright Radience throwne
From her cleare eyes, rich Iewels weare,
    They so like Diamonds shone.

The meanest weede the soyle there bare,
    Her breath did so refine,
That it with Woodbynd durst compare,
    And beard the Eglantine.

The dewe which on the tender grasse,
    The Euening had distill'd,   130
To pure Rose-water turned was,
    The shades with sweets that fill'd.

The windes were husht, no leafe so small
    At all was scene to stirre:
Whilst tuning to the waters fall,
    The small Birds sang to her.

Where she too quickly me espies,
    When I might plainely see,
A thousand Cupids from her eyes
    Shoote all at once at me.   140

Into these secret shades (quoth she)
    How dar'st thou be so bold
To enter, consecrate to me,

Or touch this hallowed mold.

Those words (quoth she) I can pronounce,
    Which to that shape can bring
Thee, which the Hunter had who once
    Sawe Dian in the Spring.

Bright Nimph againe I thus replie,
    This cannot me affright: 150
I had rather in thy presence die,
    Then liue out of thy sight.

I first vpon the Mountaines hie,
    Built Altars to thy name;
And grau'd it on the Rocks thereby,
    To propogate thy fame.

I taught the Shepheards on the Downes,
    Of thee to frame their Layes:
T'was I that fill'd the neighbouring Townes,
    With Ditties of thy praise.   160

Thy colours I deuis'd with care,
    Which were vnknowne before:
Which since that, in their braded hayre
    The Nimphes and Siluans wore.

Transforme me to what shape you can,
    I passe not what it be:
Yea what most hatefull is to man,
    So I may follow thee.

Which when she heard full pearly floods,
    I in her eyes might view: 170
(Quoth she) most welcome to these Woods,
    Too meane for one so true.

Here from the hatefull world we'll liue,
    A den of mere dispight:
To Ideots only that doth giue,
    Which be her sole delight.

To people the infernall pit,
    That more and more doth striue;
Where only villany is wit,

And Diuels only thriue. 180

Whose vilenesse vs shall neuer awe:
    But here our sports shall be:
Such as the golden world first sawe,
    Most innocent and free.

Of Simples in these Groues that growe,
    Wee'll learne the perfect skill;
The nature of each Herbe to knowe
    Which cures, and which can kill.

The waxen Pallace of the Bee,
    We seeking will surprise 190
The curious workmanship to see,
    Of her full laden thighes.

Wee'll suck the sweets out of the Combe,
    And make the gods repine:
As they doe feast in Ioues great roome,
    To see with what we dine.

Yet when there haps a honey fall,
    Wee'll lick the sirupt leaues:
And tell the Bees that their's is gall,
    To this vpon the Greaues. 200

The nimble Squirrell noting here,
    Her mossy Dray that makes,
And laugh to see the lusty Deere
    Come bounding ore the brakes.

The Spiders Webb to watch weele stand,
    And when it takes the Bee,
Weele helpe out of the Tyrants hand,
    The Innocent to free.

Sometime weele angle at the Brooke,
    The freckled Trout to take, 210
With silken Wormes, and bayte the hooke,
    Which him our prey shall make.

Of medling with such subtile tooles,
    Such dangers that enclose,
The Morrall is that painted Fooles,

Are caught with silken showes.

And when the Moone doth once appeare,
  Weele trace the lower grounds,
When Fayries in their Ringlets there
  Do daunce their nightly rounds.   220

And haue a Flocke of Turtle Doues,
  A guard on vs to keepe,
A witnesse of our honest loues,
  To watch vs till we sleepe.

Which spoke I felt such holy fires
  To ouerspred my breast,
As lent life to my Chast desires
  And gaue me endlesse rest.

By Cynthia thus doe I subsist,
  On earth Heauens onely pride,   230
Let her be mine, and let who list,
  Take all the world beside.

FINIS.

THE SHEPHEARDS SIRENA

DORILVS in sorrowes deepe,
Autumne waxing olde and chill,
As he sate his Flocks to keepe
Vnderneath an easie hill:
Chanc'd to cast his eye aside
On those fields, where he had scene,
Bright SIRENA Natures pride,
Sporting on the pleasant greene:
To whose walkes the Shepheards oft,
Came her god-like foote to finde,   10
And in places that were soft,
Kist the print there left behinde;
Where the path which she had troad,
Hath thereby more glory gayn'd,
Then in heau'n that milky rode,
Which with Nectar Hebe stayn'd:
But bleake Winters boystrous blasts,
Now their fading pleasures chid,
And so fill'd them with his wastes,
That from sight her steps were hid.   20
Silly Shepheard sad the while,
For his sweet SIRENA gone,
All his pleasures in exile:
Layd on the colde earth alone.
Whilst his gamesome cut-tayld Curre,
With his mirthlesse Master playes,
Striuing him with sport to stirre,
As in his more youthfull dayes,
DORILVS his Dogge doth chide,
Layes his well-tun'd Bagpype by,   30
And his Sheep-hooke casts aside,
There (quoth he) together lye.
When a Letter forth he tooke,
Which to him SIRENA writ,
With a deadly down-cast looke,
And thus fell to reading it.
DORILVS my deare (quoth she)
Kinde Companion of my woe,
Though we thus diuided be,
Death cannot diuorce vs so: 40
Thou whose bosome hath beene still,
Th' onely Closet of my care,
And in all my good and ill,

Euer had thy equall share:
Might I winne thee from thy Fold,
Thou shouldst come to visite me,
But the Winter is so cold,
That I feare to hazard thee:
The wilde waters are waxt hie,
So they are both deafe and dumbe,   50
Lou'd they thee so well as I,
They would ebbe when thou shouldst come;
Then my coate with light should shine,
Purer then the Vestall fire:
Nothing here but should be thine,
That thy heart can well desire:
Where at large we will relate,
From what cause our friendship grewe,
And in that the varying Fate,
Since we first each other knewe: 60
Of my heauie passed plight,
As of many a future feare,
Which except the silent night,
None but onely thou shalt heare;
My sad hurt it shall releeue,
When my thoughts I shall disclose,
For thou canst not chuse but greeue,
When I shall recount my woes;
There is nothing to that friend,
To whose close vncranied brest,   70
We our secret thoughts may send,
And there safely let it rest:
And thy faithfull counsell may,
My distressed case assist,
Sad affliction else may sway
Me a woman as it list:
Hither I would haue thee haste,
Yet would gladly haue thee stay,
When those dangers I forecast,
That may meet thee by the way,   80
Doe as thou shalt thinke it best,
Let thy knowledge be thy guide,
Liue thou in my constant breast,
Whatsoeuer shall betide.
He her Letter hauing red,
Puts it in his Scrip againe,
Looking like a man halfe dead,
By her kindenesse strangely slaine;

And as one who inly knew,
Her distressed present state, 90
And to her had still been true,
Thus doth with himselfe debate.
I will not thy face admire,
Admirable though it bee,
Nor thine eyes whose subtile fire
So much wonder winne in me:
But my maruell shall be now,
(And of long it hath bene so)
Of all Woman kind that thou
Wert ordain'd to taste of woe; 100
To a Beauty so diuine,
Paradise in little done,
O that Fortune should assigne,
Ought but what thou well mightst shun,
But my counsailes such must bee,
(Though as yet I them conceale)
By their deadly wound in me,
They thy hurt must onely heale,
Could I giue what thou do'st craue
To that passe thy state is growne, 110
I thereby thy life may saue,
But am sure to loose mine owne,
To that ioy thou do'st conceiue,
Through my heart, the way doth lye,
Which in two for thee must claue
Least that thou shouldst goe awry.
Thus my death must be a toy,
Which my pensiue breast must couer;
Thy beloued to enioy,
Must be taught thee by thy Louer. 120
Hard the Choise I haue to chuse,
To my selfe if friend I be,
I must my SIRENA loose,
If not so, shee looseth me.
Thus whilst he doth cast about,
What therein were best to doe,
Nor could yet resolue the doubt,
Whether he should stay or goe:
In those Feilds not farre away,
There was many a frolike Swaine, 130
In fresh Russets day by day,
That kept Reuells on the Plaine.
Nimble TOM, sirnam'd the Tup,

For his Pipe without a Peere,
And could tickle Trenchmore vp,
As t'would ioy your heart to heare.
RALPH as much renown'd for skill,
That the Taber touch'd so well;
For his Gittern, little GILL,
That all other did excell.   140
ROCK and ROLLO euery way,
Who still led the Rusticke Ging,
And could troule a Roundelay,
That would make the Feilds to ring,
COLLIN on his Shalme so cleare,
Many a high-pitcht Note that had,
And could make the Eechos nere
Shout as they were wexen mad.
Many a lusty Swaine beside,
That for nought but pleasure car'd,   150
Hauing DORILVS espy'd,
And with him knew how it far'd.
Thought from him they would remoue,
This strong melancholy fitt,
Or so, should it not behoue,
Quite to put him out of 's witt;
Hauing learnt a Song, which he
Sometime to Sirena sent,
Full of Iollity and glee,
When the Nimph liu'd neere to Trent   160
They behinde him softly gott,
Lying on the earth along,
And when he suspected not,
Thus the Iouiall Shepheards song.

        Neare to the Siluer Trent,
            Sirena dwelleth:
        Shee to whom Nature lent
            All that excelleth:
        By which the Muses late,
            And the neate Graces,   170
        Haue for their greater state
            Taken their places:
        Twisting an Anadem,
            Wherewith to Crowne her,
        As it belong'd to them
            Most to renowne her.
Cho.   On thy Bancke,

In a Rancke,
Let the Swanes sing her,
 And with their Musick,
 Along let them bring her.   180

Tagus and Pactolus
 Are to thee Debter,
Nor for their gould to vs
 Are they the better:
Henceforth of all the rest,
 Be thou the Riuer,
Which as the daintiest,
 Puts them downe euer,
For as my precious one,   190
 O'r thee doth trauell,
She to Pearl Parragon
 Turneth thy grauell.
Cho.   On thy Bancke,
   In a Rancke,
Let thy Swanns sing her,
 And with their Musicke,
Along let them bring her.

Our mournefull Philomell,
 That rarest Tuner,   200
Henceforth in Aperill
 Shall wake the sooner,
And to her shall complaine
 From the thicke Couer,
Redoubling euery straine
 Ouer and ouer:
For when my Loue too long
 Her Chamber keepeth;
As though it suffered wrong,
 The Morning weepeth.   210
Cho.   On thy Bancke,
   In a Rancke,
Let thy Swanes sing her,
 And with their Musick,
Along let them bring her.

Oft have I seene the Sunne
 To doe her honour.
Fix himselfe at his noone,
 To look vpon her,

And hath guilt euery Groue,   220
    Euery Hill neare her,
With his flames from aboue,
    Striuing to cheere her,
And when shee from his sight
    Hath her selfe turned,
He as it had beene night,
    In Cloudes hath mourned.
Cho.   On thy Bancke,
    In a Rancke,
Let thy Swanns sing her,   230
    And with their Musicke,
Along let them bring her.

The Verdant Meades are seene,
    When she doth view them,
In fresh and gallant Greene,
    Straight to renewe them,
And euery little Grasse
    Broad it selfe spreadeth,
Proud that this bonny Lasse
    Vpon it treadeth: 240
Nor flower is so sweete
    In this large Cincture
But it upon her feete
    Leaueth some Tincture.
Cho.   On thy Bancke,
    In a Rancke,
Let thy Swanes sing her,
    And with thy Musick,
Along let them bring her.

The Fishes in the Flood,   250
    When she doth Angle,
For the Hooke striue a good
    Them to intangle;
And leaping on the Land
    From the cleare water,
Their Scales vpon the sand,
    Lauishly scatter;
Therewith to paue the mould
    Whereon she passes,
So her selfe to behold,   260
    As in her glasses.
Cho.   On thy Bancke,

In a Ranke,
Let thy Swanns sing her,
        And with their Musicke,
Along let them bring her.

When shee lookes out by night,
        The Starres stand gazing,
Like Commets to our sight
        Fearefully blazing,   270
As wondring at her eyes
        With their much brightnesse,
Which to amaze the skies,
        Dimming their lightnesse,
The raging Tempests are Calme,
        When shee speaketh,
Such most delightsome balme
        From her lips breaketh.
Cho.   On thy Banke,
        In a Rancke, &c.   280

In all our Brittany,
        Ther's not a fayrer,
Nor can you fitt any:
        Should you compare her.
Angels her eye-lids keepe
        All harts surprizing,
Which looke whilst she doth sleepe
        Like the Sunnes rising:
She alone of her kinde
        Knoweth true measure   290
And her vnmatched mind
        Is Heauens treasure:
Cho.   On thy Bancke,
        In a Rancke
Let thy Swanes sing her,
        And with their Musick,
Along let them bring her.

Fayre Doue and Darwine cleere
        Boast yee your beauties,
To Trent your Mistres here   300
        Yet pay your duties,
My Loue was higher borne
        Tow'rds the full Fountaines,
Yet she doth Moorland scorne,

And the Peake Mountaines;
Nor would she none should dreame,
　　Where she abideth,
Humble as is the streame,
　　Which by her slydeth,
Cho.　On thy Bancke,　　　　　　　　　　　　310
　　In a Rancke,
Let thy Swannes sing her,
　　And with their Musicke,
Along let them bring her.

Yet my poore Rusticke Muse,
　　Nothing can moue her,
Nor the means I can vse,
　　Though her true Louer:
Many a long Winters night,
　　Haue I wak'd for her,　　　　　　　　　　320
Yet this my piteous plight,
　　Nothing can stirre her.
All thy Sands siluer Trent
　　Downe to the Humber,
The sighes I haue spent
　　Neuer can number.
Cho.　On thy Banke
　　In a Ranke,
Let thy Swans sing her
　　And with their Musicke　　　　　　　　　330
Along let them bring her.

Taken with this suddaine Song,
Least for mirth when he doth look
His sad heart more deeply stong,
Then the former care he tooke.
At their laughter and amaz'd,
For a while he sat aghast
But a little hauing gaz'd,
Thus he them bespake at last.
Is this time for mirth (quoth he)　　　　　　340
To a man with griefe opprest,
Sinfull wretches as you be,
May the sorrowes in my breast,
Light vpon you one by one,
And as now you mocke my woe,
When your mirth is turn'd to moane;
May your like then serue you so.

When one Swaine among the rest
Thus him merrily bespake,
Get thee vp thou arrant beast   350
Fits this season loue to make?
Take thy Sheephooke in thy hand,
Clap thy Curre and set him on,
For our fields 'tis time to stand,
Or they quickly will be gon.
Rougish Swinheards that repine
At our Flocks, like beastly Clownes,
Sweare that they will bring their Swine,
And will wroote vp all our Downes:
They their Holly whips haue brac'd,   360
And tough Hazell goades haue gott;
Soundly they your sides will baste,
If their courage faile them not.
Of their purpose if they speed,
Then your Bagpypes you may burne,
It is neither Droane nor Reed
Shepheard, that will serue your turne:
Angry OLCON sets them on,
And against vs part doth take
Euer since he was out-gone,   370
Offring Rymes with us to make.
Yet if so our Sheepe-hookes hold,
Dearely shall our Downes be bought,
For it neuer shall be told,
We our Sheep-walkes sold for naught.
And we here haue got vs Dogges,
Best of all the Westerne breed,
Which though Whelps shall lug their Hogges,
Till they make their eares to bleed:
Therefore Shepheard come away.   380
When as DORILVS arose,
Whistles Cut-tayle from his play,
And along with them he goes.

FINIS.

THE MVSES ELIZIVM

The Description of Elizium

A Paradice on earth is found,
  Though farre from vulgar sight,
Which with those pleasures doth abound
  That it Elizium hight.

Where, in Delights that neuer fade,
  The Muses lulled be,
And sit at pleasure in the shade
  Of many a stately tree,

Which no rough Tempest makes to reele
  Nor their straight bodies bowes,
Their lofty tops doe neuer feele
  The weight of winters snowes;   10

In Groues that euermore are greene,
  No falling leafe is there,
But Philomel (of birds the Queene)
  In Musicke spends the yeare.

The Merle vpon her mertle Perch,
  There to the Mavis sings,
Who from the top of some curld Berch
  Those notes redoubled rings;   20

There Daysyes damaske euery place
  Nor once their beauties lose,
That when proud Phoebus hides his face
  Themselues they scorne to close.

The Pansy and the Violet here,
  As seeming to descend,
Both from one Root, a very payre,
  For sweetnesse yet contend,

And pointing to a Pinke to tell
  Which beares it, it is loath,   30
To iudge it; but replyes for smell
  That it excels them both.

Wherewith displeasde they hang their heads
    So angry soone they grow
And from their odoriferous beds
    Their sweets at it they throw.

The winter here a Summer is,
    No waste is made by time,
Nor doth the Autumne euer misse
    The blossomes of the Prime.   40

The flower that Iuly forth doth bring
    In Aprill here is seene,
The Primrose that puts on the Spring
    In Iuly decks each Greene.

The sweets for soueraignty contend
    And so abundant be,
That to the very Earth they lend
    And Barke of euery Tree:

Rills rising out of euery Banck,
    In wild Meanders strayne,   50
And playing many a wanton pranck
    Vpon the speckled plaine,

In Gambols and lascivious Gyres
    Their time they still bestow
Nor to their Fountaines none retyres,
    Nor on their course will goe.

Those Brooks with Lillies brauely deckt,
    So proud and wanton made,
That they their courses quite neglect:
    And seeme as though they stayde,   60

Faire Flora in her state to viewe
    Which through those Lillies looks,
Or as those Lillies leand to shew
    Their beauties to the brooks.

That Phoebusin his lofty race,
    Oft layes aside his beames
And comes to coole his glowing face
    In these delicious streames;

Oft spreading Vines clime vp the Cleeues,
    Whose ripned clusters there,   70
Their liquid purple drop, which driues
    A Vintage through the yeere.

Those Cleeues whose craggy sides are clad
    With Trees of sundry sutes,
Which make continuall summer glad,
    Euen bending with their fruits,

Some ripening, ready some to fall,
    Some blossom'd, some to bloome,
Like gorgeous hangings on the wall
    Of some rich princely Roome: 80

Pomegranates, Lymons, Cytrons, so
    Their laded branches bow,
Their leaues in number that outgoe
    Nor roomth will them alow.

There in perpetuall Summers shade,
    Apolloes Prophets sit,
Among the flowres that neuer fade,
    But flowrish like their wit;

To whom the Nimphes vpon their Lyres,
    Tune many a curious lay,   90
And with their most melodious Quires
    Make short the longest day.

The thrice three Virgins heavenly Cleere,
    Their trembling Timbrels sound,
Whilst the three comely Graces there
    Dance many a dainty Round,

Decay nor Age there nothing knowes,
    There is continuall Youth,
As Time on plant or creatures growes,
    So still their strength renewth.   100

The Poets Paradice this is,
    To which but few can come;
The Muses onely bower of blisse
    Their Deare Elizium.

Here happy soules, (their blessed bowers,
    Free from the rude resort
Of beastly people) spend the houres,
    In harmelesse mirth and sport,

Then on to the Elizian plaines
    Apollo doth invite you   110
Where he prouides with pastorall straines,
    In Nimphals to delight you.

The first Nimphall

RODOPE and DORIDA.

    This Nimphall of delights doth treat,
    Choice beauties, and proportions neat,
    Of curious shapes, and dainty features
    Describd in two most perfect creatures.

When Phoebus with a face of mirth,
Had flong abroad his beames,
To blanch the bosome of the earth,
And glaze the gliding streames.
Within a goodly Mertle groue,
Vpon that hallowed day
The Nimphes to the bright Queene of loue
Their vowes were vsde to pay.
Faire Rodope and Dorida
Met in those sacred shades,   10
Then whom the Sunne in all his way,
Nere saw two daintier Maids.
And through the thickets thrild his fires,
Supposing to haue seene
The soueraigne Goddesse of desires,
Or Ioues Emperious Queene:
Both of so wondrous beauties were,
In shape both so excell,
That to be paraleld elsewhere,
No iudging eye could tell.   20
And their affections so surpasse,
As well it might be deemd,
That th' one of them the other was,
And but themselues they seem'd.
And whilst the Nimphes that neare this place,
Disposed were to play

At Barly-breake and Prison-base,
Doe passe the time away:
This peerlesse payre together set,
The other at their sport,   30
None neare their free discourse to let,
Each other thus they court,

    Dorida. My sweet, my soueraigne Rodope,
My deare delight, my loue,
That Locke of hayre thou sentst to me,
I to this Bracelet woue;
Which brighter euery day doth grow
The longer it is worne,
As its delicious fellowes doe,
Thy Temples that adorne.   40

    Rodope. Nay had I thine my Dorida,
I would them so bestow,
As that the winde vpon my way,
Might backward make them flow,
So should it in its greatst excesse
Turne to becalmed ayre,
And quite forget all boistrousnesse
To play with euery hayre.

    Dorida. To me like thine had nature giuen,
A Brow, so Archt, so cleere,   50
A Front, wherein so much of heauen
Doth to each eye appeare,
The world should see, I would strike dead
The Milky Way that's now,
And say that Nectar Hebe shed
Fell all vpon my Brow.

    Rodope. O had I eyes like Doridaes,
I would inchant the day
And make the Sunne to stand at gaze,
Till he forget his way: 60
And cause his Sister Queene of Streames,
When so I list by night;
By her much blushing at my Beames
T' eclipse her borrowed light.

    Dorida. Had I a Cheeke like Rodopes,
In midst of which doth stand,

A Groue of Roses, such as these,
In such a snowy land:
I would then make the Lilly which we now
So much for whitenesse name,   70
As drooping downe the head to bow,
And die for very shame.

    Rodope. Had I a bosome like to thine,
When I it pleas'd to show,
T' what part o' th' Skie I would incline
I would make th' Etheriall bowe,
My swannish breast brancht all with blew,
In brauery like the spring:
In Winter to the generall view
Full Summer forth should bring.   80

    Dorida. Had I a body like my deare,
Were I so straight so tall,
O, if so broad my shoulders were,
Had I a waste so small;
I would challenge the proud Queene of loue
To yeeld to me for shape,
And I should feare that Mars or Ioue
Would venter for my rape.

    Rodope. Had I a hand like thee my Gerle,
(This hand O let me kisse)   90
These Ivory Arrowes pyl'd with pearle,
Had I a hand like this;
I would not doubt at all to make,
Each finger of my hand
To taske swift Mercury to take
With his inchanting wand.

    Dorida. Had I a Theigh like Rodopes;
Which twas my chance to viewe,
When lying on yon banck at ease,
The wind thy skirt vp blew,   100
I would say it were a columne wrought
To some intent Diuine,
And for our chaste Diana sought,
A pillar for her shryne.

    Rodope. Had I a Leg but like to thine
That were so neat, so cleane,

A swelling Calfe, a Small so fine,
An Ankle, round and leane,
I would tell nature she doth misse
Her old skill; and maintaine,   110
She shewd her master peece in this,
Not to be done againe.

    Dorida. Had I that Foot hid in those shoos,
(Proportion'd to my height)
Short Heele, thin Instep, euen Toes,
A Sole so wondrous straight,
The Forresters and Nimphes at this
Amazed all should stand,
And kneeling downe, should meekely kisse
The Print left in the sand.   120

By this the Nimphes came from their sport,
All pleased wondrous well,
And to these Maydens make report
What lately them befell:
One said the dainty Lelipa
Did all the rest out-goe,
Another would a wager lay
She would outstrip a Roe;
Sayes one, how like you Florimel
There is your dainty face: 130
A fourth replide, she lik't that well,
Yet better lik't her grace,
She's counted, I confesse, quoth she,
To be our onely Pearle,
Yet haue I heard her oft to be
A melancholy Gerle.
Another said she quite mistoke,
That onely was her art,
When melancholly had her looke
Then mirth was in her heart;   140
And hath she then that pretty trick
Another doth reply,
I thought no Nimph could haue bin sick
Of that disease but I;
I know you can dissemble well
Quoth one to giue you due,
But here be some (who Ile not tell)
Can do't as well as you,
Who thus replies, I know that too,

We haue it from our Mother, 150
Yet there be some this thing can doe
More cunningly then other:
If Maydens but dissemble can
Their sorrow and ther ioy,
Their pore dissimulation than,
Is but a very toy.

The second Nimphall

LALVS, CLEON, and LIROPE.

The Muse new Courtship doth deuise,
By Natures strange Varieties,
Whose Rarieties she here relates,
And giues you Pastorall Delicates.

Lalus a Iolly youthfull Lad,
With Cleon, no lesse crown'd
With vertues; both their beings had
On the Elizian ground.
Both hauing parts so excellent,
That it a question was,
Which should be the most eminent,
Or did in ought surpasse:
This Cleon was a Mountaineer, 10
And of the wilder kinde,
And from his birth had many a yeere
Bin nurst vp by a Hinde.
And as the sequell well did show,
It very well might be;
For neuer Hart, nor Hare, nor Roe,
Were halfe so swift as he.
But Lalus in the Vale was bred,
Amongst the Sheepe and Neate,
And by these Nimphes there choicly fed, 20
With Hony, Milke, and Wheate;
Of Stature goodly, faire of speech,
And of behauiour mylde,
Like those there in the Valley rich,
That bred him of a chyld.
Of Falconry they had the skill,
Their Halkes to feed and flye,
No better Hunters ere clome Hill,
Nor hollowed to a Cry:

In Dingles deepe, and Mountains hore,
Oft with the bearded Speare
They combated the tusky Boare,
And slew the angry Beare.
In Musicke they were wondrous quaint,
Fine Aers they could deuise;
They very curiously could Paint,
And neatly Poetize;
That wagers many time were laid
On Questions that arose,
Which song the witty Lalus made,
Which Cleon should compose.
The stately Steed they manag'd well,
Of Fence the art they knew,
For Dansing they did all excell
The Gerles that to them drew;
To throw the Sledge, to pitch the Barre,
To wrestle and to Run,
They all the Youth exceld so farre,
That still the Prize they wonne.
These sprightly Gallants lou'd a Lasse,
Cald Lirope the bright,
In the whole world there scarcely was
So delicate a Wight,
There was no Beauty so diuine
That euer Nimph did grace,
But it beyond it selfe did shine
In her more heuenly face:
What forme she pleasd each thing would take
That ere she did behold,
Of Pebbles she could Diamonds make,
Grosse Iron turne to Gold:
Such power there with her presence came
Sterne Tempests she alayd,
The cruell Tiger she could tame,
She raging Torrents staid,
She chid, she cherisht, she gaue life,
Againe she made to dye,
She raisd a warre, apeasd a Strife,
With turning of her eye.
Some said a God did her beget,
But much deceiu'd were they,
Her Father was a Riuelet,
Her Mother was a Fay.
Her Lineaments so fine that were,

30

40

50

60

70

She from the Fayrie tooke,
Her Beauties and Complection cleere,
By nature from the Brooke.
These Ryualls wayting for the houre
(The weather calme and faire)
When as she vs'd to leaue her Bower
To take the pleasant ayre   80
Acosting her; their complement
To her their Goddesse done;
By gifts they tempt her to consent,
When Lalus thus begun.

    Lalus. Sweet Lirope I haue a Lambe
Newly wayned from the Damme,
Of the right kinde, it is [1]notted,
Naturally with purple spotted,
Into laughter it will put you,
To see how prettily 'twill But you;   90
When on sporting it is set,
It will beate you a Corvet,
And at euery nimble bound
Turne it selfe aboue the ground;
When tis hungry it will bleate,
From your hand to haue its meate,
And when it hath fully fed,
It will fetch Iumpes aboue your head,
As innocently to expresse
Its silly sheepish thankfullnesse,   100
When you bid it, it will play,
Be it either night or day,
This Lirope I haue for thee,
So thou alone wilt liue with me.

    Cleon. From him O turne thine eare away,
And heare me my lou'd Lirope,
I haue a Kid as white as milke,
His skin as soft as Naples silke,
His hornes in length are wondrous euen,
And curiously by nature writhen;   110
It is of th' Arcadian kinde,
Ther's not the like twixt either Inde;
If you walke, 'twill walke you by,
If you sit downe, it downe will lye,

[1] Without hornes.

It with gesture will you wooe,
And counterfeit those things you doe;
Ore each Hillock it will vault,
And nimbly doe the Summer-sault,
Upon the hinder Legs 'twill goe,
And follow you a furlong so,   120
And if by chance a Tune you roate,
'Twill foote it finely to your note,
Sceke the worlde and you may misse
To finde out such a thing as this;
This my loue I haue for thee
So thou'lt leaue him and goe with me.

    Lirope. Beleeue me Youths your gifts are rare,
And you offer wondrous faire;
Lalus for Lambe, Cleon for Kyd,
'Tis hard to iudge which most doth bid,   130
And haue you two such things in store,
And I n'er knew of them before?
Well yet I dare a Wager lay
That Brag my little Dog shall play,
As dainty tricks when I shall bid,
As Lalus Lambe, or Cleons Kid.
But t' may fall out that I may neede them
Till when yee may doe well to feed them;
Your Goate and Mutton pretty be
But Youths these are noe bayts for me,   140
Alasse good men, in vaine ye wooe,
'Tis not your Lambe nor Kid will doe.

    Lalus. I haue two Sparrowes white as Snow,
Whose pretty eyes like sparkes doe show;
In her Bosome Venus hatcht them
Where her little Cupid watcht them,
Till they too fledge their Nests forsooke
Themselues and to the Fields betooke,
Where by chance a Fowler caught them
Of whom I full dearely bought them;   150
They'll fetch you Conserue from the [2]Hip,
And lay it softly on your Lip,
Through their nibling bills they'll Chirup
And fluttering feed you with the Sirup,
And if thence you put them by

[2] The redde fruit of the smooth Bramble.

They to your white necke will flye,
And if you expulse them there
They'll hang vpon your braded Hayre;
You so long shall see them prattle
Till at length they'll fall to battle,   160
And when they haue fought their fill,
You will smile to see them bill
These birds my Lirope's shall be
So thou'lt leaue him and goe with me.

    Cleon. His Sparrowes are not worth a rush
I'le finde as good in euery bush,
Of Doues I haue a dainty paire
Which when you please to take the Air,
About your head shall gently houer
You Cleere browe from the Sunne to couer,   170
And with their nimble wings shall fan you,
That neither Cold nor Heate shall tan you,
And like Vmbrellas with their feathers
Sheeld you in all sorts of weathers:
They be most dainty Coloured things,
They haue Damask backs and Chequerd wings,
Their neckes more Various Cullours showe
Then there be mixed in the Bowe;
Venus saw the lesser Doue
And therewith was farre in Loue,   180
Offering for't her goulden Ball
For her Sonne to play withall;
These my Liropes shall be
So shee'll leaue him and goe with me.

    Lirope. Then for Sparrowes, and for Doues
I am fitted twixt my Loues,
But Lalus I take no delight
In Sparowes, for they'll scratch and bite
And though ioynd, they are euer wooing
Alwayes billing, if not doeing,   190
Twixt Venus breasts if they haue lyen
I much feare they'll infect myne;
Cleon your Doues are very dainty,
Tame Pidgeons else you know are plenty,
These may winne some of your Marrowes
I am not caught with Doues, nor Sparrowes,
I thanke ye kindly for your Coste,
Yet your labour is but loste.

Lalus. With full-leau'd Lillies I will stick
Thy braded hayre all o'r so thick,   200
That from it a Light shall throw
Like the Sunnes vpon the Snow.
Thy Mantle shall be Violet Leaues,
With the fin'st the Silkeworme weaues
As finely wouen; whose rich smell
The Ayre about thee so shall swell
That it shall haue no power to mooue.
A Ruffe of Pinkes thy Robe aboue
About thy necke so neatly set
That Art it cannot counterfet,   210
Which still shall looke so Fresh and new,
As if vpon their Roots they grew:
And for thy head Ile haue a Tyer
Of netting, made of Strawbery wyer,
And in each knot that doth compose
A Mesh, shall stick a halfe blowne Rose,
Red, damaske, white, in order set
About the sides, shall run a Fret
Of Primroses, the Tyer throughout
With Thrift and Dayses frindgd about;   220
All this faire Nimph Ile doe for thee,
So thou'lt leaue him and goe with me.

    Cleon. These be but weeds and Trash he brings,
Ile giue thee solid, costly things,
His will wither and be gone
Before thou well canst put them on;
With Currall I will haue thee Crown'd,
Whose Branches intricatly wound
Shall girt thy Temples euery way;
And on the top of euery Spray   230
Shall stick a Pearle orient and great,
Which so the wandring Birds shall cheat,
That some shall stoope to looke for Cheries,
As other for tralucent Berries.
And wondering, caught e'r they be ware
In the curld Tramels of thy hayre:
And for thy necke a Christall Chaine
Whose lincks shapt like to drops of Raine,
Vpon thy panting Breast depending,
Shall seeme as they were still descending,   240
And as thy breath doth come and goe,

So seeming still to ebbe and flow:
With Amber Bracelets cut like Bees,
Whose strange transparency who sees,
With Silke small as the Spiders Twist
Doubled so oft about thy Wrist,
Would surely thinke aliue they were,
From Lillies gathering hony there.
Thy Buskins Ivory, caru'd like Shels
Of Scallope, which as little Bels   250
Made hollow, with the Ayre shall Chime,
And to thy steps shall keepe the time:
Leaue Lalus, Lirope for me
And these shall thy rich dowry be.

    Lirope. Lalus for Flowers. Cleon for Iemmes,
For Garlands and for Diadems,
I shall be sped, why this is braue,
What Nimph can choicer Presents haue,
With dressing, brading, frowncing, flowring,
All your Iewels on me powring,   260
In this brauery being drest,
To the ground I shall be prest,
That I doubt the Nimphes will feare me,
Nor will venture to come neare me;
Neuer Lady of the May,
To this houre was halfe so gay;
All in flowers, all so sweet,
From the Crowne, beneath the Feet,
Amber, Currall, Ivory, Pearle,
If this cannot win a Gerle,   270
Ther's nothing can, and this ye wooe me,
Giue me your hands and trust ye to me,
(Yet to tell ye I am loth)
That I'le haue neither of you both;

    Lalus. When thou shalt please to stem the flood,
(As thou art of the watry brood)
I'le haue twelve Swannes more white than Snow,
Yokd for the purpose two and two,
To drawe thy Barge wrought of fine Reed
So well that it nought else shall need,   280
The Traces by which they shall hayle
Thy Barge; shall be the winding trayle
Of woodbynd; whose braue Tasseld Flowers
(The Sweetnesse of the Woodnimphs Bowres)

Shall be the Trappings to adorne,
The Swannes, by which thy Barge is borne,
Of flowred Flags I'le rob the banke
Of water-Cans and King-cups ranck
To be the Couering of thy Boate,
And on the Streame as thou do'st Floate,   290
The Naiades that haunt the deepe,
Themselues about thy Barge shall keepe,
Recording most delightfull Layes,
By Sea Gods written in thy prayse.
And in what place thou hapst to land,
There the gentle Siluery sand,
Shall soften, curled with the Aier
As sensible of thy repayre:
This my deare loue I'le doe for thee,
So Thou'lt leaue him and goe with me: 300

    Cleon. Tush Nimphe his Swannes will prove but Geese,
His Barge drinke water like a Fleece;
A Boat is base, I'le thee prouide,
A Chariot, wherein Ioue may ride;
In which when brauely thou art borne,
Thou shalt looke like the gloryous morne
Vshering the Sunne, and such a one
As to this day was neuer none,
Of the Rarest Indian Gummes,
More pretious then your Balsamummes   310
Which I by Art haue made so hard,
That they with Tooles may well be Caru'd
To make a Coach of: which shall be
Materyalls of this one for thee,
And of thy Chariot each small peece
Shall inlayd be with Amber Greece,
And guilded with the Yellow ore
Produc'd from Tagus wealthy shore;
In which along the pleasant Lawne,
With twelue white Stags thou shalt be drawne,   320
Whose brancht palmes of a stately height,
With seuerall nosegayes shall be dight;
And as thou ryd'st, thy Coach about,
For thy strong guard shall runne a Rout,
Of Estriges; whose Curled plumes,
Sen'sd with thy Chariots rich perfumes,
The scent into the Aier shall throw;
Whose naked Thyes shall grace the show;

Whilst the Woodnimphs and those bred
Vpon the mountayns, o'r thy head   330
Shall beare a Canopy of flowers,
Tinseld with drops of Aprill showers,
Which shall make more glorious showes
Then spangles, or your siluer Oas;
This bright nimph I'le doe for thee
So thou'lt leaue him and goe with me.

    Lirope. Vie and reuie, like Chapmen profer'd,
Would't be receaued what you haue offer'd;
Ye greater honour cannot doe me,
If not building Altars to me: 340
Both by Water and by Land,
Bardge and Chariot at command;
Swans vpon the Streame to rawe me,
Stags vpon the Land to drawe me,
In all this Pompe should I be seene,
What a pore thing were a Queene:
All delights in such excesse,
As but yee, who can expresse:
Thus mounted should the Nimphes me see,
All the troope would follow me,   350
Thinking by this state that I
Would asume a Deitie.
There be some in loue haue bin,
And I may commit that sinne,
And if e'r I be in loue,
With one of you I feare twill proue,
But with which I cannot tell,
So my gallant Youths farewell.

The third Nimphall

DORON. NAIJS. CLORIS. CLAIA.
DORILVS. CLOE. MERTILLA.
FLORIMEL.

With Nimphes and Forresters.

Poetick Raptures, sacred fires,
With which Apollo his inspires,
This Nimphall gives you; and withall
Obserues the Muses Festivall.

Amongst th' Elizians many mirthfull Feasts,
At which the Muses are the certaine guests,
Th' obserue one Day with most Emperiall state,
To wise Apollo which they dedicate,
The Poets God; and to his Alters bring
Th' enamel'd Brauery of the beauteous spring,
And strew their Bowers with euery precious sweet,
Which still wax fresh, most trod on with their feet;
With most choice flowers each Nimph doth brade her hayre,
And not the mean'st but bauldrick wise doth weare   10
Some goodly Garland, and the most renown'd
With curious Roseat Anadems are crown'd.
These being come into the place where they
Yearely obserue the Orgies to that day,
The Muses from their Heliconian spring
Their brimfull Mazers to the feasting bring:
When with deepe Draughts out of those plenteous Bowles,
The iocond Youth haue swild their thirsty soules,
They fall enraged with a sacred heat,
And when their braines doe once begin to sweat   20
They into braue and Stately numbers breake,
And not a word that any one doth speake
But tis Prophetick, and so strangely farre
In their high fury they transported are,
As there's not one, on any thing can straine,
But by another answred is againe
In the same Rapture, which all sit to heare;
When as two Youths that soundly liquord were,
Dorilus and Doron, two as noble swayns
As euer kept on the Elizian playns,   30
First by their signes attention hauing woonne,
Thus they the Reuels frolikly begunne.

    Doron. Come Dorilus, let vs be brave,
In lofty numbers let vs raue,
  With Rymes I will inrich thee.

    Dorilus. Content say I, then bid the base,
Our wits shall runne the Wildgoosechase,
  Spurre vp, or I will swich thee.

    Doron. The Sunne out of the East doth peepe,
And now the day begins to creepe,   40
  Vpon the world at leasure.

176

Dorilus. The Ayre enamor'd of the Greaues,
The West winde stroaks the velvit leaues
And kisses them at pleasure.

Doron. The spinners webs twixt spray and spray,
The top of euery bush make gay,
By filmy coards there dangling.

Dorilus. For now the last dayes euening dew
Euen to the full it selfe doth shew,
Each bough with Pearle bespangling.   50

Doron. O Boy how thy abundant vaine
Euen like a Flood breaks from thy braine,
Nor can thy Muse be gaged.

Dorilus. Why nature forth did neuer bring
A man that like to me can sing,
If once I be enraged.

Doron. Why Dorilus I in my skill
Can make the swiftest Streame stand still,
Nay beare back to his springing.

Dorilus. And I into a Trance most deepe   60
Can cast the Birds that they shall sleepe
When fain'st they would be singing.

Doron. Why Dorilus thou mak'st me mad,
And now my wits begin to gad,
But sure I know not whither.

Dorilus. O Doron let me hug thee then,
There neuer was two madder men,
Then let vs on together.

Doron. Hermes the winged Horse bestrid,
And thorow thick and thin he rid,   70
And floundred throw the Fountaine.

Dorilus. He spurd the Tit vntill he bled,
So that at last he ran his head
Against the forked Mountaine,

Doron. How sayst thou, but pyde Iris got

Into great Iunos Chariot,
I spake with one that saw her.

   Dorilus. And there the pert and sawcy Elfe,
Behau'd her as twere Iuno's selfe,
And made the Peacocks draw her.   80

   Doron. Ile borrow Phoebus fiery Iades,
With which about the world he trades,
And put them in my Plow.

   Dorilus. O thou most perfect frantique man,
Yet let thy rage be what it can,
Ile be as mad as thou.

   Doron. Ile to great Ioue, hap good, hap ill,
Though he with Thunder threat to kill,
And beg of him a boone.

   Dorilus. To swerue vp one of Cynthias beames,   90
And there to bath thee in the streames.
Discouerd in the Moone.

   Doron. Come frolick Youth and follow me,
My frantique boy, and Ile show thee
The Countrey of the Fayries.

   Dorilus. The fleshy Mandrake where't doth grow
In noonshade of the Mistletow,
And where the Phoenix Aryes.

   Doron. Nay more, the Swallowes winter bed,
The Caverns where the Winds are bred,   100
Since thus thou talkst of showing.

   Dorilus. And to those Indraughts Ile thee bring,
That wondrous and eternall spring
Whence th' Ocean hath its flowing.

   Doron. We'll downe to the darke house of sleepe,
Where snoring Morpheus doth keepe,
And wake the drowsy Groome.

   Dorilus. Downe shall the Dores and Windowes goe,
The Stooles vpon the Floare we'll throw,

And roare about the Roome. 110

The Muses here commanded them to stay,
Commending much the caridge of their Lay
As greatly pleasd at this their madding Bout,
To heare how brauely they had borne it out
From first to the last, of which they were right glad,
By this they found that Helicon still had
That vertue it did anciently retaine
When Orpheus Lynus and th' Ascrean Swaine
Tooke lusty Rowses, which hath made their Rimes,
To last so long to all succeeding times. 120
And now amongst this beauteous Beauie here,
Two wanton Nimphes, though dainty ones they were,
Naijs and Cloe in their female fits
Longing to show the sharpnesse of their wits,
Of the nine Sisters speciall leaue doe craue
That the next Bout they two might freely haue,
Who hauing got the suffrages of all,
Thus to their Rimeing instantly they fall.

    Naijs. Amongst you all let us see
Who ist opposes mee, 130
Come on the proudest she
To answere my dittye.

    Cloe. Why Naijs, that am I,
Who dares thy pride defie.
And that we soone shall try
Though thou be witty.

    Naijs. Cloe I scorne my Rime
Should obserue feet or time,
Now I fall, then I clime,
Where i'st I dare not. 140

    Cloe. Giue thy Invention wing,
And let her flert and fling,
Till downe the Rocks she ding,
For that I care not.

    Naijs. This presence delights me,
My freedome inuites me,
The Season excytes me,
In Rime to be merry.

Cloe. And I beyond measure,
Am rauisht with pleasure,   150
To answer each Ceasure,
Untill thou beist weary.

Naijs. Behold the Rosye Dawne,
Rises in Tinsild Lawne,
And smiling seemes to fawne,
Vpon the mountaines.

Cloe. Awaked from her Dreames,
Shooting foorth goulden Beames
Dansing vpon the Streames
Courting the Fountaines.   160

Naijs. These more then sweet Showrets,
Intice vp these Flowrets,
To trim vp our Bowrets,
Perfuming our Coats.

Cloe. Whilst the Birds billing
Each one with his Dilling
The thickets still filling
With Amorous Noets.

Naijs. The Bees vp in hony rould,
More then their thighes can hould,   170
Lapt in their liquid gould,
Their Treasure vs Bringing.

Cloe. To these Rillets purling
Vpon the stones Curling,
And oft about wherling,
Dance tow'ard their springing.

Naijs. The Wood-Nimphes sit singing,
Each Groue with notes ringing
Whilst fresh Ver is flinging
Her Bounties abroad.   180

Cloe. So much as the Turtle,
Upon the low Mertle,
To the meads fertle,
Her cares doth unload.

Naijs. Nay 'tis a world to see,
In euery bush and Tree,
The Birds with mirth and glee,
Woo'd as they woe.

Cloe. The Robin and the Wren,
Every Cocke with his Hen,
Why should not we and men,
Doe as they doe.

190

Naijs. The Faires are hopping,
The small Flowers cropping,
And with dew dropping,
Skip thorow the Greaues.

Cloe. At Barly-breake they play
Merrily all the day,
At night themselues they lay
Vpon the soft leaues.

200

Naijs. The gentle winds sally,
Vpon every Valley,
And many times dally
And wantonly sport.

Cloe. About the fields tracing,
Each other in chasing,
And often imbracing,
In amorous sort.

Naijs. And Eccho oft doth tell
Wondrous things from her Cell,
As her what chance befell,
Learning to prattle.

210

Cloe. And now she sits and mocks
The Shepherds and their flocks,
And the Heards from the Rocks
Keeping their Cattle.

When to these Maids the Muses silence cry,
For 'twas the opinion of the Company,
That were not these two taken of, that they
Would in their Conflict wholly spend the day.

220

When as the Turne to Florimel next came,
A Nimph for Beauty of especiall name,
Yet was she not so Iolly as the rest:
And though she were by her companions prest,
Yet she by no intreaty would be wrought
To sing, as by th' Elizian Lawes she ought:
When two bright Nimphes that her companions were,
And of all other onely held her deare,
Mild Claris and Mertilla, with faire speech
Their most beloued Florimel beseech,   230
T'obserue the Muses, and the more to wooe her,
They take their turnes, and thus they sing vnto her.

  Cloris. Sing, Florimel, O sing, and wee
Our whole wealth will giue to thee,
We'll rob the brim of euery Fountaine,
Strip the sweets from euery Mountaine,
We will sweepe the curled valleys,
Brush the bancks that mound our allyes,
We will muster natures dainties
When she wallowes in her plentyes,   240
The lushyous smell of euery flower
New washt by an Aprill shower,
The Mistresse of her store we'll make thee
That she for her selfe shall take thee;
Can there be a dainty thing,
That's not thine if thou wilt sing.

  Mertilla. When the dew in May distilleth,
And the Earths rich bosome filleth,
And with Pearle embrouds each Meadow,
We will make them like a widow,   250
And in all their Beauties dresse thee,
And of all their spoiles possesse thee,
With all the bounties Zephyre brings,
Breathing on the yearely springs,
The gaudy bloomes of euery Tree
In their most beauty when they be,
What is here that may delight thee,
Or to pleasure may excite thee,
Can there be a dainty thing
That's not thine if thou wilt sing.   260

But Florimel still sullenly replyes
I will not sing at all, let that suffice:

When as a Nimph one of the merry ging
Seeing she no way could be wonne to sing;
Come, come, quoth she, ye vtterly vndoe her
With your intreaties, and your reuerence to her;
For praise nor prayers, she careth not a pin;
They that our froward Florimel would winne,
Must worke another way, let me come to her,
Either Ile make her sing, or Ile vndoe her.   270

  Claia. Florimel I thus coniure thee,
  Since their gifts cannot alure thee;
  By stampt Garlick, that doth stink
  Worse then common Sewer, or Sink,
  By Henbane, Dogsbane, Woolfsbane, sweet
  As any Clownes or Carriers feet,
  By stinging Nettles, pricking Teasels
  Raysing blisters like the measels,
  By the rough Burbreeding docks,
  Rancker then the oldest Fox,   280
  By filthy Hemblock, poysning more
  Then any vlcer or old sore,
  By the Cockle in the corne,
  That smels farre worse then doth burnt horne,
  By Hempe in water that hath layne,
  By whose stench the Fish are slayne,
  By Toadflax which your Nose may tast,
  If you haue a minde to cast,
  May all filthy stinking Weeds
  That e'r bore leafe, or e'r had seeds,   290
  Florimel be giuen to thee,
  If thou'lt not sing as well as wee.

At which the Nimphs to open laughter fell,
Amongst the rest the beauteous Florimel,
(Pleasd with the spell from Claia that came,
A mirthfull Gerle and giuen to sport and game)
As gamesome growes as any of them all,
And to this ditty instantly doth fall.

  Florimel. How in my thoughts should I contriue
  The Image I am framing,   300
  Which is so farre superlatiue,
  As tis beyond all naming;
  I would Ioue of my counsell make,
  And haue his judgement in it,

But that I doubt he would mistake
How rightly to begin it,
It must be builded in the Ayre,
And tis my thoughts must doo it,
And onely they must be the stayre
From earth to mount me to it,   310
For of my Sex I frame my Lay,
Each houre, our selues forsaking,
How should I then finde out the way
To this my vndertaking,
When our weake Fancies working still,
Yet changing every minnit,
Will shew that it requires some skill,
Such difficulty's in it.
We would things, yet we know not what,
And let our will be granted,   320
Yet instantly we finde in that
Something vnthought of wanted:
Our ioyes and hopes such shadowes are,
As with our motions varry,
Which when we oft haue fetcht from farre,
With us they neuer tarry:
Some worldly crosse doth still attend,
What long we haue in spinning,
And e'r we fully get the end
We lose of our beginning.   330
Our pollicies so peevish are,
That with themselues they wrangle,
And many times become the snare
That soonest vs intangle;
For that the Loue we beare our Friends
Though nere so strongly grounded,
Hath in it certaine oblique ends
If to the bottome sounded:
Our owne well wishing making it,
A pardonable Treason;   340
For that is deriud from witt,
And vnderpropt with reason.
For our Deare selues beloued sake
(Euen in the depth of passion)
Our Center though our selues we make,
Yet is not that our station;
For whilst our Browes ambitious be
And youth at hand awayts vs,
It is a pretty thing to see

How finely Beautie cheats vs, 350
And whilst with tyme we tryfling stand
To practise Antique graces
Age with a pale and withered hand
Drawes Furowes in our faces.

When they which so desirous were before
To hear her sing; desirous are far more
To haue her cease; and call to haue her stayd
For she to much alredy had bewray'd.
And as the thrice three Sisters thus had grac'd
Their Celebration, and themselues had plac'd 360
Vpon a Violet banck, in order all
Where they at will might view the Festifall
The Nimphs and all the lusty youth that were
At this braue Nimphall, by them honored there,
To Gratifie the heauenly Gerles againe
Lastly prepare in state to entertaine
Those sacred Sisters, fairely and confer,
On each of them, their prayse particular
And thus the Nimphes to the nine Muses sung.
When as the Youth and Forresters among 370
That well prepared for this businesse were,
Become the Chorus, and thus sung they there.

    Nimphes. Clio then first of those Celestiall nine
That daily offer to the sacred shryne,
Of wise Apollo; Queene of Stories,
Thou that vindicat'st the glories
Of passed ages, and renewst
Their acts which euery day thou viewst,
And from a lethargy dost keepe
Old nodding time, else prone to sleepe. 380

    Chorus. Clio O craue of Phoebus to inspire
Vs, for his Altars with his holiest fire,
And let his glorious euer-shining Rayes
Giue life and growth to our Elizian Bayes.

    Nimphes. Melpomine thou melancholly Maid
Next, to wise Phoebus we inuoke thy ayd,
In Buskins that dost stride the Stage,
And in thy deepe distracted rage,
In blood-shed that dost take delight,
Thy obiect the most fearfull sight, 390

That louest the sighes, the shreekes, and sounds
Of horrors, that arise from wounds.

   Chorus. Sad Muse, O craue of Phoebus to inspire
Vs for his Altars, with his holiest fire,
And let his glorious euer-shining Rayes
Giue life and growth to our Elizian Bayes.

   Nimphes. Comick Thalia then we come to thee,
Thou mirthfull Mayden, onely that in glee
And loues deceits, thy pleasure tak'st,
Of which thy varying Scene that mak'st   400
And in thy nimble Sock do'st stirre
Loude laughter through the Theater,
That with the Peasant mak'st the sport,
As well as with the better sort.

   Chorus. Thalia craue of Phoebus to inspire
Vs for his Alters with his holyest fier;
And let his glorious euer-shining Rayes
Giue life, and growth to our Elizian Bayes.

   Nimphes. Euterpe next to thee we will proceed,
That first sound'st out the Musick on the Reed,   410
With breath and fingers giu'ng life,
To the shrill Cornet and the Fyfe.
Teaching euery stop and kaye,
To those vpon the Pipe that playe,
Those which Wind-Instruments we call
Or soft, or lowd, or greate, or small,

   Chorus. Euterpe aske of Phebus to inspire,
Vs for his Alters with his holyest fire
And let his glorious euer-shining Rayes
Giue life and growth to our Elizian Bayes.   420

   Nimphes. Terpsichore that of the Lute and Lyre,
And Instruments that sound with Cords and wyere,
That art the Mistres, to commaund
The touch of the most Curious hand,
When euery Quauer doth Imbrace
His like in a true Diapase,
And euery string his sound doth fill
Toucht with the Finger or the Quill.

Chorus. Terpsichore, craue Phebus to inspire
Vs for his Alters with his holyest fier   430
And let his glorious euer-shining Rayes
Giue life and growth to our Elizian Bayes.

Nimphes. Then Erato wise muse on thee we call,
In Lynes to vs that do'st demonstrate all,
Which neatly, with thy staffe and Bowe,
Do'st measure, and proportion showe;
Motion and Gesture that dost teach
That euery height and depth canst reach,
And do'st demonstrate by thy Art
What nature else would not Impart.   440

Chorus. Deare Erato craue Phebus to inspire
Vs for his Alters with his holyest fire,
And let his glorious euer-shining Rayes,
Giue life and growth to our Elizian Bayes.

Nimphes. To thee then braue Caliope we come
Thou that maintain'st, the Trumpet, and the Drum;
The neighing Steed that louest to heare,
Clashing of Armes doth please thine eare,
In lofty Lines that do'st rehearse
Things worthy of a thundring verse,   450
And at no tyme are heard to straine,
On ought that suits a Common vayne.

Chorus. Caliope, craue Phebus to inspire,
Vs for his Alters with his holyest fier,
And let his glorious euer-shining Rayes,
Giue life and growth to our Elizian Bayes.

Nimphes. Then Polyhymnia most delicious Mayd,
In Rhetoricks Flowers that art arayd,
In Tropes and Figures, richly drest,
The Fyled Phrase that louest best,   460
That art all Elocution, and
The first that gau'st to vnderstand
The force of wordes in order plac'd
And with a sweet deliuery grac'd.

Chorus. Sweet Muse perswade our Phoebus to inspire
Vs for his Altars, with his holiest fire,
And let his glorious euer shining Rayes

Giue life and growth to our Elizian Bayes.

Nimphes. Lofty Vrania then we call to thee,
To whom the Heauens for euer opened be,　　　　470
Thou th' Asterismes by name dost call,
And shewst when they doe rise and fall
Each Planets force, and dost diuine
His working, seated in his Signe,
And how the starry Frame still roules
Betwixt the fixed stedfast Poles.

Chorus. Vrania aske of Phoebus to inspire
Vs for his Altars with his holiest fire,
And let his glorious euer-shining Rayes
Giue life and growth to our Elizian Bayes.　　　　480

The fourth Nimphall

CLORIS and MERTILLA.

Chaste Cloris doth disclose the shames
Of the Felician frantique Dames,
Mertilla striues t' apease her woe,
To golden wishes then they goe.

Mertilla. Why how now Cloris, what, thy head
Bound with forsaken Willow?
Is the cold ground become thy bed?
The grasse become thy Pillow?
O let not those life-lightning eyes
In this sad vayle be shrowded,
Which into mourning puts the Skyes,
To see them ouer-clowded.

Cloris. O my Mertilla doe not praise
These Lampes so dimly burning,　　　　10
Such sad and sullen lights as these
Were onely made for mourning:
Their obiects are the barren Rocks
With aged Mosse o'r shaded;
Now whilst the Spring layes forth her Locks
With blossomes brauely braded.

Mertilla. O Cloris, Can there be a Spring,
O my deare Nimph, there may not,

Wanting thine eyes it forth to bring,
Without which Nature cannot: 20
Say what it is that troubleth thee
Encreast by thy concealing,
Speake; sorrowes many times we see
Are lesned by reuealing.

   Cloris. Being of late too vainely bent
And but at too much leisure;
Not with our Groves and Downes content,
But surfetting in pleasure;
Felicia's Fields I would goe see,
Where fame to me reported,   30
The choyce Nimphes of the world to be
From meaner beauties sorted;
Hoping that I from them might draw
Some graces to delight me,
But there such monstrous shapes I saw,
That to this houre affright me.
Throw the thick Hayre, that thatch'd their Browes,
Their eyes vpon me stared,
Like to those raging frantique Froes
For Bacchus Feasts prepared: 40
Their Bodies, although straight by kinde,
Yet they so monstrous make them,
That for huge Bags blowne vp with wind,
You very well may take them.
Their Bowels in their Elbowes are,
Whereon depend their Panches,
And their deformed Armes by farre
Made larger than their Hanches:
For their behauiour and their grace,
Which likewise should haue priz'd them,   50
Their manners were as beastly base
As th' rags that so disguisd them;
All Anticks, all so impudent,
So fashon'd out of fashion,
As blacke Cocytus vp had sent
Her Fry into this nation,
Whose monstrousnesse doth so perplex,
Of Reason and depriues me,
That for their sakes I loath my sex,
Which to this sadnesse driues me.   60

Mertilla. O my deare Cloris be not sad,
Nor with these Furies danted,
But let these female fooles be mad,
With Hellish pride inchanted;
Let not thy noble thoughts descend
So low as their affections;
Whom neither counsell can amend,
Nor yet the Gods corrections:
Such mad folks ne'r let vs bemoane,
But rather scorne their folly,   70
And since we two are here alone,
To banish melancholly,
Leaue we this lowly creeping vayne
Not worthy admiration,
And in a braue and lofty strayne,
Lets exercise our passion,
With wishes of each others good,
From our abundant treasures,
And in this iocund sprightly mood:
Thus alter we our measures.   80

Mertilla. O I could wish this place were strewd with Roses,
And that this Banck were thickly thrumd with Grasse
As soft as Sleaue, or Sarcenet euer was,
Whereon my Cloris her sweet selfe reposes.

Cloris. O that these Dewes Rosewater were for thee,
These Mists Perfumes that hang vpon these thicks,
And that the Winds were all Aromaticks,
Which, if my wish could make them, they should bee.

Mertilla. O that my Bottle one whole Diamond were,
So fild with Nectar that a Flye might sup,   90
And at one draught that thou mightst drinke it vp,
Yet a Carouse not good enough I feare.

Cloris. That all the Pearle, the Seas, or Indias haue
Were well dissolu'd, and thereof made a Lake,
Thou there in bathing, and I by to take
Pleasure to see thee cleerer than the Waue.

Mertilla. O that the Hornes of all the Heards we see,
Were of fine gold, or else that euery horne
Were like to that one of the Vnicorne,
And of all these, not one but were thy Fee.   100

Cloris. O that their Hooues were Iuory, or some thing,
Then the pur'st Iuory farre more Christalline,
Fild with the food wherewith the Gods doe dine,
To keepe thy Youth in a continuall Spring.

Mertilla. O that the sweets of all the Flowers that grow,
The labouring ayre would gather into one,
In Gardens, Fields, nor Meadowes leauing none,
And all their Sweetnesse vpon thee would throw.

Cloris. Nay that those sweet harmonious straines we heare,
Amongst the liuely Birds melodious Layes,   110
As they recording sit vpon the Sprayes,
Were houering still for Musick at thine eare.

Mertilla. O that thy name were caru'd on euery Tree,
That as these plants still great, and greater grow,
Thy name deare Nimph might be enlarged so,
That euery Groue and Coppis might speake thee.

Cloris. Nay would thy name vpon their Rynds were set,
And by the Nimphes so oft and lowdly spoken,
As that the Ecchoes to that language broken
Thy happy name might hourely counterfet.   120

Mertilla. O let the Spring still put sterne winter by,
And in rich Damaske let her Reuell still,
As it should doe if I might haue my will,
That thou mightst still walke on her Tapistry;
And thus since Fate no longer time alowes
Vnder this broad and shady Sicamore,
Where now we sit, as we haue oft before;
Those yet vnborne shall offer vp their Vowes.

The fift Nimphall

CLAIA, LELIPA, CLARINAX a Hermit.

Of Garlands, Anadems, and Wreathes,
This Nimphall nought but sweetnesse breathes,
Presents you with delicious Posies,
And with powerfull Simples closes.

Claia. See where old Clarinax is set,
His sundry Simples sorting,
From whose experience we may get
What worthy is reporting.
Then Lelipa let vs draw neere,
Whilst he his weedes is weathering,
I see some powerfull Simples there
That he hath late bin gathering.
Hail gentle Hermit, Ioue thee speed,
And haue thee in his keeping,   10
And euer helpe thee at thy need,
Be thou awake or sleeping.

Clarinax. Ye payre of most Celestiall lights,
O Beauties three times burnisht,
Who could expect such heauenly wights
With Angels features furnisht;
What God doth guide you to this place,
To blesse my homely Bower?
It cannot be but this high grace
Proceeds from some high power;   20
The houres like hand-maids still attend,
Disposed at your pleasure,
Ordayned to noe other end
But to awaite your leasure;
The Deawes drawne vp into the Aer,
And by your breathes perfumed,
In little Clouds doe houer there
As loath to be consumed:
The Aer moues not but as you please,
So much sweet Nimphes it owes you,   30
The winds doe cast them to their ease,
And amorously inclose you.

Lelipa. Be not too lauish of thy praise,
Thou good Elizian Hermit,
Lest some to heare such words as these,
Perhaps may flattery tearme it;
But of your Simples something say,
Which may discourse affoord vs,
We know your knowledge lyes that way,
With subiects you haue stor'd vs.   40

Claia. We know for Physick yours you get,
Which thus you heere are sorting,

And vpon garlands we are set,
With Wreathes and Posyes sporting:

    Lelipa. The Chaplet and the Anadem,
The curled Tresses crowning,
We looser Nimphes delight in them,
Not in your Wreathes renowning.

    Clarinax. The Garland long agoe was worne,
As Time pleased to bestow it,   50
The Lawrell onely to adorne
The Conquerer and the Poet.
The Palme his due, who vncontrould,
On danger looking grauely,
When Fate had done the worst it could,
Who bore his Fortunes brauely.
Most worthy of the Oken Wreath
The Ancients him esteemed,
Who in a Battle had from death
Some man of worth redeemed.   60
About his temples Grasse they tye,
Himselfe that so behaued
In some strong Seedge by th' Enemy,
A City that hath saued.
A Wreath of Vervaine Herhauts weare,
Amongst our Garlands named,
Being sent that dreadfull newes to beare,
Offensiue warre proclaimed.
The Signe of Peace who first displayes,
The Oliue Wreath possesses: 70
The Louer with the Myrtle Sprayes
Adornes his crisped Tresses.
In Loue the sad forsaken wight
The Willow Garland weareth:
The Funerall man befitting night,
The balefull Cipresse beareth.
To Pan we dedicate the Pine,
Whose Slips the Shepherd graceth:
Againe the Ivie and the Vine
On his, swolne Bacchus placeth.   80

    Claia. The Boughes and Sprayes, of which you tell,
By you are rightly named,
But we with those of pretious smell
And colours are enflamed;

The noble Ancients to excite
Men to doe things worth crowning,
Not vnperformed left a Rite,
To heighten their renowning:
But they that those rewards deuis'd,
And those braue wights that wore them   90
By these base times, though poorely priz'd,
Yet Hermit we adore them.
The store of euery fruitfull Field
We Nimphes at will possessing,
From that variety they yeeld
Get flowers for euery dressing:
Of which a Garland Ile compose,
Then busily attend me.
These flowers I for that purpose chose,
But where I misse amend me.   100

    Clarinax. Well Claia on with your intent,
Lets see how you will weaue it,
Which done, here for a monument
I hope with me, you'll leaue it.

    Claia. Here Damaske Roses, white and red,
Out of my lap first take I,
Which still shall runne along the thred,
My chiefest Flower this make I:
Amongst these Roses in a row,
Next place I Pinks in plenty,   110
These double Daysyes then for show,
And will not this be dainty.
The pretty Pansy then Ile tye
Like Stones some Chaine inchasing,
And next to them their neere Alye,
The purple Violet placing.
The curious choyce, Clove Iuly-flower,
Whose kinds hight the Carnation
For sweetnesse of most soueraine power
Shall helpe my Wreath to fashion.   120
Whose sundry cullers of one kinde
First from one Root derived,
Them in their seuerall sutes Ile binde,
My Garland so contriued;
A course of Cowslips then I'll stick,
And here and there though sparely
The pleasant Primrose downe Ile prick

Like Pearles, which will show rarely:
Then with these Marygolds Ile make
My Garland somewhat swelling,   130
These Honysuckles then Ile take,
Whose sweets shall helpe their smelling:
The Lilly and the Flower delice,
For colour much contenting,
For that, I them doe only prize,
They are but pore in senting:
The Daffadill most dainty is
To match with these in meetnesse;
The Columbyne compar'd to this,
All much alike for sweetnesse.   140
These in their natures onely are
Fit to embosse the border,
Therefore Ile take especiall care
To place them in their order:
Sweet-Williams, Campions, Sops-in-Wine
One by another neatly:
Thus haue I made this Wreath of mine,
And finished it featly.

    Lelipa. Your Garland thus you finisht haue,
Then as we haue attended   150
Your leasure, likewise let me craue
I may the like be friended.
Those gaudy garish Flowers you chuse,
In which our Nimphes are flaunting,
Which they at Feasts and Brydals vse,
The sight and smell inchanting:
A Chaplet me of Hearbs Ile make
Then which though yours be brauer,
Yet this of myne I'le vndertake
Shall not be short in fauour.   160
With Basill then I will begin,
Whose scent is wondrous pleasing,
This Eglantine I'le next put in,
The sense with sweetnes seasing.
Then in my Lauender I'le lay,
Muscado put among it,
And here and there a leafe of Bay,
Which still shall runne along it.
Germander, Marieram, and Tyme
Which vsed are for strewing,   170
With Hisop as an hearbe most pryme

Here in my wreath bestowing.
Then Balme and Mynt helps to make vp
My Chaplet, and for Tryall,
Costmary that so likes the Cup,
And next it Penieryall
Then Burnet shall beare vp with this
Whose leafe I greatly fansy,
Some Camomile doth not amisse,
With Sauory and some Tansy,   180
Then heere and there I'le put a sprig
Of Rosemary into it
Thus not too little or too big
Tis done if I can doe it.

    Clarinax. Claia your Garland is most gaye,
Compos'd of curious Flowers,
And so most louely Lelipa,
This Chaplet is of yours,
In goodly Gardens yours you get
Where you your laps haue laded;   190
My symples are by Nature set,
In Groues and Fields vntraded.
Your Flowers most curiously you twyne,
Each one his place supplying.
But these rough harsher Hearbs of mine,
About me rudely lying,
Of which some dwarfish Weeds there be,
Some of a larger stature,
Some by experience as we see,
Whose names expresse their nature,   200
Heere is my Moly of much fame,
In Magicks often vsed,
Mugwort and Night-shade for the same
But not by me abused;
Here Henbane, Popy, Hemblock here,
Procuring Deadly sleeping,
Which I doe minister with Feare,
Not fit for each mans keeping.
Heere holy Veruayne, and heere Dill,
Against witchcraft much auailing.   210
Here Horhound gainst the Mad dogs ill
By biting, neuer failing.
Here Mandrake that procureth loue,
In poysning philters mixed,
And makes the Barren fruitfull proue,

The Root about them fixed.
Inchaunting Lunary here lyes
In Sorceries excelling,
And this is Dictam, which we prize
Shot shafts and Darts expelling,   220
Here Saxifrage against the stone
That Powerfull is approued,
Here Dodder by whose helpe alone,
Ould Agues are remoued
Here Mercury, here Helibore,
Ould Vlcers mundifying,
And Shepheards-Purse the Flux most sore,
That helpes by the applying;
Here wholsome Plantane, that the payne
Of Eyes and Eares appeases;   230
Here cooling Sorrell that againe
We vse in hot diseases:
The medcinable Mallow here,
Asswaging sudaine Tumors,
The iagged Polypodium there,
To purge ould rotten humors,
Next these here Egremony is,
That helpes the Serpents byting,
The blessed Betony by this,
Whose cures deseruen writing: 240
This All-heale, and so nam'd of right,
New wounds so quickly healing,
A thousand more I could recyte,
Most worthy of Reuealing,
But that I hindred am by Fate,
And busnesse doth preuent me,
To cure a mad man, which of late
Is from Felicia sent me.

    Claia. Nay then thou hast inough to doe,
We pity thy enduring,   250
For they are there infected soe,
That they are past thy curing.

The sixt Nimphall

SILVIVS, HALCIVS, MELANTHVS.

A Woodman, Fisher, and a Swaine
    This Nimphall through with mirth maintaine,

Whose pleadings so the Nimphes doe please,
   That presently they giue them Bayes.

Cleere had the day bin from the dawne,
All chequerd was the Skye,
Thin Clouds like Scarfs of Cobweb Lawne
Vayld Heauen's most glorious eye.
The Winde had no more strength then this,
That leasurely it blew,
To make one leafe the next to kisse,
That closly by it grew.
The Rils that on the Pebbles playd,
Might now be heard at will;   10
This world they onely Musick made,
Else euerything was still.
The Flowers like braue embraudred Gerles,
Lookt as they much desired,
To see whose head with orient Pearles,
Most curiously was tyred;
And to it selfe the subtle Ayre,
Such souerainty assumes,
That it receiu'd too large a share
From natures rich perfumes.   20
When the Elizian Youth were met,
That were of most account,
And to disport themselues were set
Vpon an easy Mount:
Neare which, of stately Firre and Pine
There grew abundant store,
The Tree that weepeth Turpentine,
And shady Sicamore.
Amongst this merry youthfull trayne
A Forrester they had,   30
A Fisher, and a Shepheards swayne
A liuely Countrey Lad:
Betwixt which three a question grew,
Who should the worthiest be,
Which violently they pursue,
Nor stickled would they be.
That it the Company doth please
This ciuill strife to stay,
Freely to heare what each of these
For his braue selfe could say: 40
When first this Forrester (of all)
That Silvius had to name,

To whom the Lot being cast doth fall,
Doth thus begin the Game.

    Silvius. For my profession then, and for the life I lead,
All others to excell, thus for my selfe I plead;
I am the Prince of sports, the Forrest is my Fee,
He's not vpon the Earth for pleasure liues like me;
The Morne no sooner puts her rosye Mantle on,
But from my quyet Lodge I instantly am gone,   50
When the melodious Birds from euery Bush and Bryer,
Of the wilde spacious Wasts, make a continuall quire;
The motlied Meadowes then, new vernisht with the Sunne
Shute vp their spicy sweets vpon the winds that runne,
In easly ambling Gales, and softly seeme to pace,
That it the longer might their lushiousnesse imbrace:
I am clad in youthfull Greene, I other colour, scorne,
My silken Bauldrick beares my Beugle, or my Horne,
Which setting to my Lips, I winde so lowd and shrill,
As makes the Ecchoes showte from euery neighbouring Hill: 60
My Doghooke at my Belt, to which my Lyam's tyde,
My Sheafe of Arrowes by, my Woodknife at my Syde,
My Crosse-bow in my Hand, my Gaffle or my Rack
To bend it when I please, or it I list to slack,
My Hound then in my Lyam, I by the Woodmans art
Forecast, where I may lodge the goodly Hie-palm'd Hart,
To viewe the grazing Heards, so sundry times I vse,
Where by the loftiest Head I know my Deare to chuse,
And to vnheard him then, I gallop o'r the ground
Vpon my wel-breath'd Nag, to cheere my earning Hound.   70
Sometime I pitch my Toyles the Deare aliue to take,
Sometime I like the Cry, the deep-mouth'd Kennell make,
Then vnderneath my Horse, I staulke my game to strike,
And with a single Dog to hunt him hurt, I like.
The Siluians are to me true subiects, I their King,
The stately Hart, his Hind doth to my presence bring,
The Buck his loued Doe, the Roe his tripping Mate,
Before me to my Bower, whereas I sit in State.
The Dryads, Hamadryads, the Satyres and the Fawnes
Oft play at Hyde and Seeke before me on the Lawnes,   80
The frisking Fayry oft when horned Cinthia shines
Before me as I walke dance wanton Matachynes,
The numerous feathered flocks that the wild Forrests haunt
Their Siluan songs to me, in cheerefull dittyes chaunte,
The Shades like ample Sheelds, defend me from the Sunne,
Through which me to refresh the gentle Riuelets runne,

No little bubling Brook from any Spring that falls
But on the Pebbles playes me pretty Madrigals.
I' th' morne I clime the Hills, where wholsome winds do blow,
At Noone-tyde to the Vales, and shady Groues below,   90
T'wards Euening I againe the Chrystall Floods frequent,
In pleasure thus my life continually is spent.
As Princes and great Lords haue Pallaces, so I
Haue in the Forrests here, my Hall and Gallery
The tall and stately Woods, which vnderneath are Plaine,
The Groues my Gardens are, the Heath and Downes againe
My wide and spacious walkes, then say all what ye can,
The Forrester is still your only gallant man.

He of his speech scarce made an end,
But him they load with prayse,   100
The Nimphes most highly him commend,
And vow to giue him Bayes:
He's now cryde vp of euery one,
And who but onely he,
The Forrester's the man alone,
The worthyest of the three.
When some then th' other farre more stayd,
Wil'd them a while to pause,
For there was more yet to be sayd,
That might deserve applause,   110
When Halcius his turne next plyes,
And silence hauing wonne,
Roome for the fisher man he cryes,
And thus his Plea begunne.

   Halcius. No Forrester, it so must not be borne away,
But heare what for himselfe the Fisher first can say,
The Chrystall current Streames continually I keepe,
Where euery Pearle-pau'd Foard, and euery Blew-eyd deepe
With me familiar are; when in my Boate being set,
My Oare I take in hand, my Augle and my Net   120
About me; like a Prince my selfe in state I steer,
Now vp, now downe the Streame, now am I here, now ther,
The Pilot and the Fraught my selfe; and at my ease
Can land me where I list, or in what place I please,
The Siluer-scaled Sholes, about me in the Streames,
As thick as ye discerne the Atoms in the Beames,
Neare to the shady Banck where slender Sallowes grow,
And Willows their shag'd tops downe t'wards the waters bow
I shove in with my Boat to sheeld me from the heat,

Where chusing from my Bag, some prou'd especiall bayt,   130
The goodly well growne Trout I with my Angle strike,
And with my bearded Wyer I take the rauenous Pike,
Of whom when I haue hould, he seldome breakes away
Though at my Lynes full length, soe long I let him play
Till by my hand I finde he well-nere wearyed be,
When softly by degrees I drawe him vp to me.
The lusty Samon to, I oft with Angling take,
Which me aboue the rest most Lordly sport doth make,
Who feeling he is caught, such Frisks and bounds doth fetch,
And by his very strength my Line soe farre doth stretch,   140
As draws my floating Corcke downe to the very ground,
And wresting at my Rod, doth make my Boate turne round.
I neuer idle am, some tyme I bayt my Weeles,
With which by night I take the dainty siluer Eeles,
And with my Draughtnet then, I sweepe the streaming Flood,
And to my Tramell next, and Cast-net from the Mud,
I beate the Scaly brood, noe hower I idely spend,
But wearied with my worke I bring the day to end:
The Naijdes and Nymphes that in the Riuers keepe,
Which take into their care, the store of euery deepe,   150
Amongst the Flowery flags, the Bullrushes and Reed,
That of the Spawne haue charge (abundantly to breed)
Well mounted vpon Swans, their naked bodys lend
To my discerning eye, and on my Boate attend,
And dance vpon the Waues, before me (for my sake)
To th' Musick the soft wynd vpon the Reeds doth make
And for my pleasure more, the rougher Gods of Seas
From Neptune's Court send in the blew Neriades,
Which from his bracky Realme vpon the Billowes ride
And beare the Riuers backe with euery streaming Tyde,   160
Those Billowes gainst my Boate, borne with delightfull Gales,
Oft seeming as I rowe to tell me pretty tales,
Whilst Ropes of liquid Pearle still load my laboring Oares,
As streacht vpon the Streame they stryke me to the Shores:
The silent medowes seeme delighted with my Layes,
As sitting in my Boate I sing my Lasses praise,
Then let them that like, the Forrester vp cry,
Your noble Fisher is your only man say I.

This speech of Halcius turn'd the Tyde,
And brought it so about,   170
That all vpon the Fisher cryde,
That he would beare it out;
Him for the speech he made, to clap

Who lent him not a hand,
And said t'would be the Waters hap,
Quite to put downe the Land.
This while Melanthus silent sits,
(For so the Shepheard hight)
And hauing heard these dainty wits,
Each pleading for his right;   180
To heare them honor'd in this wise,
His patience doth prouoke,
When for a Shepheard roome he cryes,
And for himselfe thus spoke.

    Melanthus. Well Fisher you haue done, and Forrester for you
Your Tale is neatly tould, s'are both's to giue you due,
And now my turne comes next, then heare a Shepherd speak:
My watchfulnesse and care giues day scarce leaue to break,
But to the Fields I haste, my folded flock to see,
Where when I finde, nor Woolfe, nor Fox, hath iniur'd me,   190
I to my Bottle straight, and soundly baste my Throat,
Which done, some Country Song or Roundelay I roate
So merrily; that to the musick that I make,
I Force the Larke to sing ere she be well awake;
Then Baull my cut-tayld Curre and I begin to play,
He o'r my Shephooke leapes, now th'one, now th'other way,
Then on his hinder feet he doth himselfe aduance,
I tune, and to my note, my liuely Dog doth dance,
Then whistle in my Fist, my fellow Swaynes to call,
Downe goe our Hooks and Scrips, and we to Nine-holes fall,   200
At Dust-point, or at Quoyts, else are we at it hard,
All false and cheating Games, we Shepheards are debard;
Suruaying of my sheepe if Ewe or Wether looke
As though it were amisse, or with my Curre, or Crooke
I take it, and when once I finde what it doth ayle,
It hardly hath that hurt, but that my skill can heale;
And when my carefull eye, I cast vpon my sheepe
I sort them in my Pens, and sorted soe I keepe:
Those that are bigst of Boane, I still reserue for breed,
My Cullings I put off, or for the Chapman feed.   210
When the Euening doth approach I to my Bagpipe take,
And to my Grazing flocks such Musick then I make,
That they forbeare to feed; then me a King you see,
I playing goe before, my Subiects followe me,
My Bell-weather most braue, before the rest doth stalke,
The Father of the flocke, and after him doth walke
My writhen-headed Ram, with Posyes crowned in pride

Fast to his crooked hornes with Rybands neatly ty'd
And at our Shepheards Board that's cut out of the ground,
My fellow Swaynes and I together at it round,   220
With Greencheese, clouted Cream, with Flawns, and Custards, stord,
Whig, Sider, and with Whey, I domineer a Lord,
When shering time is come I to the Riuer driue,
My goodly well-fleec'd Flocks: (by pleasure thus I thriue)
Which being washt at will; vpon the shering day,
My wooll I foorth in Loaks, fit for the wynder lay,
Which vpon lusty heapes into my Coate I heaue,
That in the Handling feeles as soft as any Sleaue,
When euery Ewe two Lambes, that yeaned hath that yeare,
About her new shorne neck a Chaplet then doth weare;   230
My Tarboxe, and my Scrip, my Bagpipe, at my back,
My Sheephooke in my hand, what can I say I lacke;
He that a Scepter swayd, a sheephooke in his hand,
Hath not disdaind to haue, for Shepheards then I stand;
Then Forester and you my Fisher cease your strife
I say your Shepheard leads your onely merry life,

They had not cryd the Forester,
And Fisher vp before,
So much: but now the Nimphes preferre,
The Shephard ten tymes more,   240
And all the Ging goes on his side,
Their Minion him they make,
To him themselues they all apply'd,
And all his partie take;
Till some in their discretion cast,
Since first the strife begunne,
In all that from them there had past
None absolutly wonne;
That equall honour they should share;
And their deserts to showe,   250
For each a Garland they prepare,
Which they on them bestowe,
Of all the choisest flowers that weare,
Which purposly they gather,
With which they Crowne them, parting there,
As they came first together.

The seuenth Nimphall

FLORIMEL, LELIPA, NAIJS, CODRVS a Feriman.

The Nimphes, the Queene of loue pursue,
Which oft doth hide her from their view:
But lastly from th' Elizian Nation,
She banisht is by Proclamation.

Florimel. Deare Lelipa, where hast thou bin so long,
Was't not enough for thee to doe me wrong;
To rob me of thy selfe, but with more spight
To take my Naijs from me, my delight?
Yee lazie Girles, your heads where haue ye layd,
Whil'st Venus here her anticke prankes hath playd?

Lelipa. Nay Florimel, we should of you enquire,
The onely Mayden, whom we all admire
For Beauty, Wit, and Chastity, that you
Amongst the rest of all our Virgin crue,   10
In quest of her, that you so slacke should be,
And leaue the charge to Naijs and to me.

Florimel. Y'are much mistaken Lelipa, 'twas I,
Of all the Nimphes, that first did her descry,
At our great Hunting, when as in the Chase
Amongst the rest, me thought I saw one face
So exceeding faire, and curious, yet vnknowne
That I that face not possibly could owne.
And in the course, so Goddesse like a gate,
Each step so full of maiesty and state;   20
That with my selfe, I thus resolu'd that she
Lesse then a Goddesse (surely) could not be:
Thus as Idalia, stedfastly I ey'd,
A little Nimphe that kept close by her side
I noted, as vnknowne as was the other,
Which Cupid was disguis'd so by his mother.
The little purblinde Rogue, if you had seene,
You would haue thought he verily had beene
One of Diana's Votaries so clad,
He euery thing so like a Huntresse had: 30
And she had put false eyes into his head,
That very well he might vs all haue sped.
And still they kept together in the Reare,
But as the Boy should haue shot at the Deare,

He shot amongst the Nimphes, which when I saw,
Closer vp to them I began to draw;
And fell to hearken, when they naught suspecting,
Because I seem'd them vtterly neglecting,
I heard her say, my little Cupid too't,
Now Boy or neuer, at the Beuie shoot,   40
Haue at them Venus quoth the Boy anon,
I'le pierce the proud'st, had she a heart of stone:
With that I cryde out, Treason, Treason, when
The Nimphes that were before, turning agen
To vnderstand the meaning of this cry,
They out of sight were vanish't presently.
Thus but for me, the Mother and the Sonne,
Here in Elizium, had vs all vndone.

    Naijs. Beleeue me, gentle Maide, 'twas very well,
But now heare me my beauteous Florimel,   50
Great Mars his Lemman being cryde out here,
She to Felicia goes, still to be neare
Th' Elizian Nimphes, for at vs is her ayme,
The fond Felicians are her common game.
I vpon pleasure idly wandring thither,
Something worth laughter from those fooles to gather,
Found her, who thus had lately beene surpriz'd,
Fearing the like, had her faire selfe disguis'd
Like an old Witch, and gaue out to haue skill
In telling Fortunes either good or ill;   60
And that more nearly she with them might close,
She cut the Cornes, of dainty Ladies Toes:
She gaue them Phisicke, either to coole or mooue them,
And powders too to make their sweet Hearts loue them:
And her sonne Cupid, as her Zany went,
Carrying her boxes, whom she often sent
To know of her faire Patients how they slept.
By which meanes she, and the blinde Archer crept
Into their fauours, who would often Toy,
And tooke delight in sporting with the Boy;   70
Which many times amongst his waggish tricks,
These wanton Wenches in the bosome prickes;
That they before which had some franticke fits,
Were by his Witchcraft quite out of their wits.
Watching this Wisard, my minde gaue me still
She some Impostor was, and that this skill
Was counterfeit, and had some other end.
For which discouery, as I did attend,

Her wrinckled vizard being very thin,
My piercing eye perceiu'd her cleerer skin   80
Through the thicke Riuels perfectly to shine;
When I perceiu'd a beauty so diuine,
As that so clouded, I began to pry
A little nearer, when I chanc't to spye
That pretty Mole vpon her Cheeke, which when
I saw; suruaying euery part agen,
Vpon her left hand, I perceiu'd the skarre
Which she receiued in the Troian warre;
Which when I found, I could not chuse but smile.
She, who againe had noted me the while,   90
And, by my carriage, found I had descry'd her,
Slipt out of sight, and presently doth hide her.

    Lelipa. Nay then my dainty Girles, I make no doubt
But I my selfe as strangely found her out
As either of you both; in Field and Towne,
When like a Pedlar she went vp and downe:
For she had got a pretty handsome Packe,
Which she had fardled neatly at her backe:
And opening it, she had the perfect cry,
Come my faire Girles, let's see, what will you buy.   100
Here be fine night Maskes, plastred well within,
To supple wrinckles, and to smooth the skin:
Heer's Christall, Corall, Bugle, Iet, in Beads,
Cornelian Bracelets for my dainty Maids:
Then Periwigs and Searcloth-Gloues doth show,
To make their hands as white as Swan or Snow:
Then takes she forth a curious gilded boxe,
Which was not opened but by double locks;
Takes them aside, and doth a Paper spred,
In which was painting both for white and red: 110
And next a piece of Silke, wherein there lyes
For the decay'd, false Breasts, false Teeth, false Eyes
And all the while shee's opening of her Packe,
Cupid with's wings bound close downe to his backe:
Playing the Tumbler on a Table gets,
And shewes the Ladies many pretty feats.
I seeing behinde him that he had such things,
For well I knew no boy but he had wings,
I view'd his Mothers beauty, which to me
Lesse then a Goddesse said, she could not be: 120
With that quoth I to her, this other day,
As you doe now, so one that came this way,

Shew'd me a neate piece, with the needle wrought,
How Mars and Venus were together caught
By polt-foot Vulcan in an Iron net;
It grieu'd me after that I chanc't to let,
It to goe from me: whereat waxing red,
Into her Hamper she hung downe her head,
As she had stoup't some noueltie to seeke,
But 'twas indeed to hide her blushing Cheeke: 130
When she her Trinkets trusseth vp anon,
E'r we were 'ware, and instantly was gone.

  Florimel. But hearke you Nimphes, amongst our idle prate,
Tis current newes through the Elizian State,
That Venus and her Sonne were lately seene
Here in Elizium, whence they oft haue beene
Banisht by our Edict, and yet still merry,
Were here in publique row'd o'r at the Ferry,
Where as 'tis said, the Ferryman and she
Had much discourse, she was so full of glee,   140
Codrus much wondring at the blind Boyes Bow.

  Naijs. And what it was, that easly you may know,
Codrus himselfe comes rowing here at hand.

  Lelipa. Codrus Come hither, let your Whirry stand,
I hope vpon you, ye will take no state
Because two Gods haue grac't your Boat of late;
Good Ferry-man I pray thee let vs heare
What talke ye had, aboard thee whilst they were.

  Codrus. Why thus faire Nimphes.
As I a Fare had lately past,   150
And thought that side to ply,
I heard one as it were in haste;
A Boate, a Boate, to cry,
Which as I was aboute to bring,
And came to view my Fraught,
Thought I; what more then heauenly thing,
Hath fortune hither brought.
She seeing mine eyes still on her were,
Soone, smilingly, quoth she;
Sirra, looke to your Roother there,   160
Why lookst thou thus at me?
And nimbly stept into my Boat,
With her a little Lad

Naked and blind, yet did I note,
That Bow and Shafts he had,
And two Wings to his Shoulders fixt,
Which stood like little Sayles,
With farre more various colours mixt,
Then be your Peacocks Tayles;
I seeing this little dapper Elfe,   170
Such Armes as these to beare,
Quoth I thus softly to my selfe,
What strange thing haue we here,
I neuer saw the like thought I:
Tis more then strange to me,
To haue a child haue wings to fly,
And yet want eyes to see;
Sure this is some deuised toy,
Or it transform'd hath bin,
For such a thing, halfe Bird, halfe Boy,   180
I thinke was neuer seene;
And in my Boat I turnd about,
And wistly viewd the Lad,
And cleerely saw his eyes were out,
Though Bow and Shafts he had.
As wistly she did me behold,
How likst thou him, quoth she,
Why well, quoth I; and better should,
Had he but eyes to see.
How sayst thou honest friend, quoth she,   190
Wilt thou a Prentice take,
I thinke in time, though blind he be,
A Ferry-man hee'll make;
To guide my passage Boat quoth I,
His fine hands were not made,
He hath beene bred too wantonly
To vndertake my trade;
Why helpe him to a Master then,
Quoth she, such Youths be scant,
It cannot be but there be men   200
That such a Boy do want.
Quoth I, when you your best haue done,
No better way you'll finde,
Then to a Harper binde your Sonne,
Since most of them are blind.
The louely Mother and the Boy,
Laught heartily thereat,
As at some nimble iest or toy,

To heare my homely Chat.
Quoth I, I pray you let me know, 210
Came he thus first to light,
Or by some sicknesse, hurt, or blow,
Depryued of his sight;
Nay sure, quoth she, he thus was borne,
Tis strange borne blind, quoth I,
I feare you put this as a scorne
On my simplicity;
Quoth she, thus blind I did him beare,
Quoth I, if't be no lye,
Then he 's the first blind man Ile sweare, 220
Ere practisd Archery,
A man, quoth she, nay there you misse,
He 's still a Boy as now,
Nor to be elder then he is,
The Gods will him alow;
To be no elder then he is,
Then sure he is some sprite
I straight replide, againe at this,
The Goddesse laught out right;
It is a mystery to me, 230
An Archer and yet blinde;
Quoth I againe, how can it be,
That he his marke should finde;
The Gods, quoth she, whose will it was
That he should want his sight,
That he in something should surpasse,
To recompence their spight,
Gaue him this gift, though at his Game
He still shot in the darke,
That he should haue so certaine ayme, 240
As not to misse his marke.
By this time we were come a shore,
When me my Fare she payd,
But not a word she vttered more,
Nor had I her bewrayd,
Of Venus nor of Cupid I
Before did neuer heare,
But that Fisher comming by
Then, told me who they were.

Florimel. Well: against them then proceed 250
As before we haue decreed,
That the Goddesse and her Child,

Be for euer hence exild,
Which Lelipa you shall proclaime
In our wise Apollo's name.

   Lelipa. To all th' Elizian Nimphish Nation,
Thus we make our Proclamation,
Against Venus and her Sonne
For the mischeefe they haue done,
After the next last of May,   260
The fixt and peremtory day,
If she or Cupid shall be found
Vpon our Elizian ground,
Our Edict, meere Rogues shall make them,
And as such, who ere shall take them,
Them shall into prison put,
Cupids wings shall then be cut,
His Bow broken, and his Arrowes
Giuen to Boyes to shoot at Sparrowes,
And this Vagabund be sent,   270
Hauing had due punishment
To mount Cytheron, which first fed him:
Where his wanton Mother bred him,
And there out of her protection
Dayly to receiue correction;
Then her Pasport shall be made,
And to Cyprus Isle conuayd,
And at Paphos in her Shryne,
Where she hath been held diuine,
For her offences found contrite,   280
There to liue an Anchorite.

The eight Nimphall

MERTILLA, CLAIA, CLORIS.

   A Nimph is marryed to a Fay,
Great preparations for the Day,
All Rites of Nuptials they recite you
To the Brydall and inuite you.

   Mertilla. But will our Tita wed this Fay?

   Claia. Yea, and to morrow is the day.

Mertilla. But why should she bestow her selfe
Vpon this dwarfish Fayry Elfe?

Claia. Why by her smalnesse you may finde,
That she is of the Fayry kinde,
And therefore apt to chuse her make
Whence she did her begining take:
Besides he 's deft and wondrous Ayrye,
And of the noblest of the Fayry,   10
Chiefe of the Crickets of much fame,
In Fayry a most ancient name.
But to be briefe, 'tis cleerely done,
The pretty wench is woo'd and wonne.

Cloris. If this be so, let vs prouide
The Ornaments to fit our Bryde.
For they knowing she doth come
From vs in Elizium,
Queene Mab will looke she should be drest
In those attyres we thinke our best,   20
Therefore some curious things lets giue her,
E'r to her Spouse we her deliuer.

Mertilla. Ile haue a Iewell for her eare,
(Which for my sake Ile haue her weare)
'T shall be a Dewdrop, and therein
Of Cupids I will haue a twinne,
Which strugling, with their wings shall break
The Bubble, out of which shall leak,
So sweet a liquor as shall moue
Each thing that smels, to be in loue.   30

Claia. Beleeue me Gerle, this will be fine,
And to this Pendant, then take mine;
A Cup in fashion of a Fly,
Of the Linxes piercing eye,
Wherein there sticks a Sunny Ray
Shot in through the cleerest day,
Whose brightnesse Venus selfe did moue,
Therein to put her drinke of Loue,
Which for more strength she did distill,
The Limbeck was a Phoenix quill,   40
At this Cups delicious brinke,
A Fly approching but to drinke,
Like Amber or some precious Gumme

It transparant doth become.

    Cloris. For Iewels for her eares she's sped,
But for a dressing for her head
I thinke for her I haue a Tyer,
That all Fayryes shall admyre,
The yellowes in the full-blowne Rose,
Which in the top it doth inclose   50
Like drops of gold Oare shall be hung;
Vpon her Tresses, and among
Those scattered seeds (the eye to please)
The wings of the Cantharides:
With some o' th' Raine-bow that doth raile
Those Moons in, in the Peacocks taile:
Whose dainty colours being mixt
With th' other beauties, and so fixt,
Her louely Tresses shall appeare,
As though vpon a flame they were.   60
And to be sure she shall be gay,
We'll take those feathers from the Iay;
About her eyes in Circlets set,
To be our Tita's Coronet.

    Mertilla. Then dainty Girles I make no doubt,
But we shall neatly send her out:
But let's amongst our selues agree,
Of what her wedding Gowne shall be.

    Claia. Of Pansie, Pincke, and Primrose leaues,
Most curiously laid on in Threaues: 70
And all embroydery to supply,
Powthred with flowers of Rosemary:
A trayle about the skirt shall runne,
The Silkewormes finest, newly spunne;
And euery Seame the Nimphs shall sew
With th' smallest of the Spinners Clue:
And hauing done their worke, againe
These to the Church shall beare her Traine:
Which for our Tita we will make
Of the cast slough of a Snake,   80
Which quiuering as the winde doth blow,
The Sunne shall it like Tinsell shew.

    Cloris. And being led to meet her mate,
To make sure that she want no state,

Moones from the Peacockes tayle wee'll shred,
With feathers from the Pheasants head:
Mix'd with the plume of (so high price,)
The precious bird of Paradice.
Which to make vp, our Nimphes shall ply
Into a curious Canopy.   90
Borne o're her head (by our enquiry)
By Elfes, the fittest of the Faery.

    Mertilla. But all this while we haue forgot
Her Buskins, neighbours, haue we not?

    Claia. We had, for those I'le fit her now,
They shall be of the Lady-Cow:
The dainty shell vpon her backe
Of Crimson strew'd with spots of blacke;
Which as she holds a stately pace,
Her Leg will wonderfully grace.   100

    Cloris. But then for musicke of the best,
This must be thought on for the Feast.

    Mertilla. The Nightingale of birds most choyce,
To doe her best shall straine her voyce;
And to this bird to make a Set,
The Mauis, Merle, and Robinet;
The Larke, the Lennet, and the Thrush,
That make a Quier of euery Bush.
But for still musicke, we will keepe
The Wren, and Titmouse, which to sleepe   110
Shall sing the Bride, when shee's alone
The rest into their chambers gone.
And like those vpon Ropes that walke
On Gossimer, from staulke to staulke,
The tripping Fayry tricks shall play
The euening of the wedding day.

    Claia. But for the Bride-bed, what were fit,
That hath not beene talk'd of yet.

    Cloris. Of leaues of Roses white and red,
Shall be the Couering of her bed: 120
The Curtaines, Valence, Tester, all,
Shall be the flower Imperiall,
And for the Fringe, it all along

With azure Harebels shall be hung:
Of Lillies shall the Pillowes be,
With downe stuft of the Butterflee.

    Mertilla. Thus farre we handsomely haue gone,
Now for our Prothalamion
Or Marriage song of all the rest,
A thing that much must grace our feast.   130
Let vs practise then to sing it,
Ere we before th' assembly bring it:
We in Dialogues must doe it,
The my dainty Girles set to it.

    Claia. This day must Tita marryed be,
Come Nimphs this nuptiall let vs see.
Mertilla. But is it certaine that ye say,
Will she wed the Noble Faye?

    Cloris. Sprinckle the dainty flowers with dewes,
Such as the Gods at Banquets vse: 140
Let Hearbs and Weeds turne all to Roses,
And make proud the posts with posies:
Shute your sweets into the ayre,
Charge the morning to be fayre.

    Claia.   } For our Tita is this day,
    Mertilla. } To be married to a Faye.

    Claia. By whom then shall our Bride be led
To the Temple to be wed.

    Mertilla. Onely by your selfe and I,
Who that roomth should else supply?   150

    Cloris. Come bright Girles, come altogether,
And bring all your offrings hither,
Ye most braue and Buxome Beuye,
All your goodly graces Leuye,
Come in Maiestie and state
Our Brydall here to celebrate.

    Mertilla. } For our Tita is this day,
    Claia.   } Married to a noble Faye.

Claia. Whose lot wilt be the way to strow
On which to Church our Bride must goe?   160

Mertilla. That I think as fit'st of all,
To liuely Lelipa will fall.

Cloris. Summon all the sweets that are,
To this nuptiall to repayre;
Till with their throngs themselues they smother,
Strongly styfling one another;
And at last they all consume,
And vanish in one rich perfume.

Mertilla. } For our Tita is this day,
Claia.   } Married to a noble Faye.   170

Mertilla. By whom must Tita married be,
'Tis fit we all to that should see?

Claia. The Priest he purposely doth come,
Th' Arch Flamyne of Elizium.

Cloris. With Tapers let the Temples shine,
Sing to Himen, Hymnes diuine:
Load the Altars till there rise
Clouds from the burnt sacrifice;
With your Sensors fling aloofe
Their smels, till they ascend the Roofe.   180

Mertilla. } For our Tita is this day,
Claia.   } Married to a noble Fay.

Mertilla. But comming backe when she is wed,
Who breakes the Cake aboue her head.

Claia. That shall Mertilla, for shee's tallest,
And our Tita is the smallest.

Cloris. Violins, strike vp aloud,
Ply the Gitterne, scowre the Crowd,
Let the nimble hand belabour
The whistling Pipe, and drumbling Taber: 190
To the full the Bagpipe racke,
Till the swelling leather cracke.

Mertilla. } For our Tita is this day,
Claia.   } Married to a noble Fay.

Claia. But when to dyne she takes her seate
What shall be our Tita's meate?

Mertilla. The Gods this Feast, as to begin,
Haue sent of their Ambrosia in.

Cloris. Then serue we vp the strawes rich berry,
The Respas, and Elizian Cherry: 200
The virgin honey from the flowers
In Hibla, wrought in Flora's bowers:
Full Bowles of Nectar, and no Girle
Carouse but in dissolued Pearle.

Mertilla. } For our Tita is this day,
Claia.   } Married to a noble Fay.

Claia. But when night comes, and she must goe
To Bed, deare Nimphes what must we doe?

Mertilla. In the Posset must be brought,
And Poynts be from the Bridegroome caught.   210

Cloris. In Maskes, in Dances, and delight,
And reare Banquets spend the night:
Then about the Roome we ramble,
Scatter Nuts, and for them scramble:
Ouer Stooles, and Tables tumble,
Neuer thinke of noyse nor rumble.

Mertilla. } For our Tita is this day,
Claia.   } Married to a noble Fay.

The ninth Nimphall

MVSES and NIMPHS.

The Muses spend their lofty layes,
Vpon Apollo and his prayse;
The Nimphs with Gems his Alter build,
This Nimphall is with Phoebus fild.

A Temple of exceeding state,
The Nimphes and Muses rearing,
Which they to Phoebus dedicate,
Elizium euer cheering:
These Muses, and those Nimphes contend
This Phane to Phoebus offring,
Which side the other should transcend,
These praise, those prizes proffering,
And at this long appointed day,
Each one their largesse bringing,   10
Those nine faire Sisters led the way
Thus to Apollo singing.

    The Muses. Thou youthfull God that guid'st the howres,
The Muses thus implore thee,
By all those Names, due to thy powers,
By which we still adore thee.
Sol, Tytan, Delius, Cynthius, styles
Much reuerence that have wonne thee,
Deriu'd from Mountaines as from Iles
Where worship first was done thee.   20
Rich Delos brought thee forth diuine,
Thy Mother thither driven,
At Delphos thy most sacred shrine,
Thy Oracles were giuen.
In thy swift course from East to West,
They minutes misse to finde thee,
That bear'st the morning on thy breast,
And leau'st the night behinde thee.
Vp to Olimpus top so steepe,
Thy startling Coursers currying;   30
Thence downe to Neptunes vasty deepe,
Thy flaming Charriot hurrying.
Eos, Ethon, Phlegon, Pirois, proud,
[1]Their lightning Maynes aduancing:
Breathing forth fire on euery cloud
Vpon their Iourney prancing.
Whose sparkling hoofes, with gold for speed
Are shod, to scape all dangers,
Where they upon Ambrosia feed,
In their celestiall Mangers.   40
[2]Bright Colatina, that of hils

---

[1] The horses drawing the Chariot of the Sunne.
[2] The mountains first saluting the Sunne at his rising.

Is Goddesse, and hath keeping
Her Nimphes, the cleere Oreades wils
T'attend thee from thy sleeping.
Great [3]Demogorgon feeles thy might,
His Mynes about him heating:
Who through his bosome dart'st thy light,
Within the Center sweating.
If thou but touch thy golden Lyre,
Thou Minos mou'st to heare thee: 50
[4]The Rockes feele in themselues a fire,
And rise vp to come neere thee.
'Tis thou that Physicke didst deuise
Hearbs by their natures calling:
Of which some opening at thy Rise,
And closing at thy falling.
Fayre Hyacinth thy most lou'd Lad,
That with the sledge thou sluest;
Hath in a flower the life he had,
Whose root thou still renewest,   60
Thy Daphne thy beloued Tree,
That scornes thy Fathers Thunder,
And thy deare Clitia yet we see,
[5]Not time from thee can sunder;
From thy bright Bow that Arrow flew
(Snatcht from thy golden Quiver)
Which that fell Serpent Python slew,
Renowning thee for euer.
The Actian and the Pythian Games
[6]Deuised were to praise thee,   70
With all th' Apolinary names
That th' Ancients thought could raise thee.
A Shryne vpon this Mountaine hie,
To thee we'll haue erected,
Which thou the God of Poesie
Must care to haue protected:
With thy loud Cinthus that shall share,
With all his shady Bowers,
Nor Licia's Cragus shall compare
With this, for thee, of ours.   80

---

[3] Supposed the God of earth.
[4] One of the Iudges of hell.
[5] A Nimph lou'd of Apollo, and by him changed into a flower.
[6] Playes or Games in honor of Apollo.

Thus hauing sung, the Nimphish Crue
Thrust in amongst them thronging,
Desiring they might haue the due
That was to them belonging.
Quoth they, ye Muses as diuine,
Are in his glories graced,
But it is we must build the Shryne
Wherein they must be placed;
Which of those precious Gemmes we'll make
That Nature can affoord vs,   90
Which from that plenty we will take,
Wherewith we here have stor'd vs:
O glorious Phoebus most diuine,
Thine Altars then we hallow.
And with those stones we build a Shryne
To thee our wise Apollo.

    The Nimphes. No Gem, from Rocke, Seas, running streames,
(Their numbers let vs muster)
But hath from thy most powerfull beames
The Vertue and the Lustre;   100
The Diamond, the King of Gemmes,
The first is to be placed,
That glory is of Diadems,
Them gracing, by them graced:
In whom thy power the most is seene,
The raging fire refelling:
The Emerauld then, most deepely greene,
For beauty most excelling,
Resisting poyson often prou'd
By those about that beare it.   110
The cheerfull Ruby then, much lou'd,
That doth reuiue the spirit,
Whose kinde to large extensure growne
The colour so enflamed,
Is that admired mighty stone
The Carbunckle that's named,
Which from it such a flaming light
And radiency eiecteth,
That in the very dark'st of night
The eye to it directeth.   120
The yellow Iacynth, strengthening Sense,
Of which who hath the keeping,
No Thunder hurts nor Pestilence,
And much prouoketh sleeping:

The Chrisolite, that doth resist
Thirst, proued, neuer failing,
The purple colored Amatist,
'Gainst strength of wine prevailing;
The verdant gay greene Smaragdus,
Most soueraine ouer passion: 130
The Sardonix approu'd by vs
To master Incantation.
Then that celestiall colored stone
The Saphyre, heauenly wholly,
Which worne, there wearinesse is none,
And cureth melancholly:
The Lazulus, whose pleasant blew
With golden vaines is graced;
The Iaspis, of so various hew,
Amongst our other placed;   140
The Onix from the Ancients brought,
Of wondrous Estimation,
Shall in amongst the rest be wrought
Our sacred Shryne to fashion;
The Topas, we'll stick here and there,
And sea-greene colored Berill,
And Turkesse, which who haps to beare
Is often kept from perill,
To Selenite, of Cynthia's light,
So nam'd, with her still ranging,   150
Which as she wanes or waxeth bright
Its colours so are changing.
With Opalls, more then any one,
We'll deck thine Altar fuller,
For that of euery precious stone,
It doth retaine some colour;
With bunches of Pearle Paragon
Thine Altars vnderpropping,
Whose base is the Cornelian,
Strong bleeding often stopping: 160
With th' Agot, very oft that is
Cut strangely in the Quarry,
As Nature ment to show in this,
How she her selfe can varry:
With worlds of Gems from Mines and Seas
Elizium well might store vs:
But we content our selues with these
That readiest lye before vs:
And thus O Phoebus most diuine

Thine Altars still we hallow,   170
And to thy Godhead reare this Shryne
Our onely wise Apollo.

The tenth Nimphall

NAIIS, CLAIA, CORBILVS, SATYRE.

A Satyre on Elizium lights,
Whose vgly shape the Nimphes affrights,
Yet when they heare his iust complaint,
They make him an Elizian Saint.

Corbilus.

What; breathles Nimphs? bright Virgins let me know
What suddaine cause constraines ye to this haste?
What haue ye seene that should affright ye so?
What might it be from which ye flye so fast?
I see your faces full of pallid feare,
As though some perill followed on your flight;
Take breath a while, and quickly let me heare
Into what danger ye haue lately light.

Naijs. Neuer were poore distressed Gerles so glad,
As when kinde, loued Corbilus we saw,   10
When our much haste vs so much weakned had,
That scarcely we our wearied breathes could draw,
In this next Groue vnder an aged Tree,
So fell a monster lying there we found,
As till this day, our eyes did neuer see,
Nor euer came on the Elizian ground.
Halfe man, halfe Goate, he seem'd to vs in show,
His vpper parts our humane shape doth beare,
But he's a very perfect Goat below,
His crooked Cambrils arm'd with hoofe and hayre.   20

Claia. Through his leane Chops a chattering he doth make
Which stirres his staring beastly driueld Beard,
And his sharpe hornes he seem'd at vs to shake,
Canst thou then blame vs though we are afeard.

Corbilus. Surely it seemes some Satyre this should be,
Come and goe back and guide me to the place,
Be not affraid, ye are safe enough with me,

Silly and harmlesse be their Siluan Race.

    Claia. How Corbilus; a Satyre doe you say?
How should he ouer high Parnassus hit?   30
Since to these fields there's none can finde the way,
But onely those the Muses will permit.

    Corbilus. 'Tis true; but oft, the sacred Sisters grace
The silly Satyre, by whose plainnesse, they
Are taught the worlds enormities to trace,
By beastly mens abhominable way;
Besyde he may be banisht his owne home
By this base time, or be so much distrest,
That he the craggy by-clift Hill hath clome
To finde out these more pleasant Fields of rest.   40

    Naijs. Yonder he sits, and seemes himselfe to bow
At our approach, what doth our presence awe him?
Me thinks he seemes not halfe so vgly now,
As at the first, when I and Claia saw him.

    Corbilus. 'Tis an old Satyre, Nimph, I now discerne,
Sadly he sits, as he were sick or lame,
His lookes would say, that we may easly learne
How, and from whence, he to Elizium came.
Satyre, these Fields, how cam'st thou first to finde?
What Fate first show'd thee this most happy store?   50
When neuer any of thy Siluan kinde
Set foot on the Elizian earth before?

    Satyre. O neuer aske, how I came to this place,
What cannot strong necessity finde out?
Rather bemoane my miserable case,
Constrain'd to wander this wide world about:
With wild Silvanus and his woody crue,
In Forrests I, at liberty and free,
Liu'd in such pleasure as the world ne'r knew,
Nor any rightly can conceiue but we.   60
This iocond life we many a day enioy'd,
Till this last age, those beastly men forth brought,
That all those great and goodly Woods destroy'd.
Whose growth their Grandsyres, with such sufferance sought,
That faire Felicia which was but of late,
Earth's Paradice, that neuer had her Peere,
Stands now in that most lamentable state,

That not a Siluan will inhabit there;
Where in the soft and most delicious shade,
In heat of Summer we were wont to play,   70
When the long day too short for vs we made,
The slyding houres so slyly stole away;
By Cynthia's light, and on the pleasant Lawne,
The wanton Fayry we were wont to chase,
Which to the nimble clouen-footed Fawne,
Vpon the plaine durst boldly bid the base.
The sportiue Nimphes, with shouts and laughter shooke
The Hils and Valleyes in their wanton play,
Waking the Ecchoes, their last words that tooke,
Till at the last, they lowder were then they.   80
The lofty hie Wood, and the lower spring,
Sheltring the Deare, in many a suddaine shower;
Where Quires of Birds, oft wonted were to sing,
The flaming Furnace wholly doth deuoure;
Once faire Felicia, but now quite defac'd,
Those Braueries gone wherein she did abound,
With dainty Groues, when she was highly grac'd
With goodly Oake, Ashe, Elme, and Beeches croun'd:
But that from heauen their iudgement blinded is,
In humane Reason it could neuer be,   90
But that they might haue cleerly seene by this,
Those plagues their next posterity shall see.
The little Infant on the mothers Lap
For want of fire shall be so sore distrest,
That whilst it drawes the lanke and empty Pap,
The tender lips shall freese vnto the breast;
The quaking Cattle which their Warmstall want,
And with bleake winters Northerne winde opprest,
Their Browse and Stouer waxing thin and scant,
The hungry Groues shall with their Caryon feast.   100
Men wanting Timber wherewith they should build,
And not a Forrest in Felicia found,
Shall be enforc'd vpon the open Field,
To dig them caues for houses in the ground:
The Land thus rob'd, of all her rich Attyre,
Naked and bare her selfe to heauen doth show,
Begging from thence that Ioue would dart his fire
Vpon those wretches that disrob'd her so;
This beastly Brood by no meanes may abide
The name of their braue Ancestors to heare,   110
By whom their sordid slauery is descry'd,
So vnlike them as though not theirs they were,

Nor yet they sense, nor vnderstanding haue,
Of those braue Muses that their Country song,
But with false Lips ignobly doe depraue
The right and honour that to them belong;
This cruell kinde thus Viper-like deuoure
That fruitfull soyle which them too fully fed;
The earth doth curse the Age, and euery houre
Againe, that it these viprous monsters bred.   120
I seeing the plagues that shortly are to come
Vpon this people cleerely them forsooke:
And thus am light into Elizium,
To whose straite search I wholly me betooke.

    Naijs. Poore silly creature, come along with vs,
Thou shalt be free of the Elizian fields:
Be not dismaid, nor inly grieued thus,
This place content in all abundance yeelds.
We to the cheerefull presence will thee bring,
Of Ioues deare Daughters, where in shades they sit,   130
Where thou shalt heare those sacred Sisters sing,
Most heauenly Hymnes, the strength and life of wit:

    Claia. Where to the Delphian God vpon their Lyres
His Priests seeme rauisht in his height of praise:
Whilst he is crowning his harmonious Quiers
With circling Garlands of immortall Bayes.

    Corbilus. Here liue in blisse, till thou shalt see those slaues,
Who thus set vertue and desert at nought:
Some sacrific'd vpon their Grandsires graues,
And some like beasts in markets sold and bought.   140
Of fooles and madmen leaue thou then the care,
That haue no vnderstanding of their state:
For whom high heauen doth so iust plagues prepare,
That they to pitty shall conuert thy hate.
And to Elizium be thou welcome then,
Vntill those base Felicians thou shalt heare,
By that vile nation captiued againe,
That many a glorious age their captiues were.

SONGS FROM THE 'SHEPHERD'S GARLAND'

[From the Edition of 1593]

The Gods delight, the heauens hie spectacle,
Earths greatest glory, worlds rarest miracle.

Fortunes fay'rst mistresse, vertues surest guide,
Loues Gouernesse, and natures chiefest pride.

Delights owne darling, honours cheefe defence,
Chastities choyce, and wisdomes quintessence.

Conceipts sole Riches, thoughts only treasure,
Desires true hope, Ioyes sweetest pleasure.

Mercies due merite, valeurs iust reward,
Times fayrest fruite, fames strongest guarde.   10

Yea she alone, next that eternall he,
The expresse Image of eternitie.

From Eclogue ij

Tell me fayre flocke, (if so you can conceaue)
The sodaine cause of my night-sunnes eclipse,
If this be wrought me my light to bereaue,
By Magick spels, from some inchanting lips
Or vgly Saturne from his combust sent,
This fatall presage of deaths dreryment.

Oh cleerest day-starre, honored of mine eyes,
Yet sdaynst mine eyes should gaze vpon thy light,
Bright morning sunne, who with thy sweet arise,
Expell'st the clouds of my harts lowring night,   10
Goddes reiecting sweetest sacrifice,
Of mine eyes teares ay offered to thine eyes.

May purest heauens scorne my soules pure desires?
Or holy shrines hate Pilgrims orizons?
May sacred temples gaynsay sacred prayers?
Or Saints refuse the poores deuotions?
Then Orphane thoughts with sorrow be you waind,
When loues Religion shalbe thus prophayn'd.

Yet needes the earth must droope with visage sad,
When siluer dewes been turn'd to bitter stormes,   20
The Cheerful Welkin, once in sables clad,
Her frownes foretell poore humaine creatures harmes.
And yet for all to make amends for this,
The clouds sheed teares, and weepen at my misse.

From Eclogue iij

O thou fayre siluer Thames: O cleerest chrystall flood,
Beta alone the Phenix is, of all thy watery brood,
    The Queene of Virgins onely she:
    And thou the Queene of floods shalt be:
Let all thy Nymphes be ioyfull then to see this happy day,
Thy Beta now alone shalbe the subiect of my laye.

With daintie and delightsome straines of sweetest virelayes:
Come louely shepheards sit we down and chant our Betas prayse:
    And let vs sing so rare a verse,
    Our Betas prayses to rehearse,   10
That little Birds shall silent be, to heare poore shepheards sing,
And riuers backward bend their course, and flow vnto the spring.

Range all thy swannes faire Thames together on a rancke,
And place them duely one by one, vpon thy stately banck,
    Then set together all agood,
    Recording to the siluer flood,
And craue the tunefull Nightingale to helpe you with her lay,
The Osel and the Throstlecocke, chiefe musicke of our maye.

O! see what troups of Nimphs been sporting on the strands,
And they been blessed Nimphs of peace, with Oliues in their hands. 20
    How meryly the Muses sing,
    That all the flowry Medowes ring,
And Beta sits vpon the banck, in purple and in pall,
And she the Queene of Muses is, and weares the Corinall.

Trim vp her Golden tresses with Apollos sacred tree,
O happy sight vnto all those that loue and honor thee,
    The Blessed Angels haue prepar'd,
    A glorious Crowne for thy reward,
Not such a golden Crowne as haughty Cæsar weares,
But such a glittering starry Crowne as Ariadne beares.   30

Make her a goodly Chapilet of azur'd Colombine,
And wreath about her Coronet with sweetest Eglentine:
  Bedeck our Beta all with Lillies,
  And the dayntie Daffadillies,
With Roses damask, white, and red, and fairest flower delice,
With Cowslips of Jerusalem, and cloues of Paradice.

O thou fayre torch of heauen, the days most dearest light,
And thou bright shyning Cinthya, the glory of the night:
  You starres the eyes of heauen,
  And thou the glyding leuen,   40
And thou O gorgeous Iris with all strange Colours dyd,
When she streams foorth her rayes, then dasht is all your pride.

See how the day stands still, admiring of her face,
And time loe stretcheth foorth her armes, thy Beta to imbrace,
  The Syrens sing sweete layes,
  The Trytons sound her prayse,
Goe passe on Thames and hie thee fast vnto the Ocean sea,
And let thy billowes there proclaime thy Betas holy-day.

And water thou the blessed roote of that greene Oliue tree,
With whose sweete shadow, al thy bancks with peace preserued be, 50
  Lawrell for Poets and Conquerours,
  And mirtle for Loues Paramours:
That fame may be thy fruit, the boughes preseru'd by peace,
And let the mournful Cipres die, now stormes and tempest cease.

Wee'l straw the shore with pearle where Beta walks alone,
And we wil paue her princely Bower with richest Indian stone,
  Perfume the ayre and make it sweete,
  For such a Goddesse it is meete,
For if her eyes for purity contend with Titans light,
No maruaile then although they so doe dazell humaine sight.   60

Sound out your trumpets then, from London's stately towres,
To beate the stormie windes a back and calme the raging showres,
  Set too the Cornet and the flute,
  The Orpharyon and the Lute,
And tune the Taber and the Pipe, to the sweet violons,
And moue the thunder in the ayre, with lowdest Clarions.

Beta long may thine Altars smoke, with yeerely sacrifice,
And long thy sacred Temples may their Saboths solemnize,
  Thy shepheards watch by day and night,

Thy Mayds attend the holy light,   70
And thy large empyre stretch her armes from east vnto the west,
And thou vnder thy feet mayst tread, that foule seuen-headed beast.

From Eclogue iv

Melpomine put on thy mourning Gaberdine,
And set thy song vnto the dolefull Base,
And with thy sable vayle shadow thy face,
        with weeping verse,
        attend his hearse,
Whose blessed soule the heauens doe now enshrine.

Come Nymphs and with your Rebecks ring his knell,
Warble forth your wamenting harmony,
And at his drery fatall obsequie,
        with Cypres bowes,   10
        maske your fayre Browes,
And beat your breasts to chyme his burying peale.

Thy birth-day was to all our ioye, the euen,
And on thy death this dolefull song we sing,
Sweet Child of Pan, and the Castalian spring,
        vnto our endless mone,
        from vs why art thou gone,
To fill vp that sweete Angels quier in heauen.

O whylome thou thy lasses dearest loue,
When with greene Lawrell she hath crowned thee,   20
Immortal mirror of all Poesie:
        the Muses treasure,
        the Graces pleasure,
Reigning with Angels now in heauen aboue.

Our mirth is now depriu'd of all her glory,
Our Taburins in dolefull dumps are drownd.
Our viols want their sweet and pleasing sound,
        our melodie is mar'd
and we of ioyes debard,
O wicked world so mutable and transitory.   30

O dismall day, bereauer of delight,
O stormy winter, sourse of all our sorrow,
O most vntimely and eclipsed morrow,
        to rob us quite,

of all delight,
Darkening that starre which euer shone so bright.

Oh Elphin, Elphin, Though thou hence be gone,
In spight of death yet shalt thou liue for aye,
Thy Poesie is garlanded with Baye:
    and still shalt blaze
    thy lasting prayse:
Whose losse poore shepherds euer shall bemone.

Come Girles, and with Carnations decke his graue,
With damaske Roses and the hyacynt:
Come with sweete Williams, Marioram and Mynt,
    with precious Balmes,
    with hymnes and psalmes,
This funerall deserues no lesse at all to haue.

But see where Elphin sits in fayre Elizia,
Feeding his flocke on yonder heauenly playne,
Come and behold, you louely shepheards swayne,
    piping his fill
    on yonder hill,
Tasting sweete Nectar, and Ambrosia.

40

50

From Eclogue vij

Borrill.

Oh spightfull wayward wretched loue,
Woe to Venus which did nurse thee,
Heauens and earth thy plagues doe proue,
Gods and men haue cause to curse thee.
Thoughts griefe, hearts woe,
Hopes paine, bodies languish,
Enuies rage, sleepes foe,
Fancies fraud, soules anguish,
Desires dread, mindes madnes,
Secrets bewrayer, natures error,
Sights deceit, sullens sadnes,
Speeches expence, Cupids terror,
Malcontents melancholly,
Liues slaughter, deaths nurse,
Cares slaue, dotard's folly,
Fortunes bayte, world's curse,
Lookes theft, eyes blindnes,

10

Selfes will, tongues treason,
Paynes pleasure, wrongs kindnes,
Furies frensie, follies reason: 20
With cursing thee as I began,
Neither God, neither man,
Neither Fayrie, neither Feend.

Batte.

Loue is the heauens fayre aspect,
    loue is the glorie of the earth,
Loue only doth our liues direct,
    loue is our guyder from our birth,

Loue taught my thoughts at first to flie,
    loue taught mine eyes the way to loue,
Loue raysed my conceit so hie,   30
    loue framd my hand his arte to proue.

Loue taught my Muse her perfect skill,
    loue gaue me first to Poesie:
Loue is the Soueraigne of my will,
    loue bound me first to loyalty.

Loue was the first that fram'd my speech,
    loue was the first that gaue me grace:
Loue is my life and fortunes leech,
    loue made the vertuous giue me place.

Loue is the end of my desire,   40
    loue is the loadstarre of my loue,
Loue makes my selfe, my selfe admire,
    loue seated my delights aboue.

Loue placed honor in my brest,
    loue made me learnings fauoret,
Loue made me liked of the best,
    loue first my minde on virtue set.

Loue is my life, life is my loue,
    loue is my whole felicity,
Loue is my sweete, sweete is my loue,   50
    I am in loue, and loue in mee.

From Eclogue viij

Farre in the countrey of Arden
There wond a knight hight Cassemen,
    as bolde as Isenbras:
Fell was he and eger bent,
In battell and in Tournament,
    as was the good sir Topas.
He had as antique stories tell,
A daughter cleaped Dowsabell,
    a mayden fayre and free:
And for she was her fathers heire,   10
Full well she was ycond the leyre,
    of mickle curtesie.
The silke wel couth she twist and twine,
And make the fine Marchpine,
    and with the needle werke,
And she couth helpe the priest to say
His Mattens on a holyday,
    and sing a Psalme in Kirke.
She ware a frocke of frolicke greene,
Might well beseeme a mayden Queene,   20
    which seemly was to see.
A hood to that so neat and fine,
In colour like the colombine,
    ywrought full featously.
Her feature all as fresh aboue,
As is the grasse that grows by Doue,
    as lyth as lasse of Kent:
Her skin as soft as Lemster wooll,
As white as snow on peakish hull,
    or Swanne that swims in Trent.   30
This mayden in a morne betime,
Went forth when May was in her prime,
    to get sweet Cetywall,
The hony-suckle, the Harlocke,
The Lilly and the Lady-smocke,
    to decke her summer hall.
Thus as she wandred here and there,
Ypicking of the bloomed Breere,
    she chanced to espie
A shepheard sitting on a bancke,   40
Like Chanteclere he crowed crancke,
    and pip'd with merrie glee:
He leard his sheepe as he him list,

When he would whistle in his fist,
   to feede about him round:
Whilst he full many a caroll sung,
Vntill the fields and medowes rung,
   and that the woods did sound:
In fauour this same shepheards swayne,
Was like the bedlam Tamburlayne,   50
   which helde prowd Kings in awe:
But meeke he was as Lamb mought be,
Ylike that gentle Abel he,
   whom his lewd brother slaw.
This shepheard ware a sheepe gray cloke,
Which was of the finest loke,
   that could be cut with sheere,
His mittens were of Bauzens skinne,
His cockers were of Cordiwin
   his hood of Meniueere.   60
His aule and lingell in a thong,
His tar-boxe on his broad belt hong,
   his breech of Coyntrie blew:
Full crispe and curled were his lockes,
His browes as white as Albion rockes,
   so like a louer true.
And pyping still he spent the day,
So mery as the Popingay:
   which liked Dowsabell,
That would she ought or would she nought,   70
This lad would neuer from her thought:
   she in loue-longing fell,
At length she tucked vp her frocke,
White as the Lilly was her smocke,
   she drew the shepheard nie,
But then the shepheard pyp'd a good,
That all his sheepe forsooke their foode,
   to heare his melodie.
Thy sheepe quoth she cannot be leane,
That haue a iolly shepheards swayne,   80
   the which can pipe so well.
Yea but (sayth he) their shepheard may,
Jf pyping thus he pine away,
   in loue of Dowsabell.
Of loue fond boy take thou no keepe,
Quoth she, looke well vnto thy sheepe,
   lest they should hap to stray.
Quoth he, so had I done full well,

Had I not seene fayre Dowsabell,
    come forth to gather Maye. 90
With that she gan to vaile her head,
Her cheekes were like the Roses red,
    but not a word she sayd.
With that the shepheard gan to frowne,
He threw his pretie pypes adowne,
    and on the ground him layd.
Sayth she, I may not stay till night,
And leaue my summer hall vndight,
    and all for long of thee.
My Coate sayth he, nor yet my foulde, 100
Shall neither sheepe nor shepheard hould,
    except thou fauour me.
Sayth she yet leuer I were dead,
Then I should lose my maydenhead,
    and all for loue of men:
Sayth he yet are you too vnkind,
If in your heart you cannot finde,
    to loue vs now and then:
And J to thee will be as kinde,
As Colin was to Rosalinde, 110
    of curtesie the flower;
Then will I be as true quoth she,
As euer mayden yet might be,
    vnto her Paramour:
With that she bent her snowe-white knee,
Downe by the shepheard kneeled shee,
    and him she sweetely kist.
With that the shepheard whoop'd for ioy,
Quoth he, ther's neuer shepheards boy,
    that euer was so blist. 120

[From the Edition of 1605]

From Eclogue ij

Then this great Vniuerse no lesse,
Can serue her prayses to expresse:
Betwixt her eies the poles of Loue,
The host of heauenly beautyes moue,
Depainted in their proper stories,
As well the fixd as wandring glories,
Which from their proper orbes not goe,
Whether they gyre swift or slowe:
Where from their lips, when she doth speake,
The musick of those sphears do breake,   10
Which their harmonious motion breedeth:
From whose cheerfull breath proceedeth:
That balmy sweetnes that giues birth
To euery ofspring of the earth.
Her shape and cariage of which frame
In forme how well shee beares the same,
Is that proportion heauens best treasure,
Whereby it doth all poyze and measure,
So that alone her happy sight
Conteynes perfection and delight.   20

From Eclogue ij

Vppon a bank with roses set about,
Where pretty turtles ioyning bil to bill,
And gentle springs steale softly murmuring out
Washing the foote of pleasures sacred hill:
There little loue sore wounded lyes,
His bowe and arowes broken,
Bedewd with teares from Venus eyes
Oh greeuous to be spoken.

Beare him my hart slaine with her scornefull eye
Where sticks the arrowe that poore hart did kill,   10
With whose sharp pile request him ere he die,
About the same to write his latest will,
And bid him send it backe to mee,
At instant of his dying,
That cruell cruell shee may see
My faith and her denying.

His chappell be a mournefull Cypresse Shade,
And for a chauntry Philomels sweet lay,
Where prayers shall continually be made
By pilgrim louers passing by that way.   20
With Nymphes and shepheards yearly moane
His timeles death beweeping,
In telling that my hart alone
Hath his last will in keeping.

[From the Edition of 1606]

From Eclogue vij

Now fye vpon thee wayward loue,
Woe to Venus which did nurse thee,
Heauen and earth thy plagues doe proue,
Gods and men haue cause to curse thee.
What art thou but th' extreamst madnesse,
Natures first and only error
That consum'st our daies in sadnesse,
By the minds Continuall terror:
Walking in Cymerian blindnesse,
In thy courses voy'd of reason.   10
Sharp reproofe thy only kindnesse,
In thy trust the highest treason?
Both the Nymph and ruder swaine,
Vexing with continuall anguish,
Which dost make the ould complaine
And the young to pyne and languishe,
Who thee keepes his care doth nurse,
That seducest all to folly,
Blessing, bitterly doest curse,
Tending to destruction wholly: 20
Thus of thee as I began,
So againe I make an end,
Neither god neither man,
Neither faiery, neither feend.

BATTE.

What is Loue but the desire
Of the thing that fancy pleaseth?
A holy and resistlesse fier,
Weake and strong alike that ceaseth,
Which not heauen hath power to let,
Nor wise nature cannot smother,   30
Whereby Phoebus doth begette
On the vniuersall mother.
That the euerlasting Chaine,
Which together al things tied,
And vnmooued them retayne
And by which they shall abide:
That concent we cleerely find,
All things doth together drawe,

And so strong in euery kinde,
Subiects them to natures law.   40
Whose hie virtue number teaches
In which euery thing dooth mooue,
From the lowest depth that reaches
To the height of heauen aboue:
Harmony that wisely found,
When the cunning hand doth strike
Whereas euery amorous sound,
Sweetly marryes with his like.
The tender cattell scarcely take
From their damm's the feelds to proue,   50
But ech seeketh out a make,
Nothing liues that doth not loue:
Not soe much as but the plant
As nature euery thing doth payre,
By it if the male it want
Doth dislike and will not beare:
Nothing then is like to loue
In the which all creatures be.
From it nere let me remooue
Nor let it remooue from me.   60

From Eclogue ix

BATTE.

> Gorbo, as thou cam'st this waye
> By yonder little hill,
> Or as thou through the fields didst straye
> Sawst thou my Daffadill?
>
> Shee's in a frock of Lincolne greene
> The colour maides delight
> And neuer hath her beauty seen
> But through a vale of white.
>
> Then Roses richer to behold
> That trim vp louers bowers,   10
> The Pansy and the Marigould
> Tho Phoebus Paramours.

Gorbo.   Thou well describ'st the Daffadill
> It is not full an hower
> Since by the spring neare yonder hill

I saw that louely flower.

Batte. Yet my faire flower thou didst not meet,
   Nor news of her didst bring,
   And yet my Daffadill more sweete,
   Then that by yonder spring.   20

Gorbo. I saw a shepheard that doth keepe
   In yonder field of Lillies,
   Was making (as he fed his sheepe)
   A wreathe of Daffadillies.

Batte. Yet Gorbo thou delud'st me stil
   My flower thou didst not see,
   For know my pretie Daffadill
   Is worne of none but me.

   To shew it selfe but neare her seate,
   No Lilly is so bould,   30
   Except to shade her from the heate,
   Or keepe her from the colde:

Gorbo. Through yonder vale as I did passe,
   Descending from the hill,
   I met a smerking bony lasse,
   They call her Daffadill:

   Whose presence as along she went,
   The prety flowers did greet,
   As though their heads they downward bent,
   With homage to her feete.   40

   And all the shepheards that were nie,
   From toppe of euery hill,
   Vnto the vallies lowe did crie,
   There goes sweet Daffadill.

Gorbo. I gentle shepheard, now with ioy
   Thou all my flockes dost fill,
   That's she alone kind shepheards boy,
   Let vs to Daffadill.

From Eclogue ix

Motto.	Tell me thou skilfull shepheards swayne,
	Who's yonder in the vally set?
Perkin.	O it is she whose sweets do stayne,
	The Lilly, Rose, or violet.

Motto.   Why doth the Sunne against his kind,
     Stay his bright Chariot in the skies,
Perkin.   He pawseth almost stroken blind,
     With gazing on her heauenly eies:

Motto.   Why doe thy flocks forbeare their foode,
     Which somtyme was their chiefe delight,   10
Perkin.   Because they neede no other good,
     That liue in presence of her sight:

Motto.   How com those flowers to florish still,
     Not withering with sharpe winters breath?
Perkin.   She hath robd nature of her skill,
     And comforts all things with her breath:

Motto.   Why slide these brookes so slow away,
     As swift as the wild Roe that were,
Perkin.   O muse not shepheard that they stay,
     When they her heauenly voice do heare.   20

Motto.   From whence com all these goodly swayns
     And lonely nimphs attir'd in greene,
Perkin.   From gathering garlands on the playnes,
     To crowne thy Siluia shepheards queen.

Motto.   The sun that lights this world below,
     Flocks, Brooks and flowers, can witnesse bear,
Perkin.   These shepheards, and these nymphs do know,
     Thy Syluia is as chast, as fayre.

From Eclogue ix

Rowland. Of her pure eyes (that now is seen)
Chorus.   Help vs to sing that be her faithful swains
Row: O she alone the shepheards Queen,
Cho: Her Flocke that leades,
     The goddesse of these medes,
     These mountaines and these plaines.

Row:	Those eyes of hers that are more cleere,	
Cho:	Then silly shepheards can in song expresse,	
Row:	Then be his beams that rule the yeare,	
Cho:	Fy on that prayse,	10
	In striuing things to rayse:	
	That doth but make them lesse.	

Row:	That doe the flowery spring prolong,	
Cho:	So much the earth doth in her presence ioy,	
Row:	And keeps the plenteous summer young:	
Cho:	And doth asswage	
	The wrathfull winters rage	
	That would our flocks destroy.	

Row:	Ioue saw her brest that naked lay,	
Cho:	A sight alone was fit for Ioue to see:	20
Row:	And swore it was the milkie way,	
Cho:	Of all most pure,	
	The path (we vs assure)	
	Vnto Ioues court to be.	

Row:	He saw her tresses hanging downe.	
Cho:	That too and fro were mooued with the ayre,	
Row:	And sayd that Ariadnes crowne,	
Cho:	With those compar'd:	
	The gods should not regard	
	Nor Berenices hayre.	30

Row:	When she hath watch'd my flockes by night,	
Cho:	O happie were the flockes that she did keepe:	
Row:	They neuer needed Cynthia's light,	
Cho:	That soone gaue place,	
	Amazed with her grace,	
	That did attend thy sheepe.	

Row:	Aboue where heauens hie glories are,	
Cho:	When as she shall be placed in the skies,	
Row:	She shall be calld the shepheards starre,	
Cho:	And euermore,	40
	We shepheards will adore,	
	Her setting and her rise.	

APPENDIX

In this Appendix, I have collected certain fugitive pieces of Drayton's; chiefly commendatory verses prefixed to various friends' books. The first song is from England's Helicon, and is, I think, too pretty to be lost. Three of the commendatory poems are in sonnet-form, and their inclusion brings us nearer the whole number published by Drayton; of which there are doubtless a few still lacking. But I have tried to make the collection of sonnets as complete as possible.

From England's Helicon (1600) p. 97.

Rowlands Madrigall.

Faire Loue rest thee heere,
Neuer yet was morne so cleere,
Sweete be not vnkinde,
Let me thy fauour finde,
     Or else for loue I die.

Harke this pretty bubling spring,
How it makes the Meadowes ring,
Loue now stand my friend,
Heere let all sorrow end,
     And I will honour thee.   10

See where little Cupid lyes,
Looking babies in her eyes.
Cupid helpe me now,
Lend to me thy bowe,
     To wound her that wounded me.

Heere is none to see or tell,
All our flocks are feeding by,
This Banke with Roses spred,
Oh it is a dainty bed,
     Fit for my Loue and me.   20

Harke the birds in yonder Groaue,
How they chaunt vnto my Loue,
Loue be kind to me,
As I haue beene to thee,
     For thou hast wonne my hart.

Calme windes blow you faire,
Rock her thou gentle ayre,
O the morne is noone,
The euening comes too soone,
    To part my Loue and me. 30

The Roses and thy lips doo meete,
Oh that life were halfe so sweete,
Who would respect his breath,
That might die such a death,
    Oh that life thus might die.

All the bushes that be neere,
With sweet Nightingales beset,
Hush sweete and be still,
Let them sing their fill,
    There's none our ioyes to let. 40

Sunne why doo'st thou goe so fast?
Oh why doo'st thou make such hast?
It is too early yet,
So soone from ioyes to flit
    Why art thou so vnkind?

See my little Lambkins runne,
Looke on them till I haue done,
Hast not on the night,
To rob me of her light,
    That liue but by her eyes. 50

Alas, sweete Loue, we must depart,
Harke, my dogge begins to barke,
Some bodie's comming neere,
They shall not find vs heere,
    For feare of being chid.

Take my Garland and my Gloue,
Weare it for my sake my Loue,
To morrow on the greene,
Thou shalt be our Sheepheards Queene,
    Crowned with Roses gay. 60

Mich. Drayton.

FINIS.

From T. Morley's First Book of Ballets (1595).

Mr. M.D. to the Author.

Such was old Orpheus cunning,
That sencelesse things drew neere him,
And heards of beasts to heare him,
The stock, the stone, the Oxe, the Asse came running,
Morley! but this enchaunting
To thee, to be the Musick-God is wanting.
And yet thou needst not feare him;
Draw thou the Shepherds still and Bonny lasses,
And enuie him not stocks, stones, Oxen, Asses.

Prefixed to Christopher Middleton's Legend of Humphrey Duke of Gloucester (1600).

To his friend, Master Chr. M. his Booke.

Like as a man, on some aduenture bound
His honest friendes, their kindnes to expresse,
T'incourage him of whome the maine is own'd;
Some venture more, and some aduenture lesse,
That if the voyage (happily) be good:
They his good fortune freely may pertake;
If otherwise it perrish in the flood,
Yet like good friends theirs perish'd for his sake.
On thy returne I put this little forth,
My chaunce with thine indifferently to proue,
Which though (I know) not fitting with thy worth,
Accept it yet since it proceedes from loue;
    And if thy fortune prosper, I may see
    I haue some share, though most returne to thee.

Mich. Drayton.

Prefixed to John Davies of Hereford; Holy Roode (1609).

To M. IOHN DAVIES, my good friend.

Such men as hold intelligence with Letters,
And in that nice and Narrow way of Verse,
As oft they lend, so oft they must be Debters,
If with the Muses they will haue commerce:
Seldome at Stawles, me, this way men rehearse,

To mine Inferiours, not unto my Betters:
He stales his Lines that so doeth them disperse;
I am so free, I loue not Golden-fetters.
And many Lines fore Writers, be but Setters
To them which cheate with Papers; which doth pierse,
Our Credits: when we shew our selues Abetters:
To those that wrong our knowledge: we rehearse
    Often (my good Iohn; and I loue) thy Letters;
    Which lend me Credit, as I lend my Verse.

Michael Drayton.

Prefixed to Sir David Murray's Sophonisba &c. (1611).
To my kinde friend Da: Murray.

In new attire (and put most neatly on)
Thou Murray mak'st thy passionate Queene apeare,
As when she sat on the Numidian throne,
Deck'd with those Gems that most refulgent were.
So thy stronge muse her maker like repaires,
That from the ruins of her wasted vrne,
Into a body of delicious ayres:
Againe her spirit doth transmigrated turne,
That scortching soile which thy great subiect bore,
Bred those that coldly but exprest her merit,
But breathing now vpon our colder shore,
Here shee hath found a noble fiery spirit,
    Both there, and here, so fortunate for Fame,
    That what she was, she's euery where the same.

M. DRAYTON.

Among the Panegyrical Verses before Coryat's Crudities (1611).

Incipit Michael Drayton.

A briefe Prologue to the verses following.

Deare Tom, thy booke was like to come to light,
Ere I could gaine but one halfe howre to write;
They go before whose wits are at their noones,
And I come after bringing Salt and Spoones.

Many there be that write before thy Booke,
For whom (except here) who could euer looke?

Thrice happy are all wee that had the Grace
To haue our names set in this liuing place.
Most worthy man, with thee it is euen thus,
As men take Dottrels, so hast thou ta'n vs.
Which as a man his arme or leg doth set,
So this fond Bird will likewise counterfeit:
Thou art the Fowler, and doest shew vs shapes
And we are all thy Zanies, thy true Apes.　　　　　　10
I saw this age (from what it was at first)
Swolne, and so bigge, that it was like to burst,
Growne so prodigious, so quite out of fashion,
That who will thriue, must hazard his damnation:
Sweating in panges, sent such a horrid mist,
As to dim heauen: I looked for Antichrist
Or some new set of Diuels to sway hell,
Worser then those, that in the Chaos fell:
Wondring what fruit it to the world would bring,
At length it brought forth this: O most strange thing;　　　20
And with sore throwes, for that the greatest head
Euer is hard'st to be deliuered.
By thee wise Coryate we are taught to know,
Great, with great men which is the way to grow.
For in a new straine thou com'st finely in,
Making thy selfe like those thou mean'st to winne:
Greatnesse to me seem'd euer full of feare,
Which thou found'st false at thy arriuing there,
Of the Bermudas, the example such,
Where not a ship vntill this time durst touch;　　　　　30
Kep't as suppos'd by hels infernall dogs,
Our Fleet found their most honest wyld courteous hogs.
Liue vertuous Coryate, and for euer be
Lik'd of such wise men, as are most like thee.

Explicit Michael Drayton.

Prefixed to William Browne's Britannia's Pastorals (1613).

To his Friend the AVTHOR.

Driue forth thy Flocke, young Pastor, to that Plaine,
Where our old Shepheards wont their flocks to feed;
To those cleare walkes, where many a skilfull Swaine
To'ards the calme eu'ning, tun'd his pleasant Reede,
Those, to the Muses once so sacred, Downes,
As no rude foote might there presume to stand:

(Now made the way of the vnworthiest Clownes,
Dig'd and plow'd vp with each vnhallowed hand)
If possible thou canst, redeeme those places,
Where, by the brim of many a siluer Spring,   10
The learned Maydens, and delightfull Graces
Often haue sate to heare our Shepheards sing:
Where on those Pines the neighb'ring Groues among,
(Now vtterly neglected in these dayes)
Our Garlands, Pipes, and Cornamutes were hong
The monuments of our deserued praise.
So may thy Sheepe like, so thy Lambes increase,
And from the Wolfe feede euer safe and free!
So maist thou thriue, among the learned prease,
As thou young Shepheard art belou'd of mee!   20

Prefixed to Chapman's Translation of Hesiod's Georgics (1618).

To my worthy friend Mr. George Chapman, and his translated Hesiod.

Chapman; We finde by thy past-prized fraught,
What wealth thou dost vpon this Land conferre;
Th'olde Grecian Prophets hither that hast brought,
Of their full words the true interpreter:
And by thy trauell, strongly hast exprest
The large dimensions of the English tongue;
Deliuering them so well, the first and best,
That to the world in Numbers euer sung.
Thou hast vnlock'd the treasury, wherein
All Art, and knowledge haue so long been hidden: 10
Which, till the gracefull Muses did begin
Here to inhabite, was to vs forbidden.
    In blest Elizivm (in a place most fit)
Vnder that tree due to the Delphian God,
Musæus, and that Iliad Singer sit,
And neare to them that noble Hesiod,
Smoothing their rugged foreheads; and do smile,
After so many hundred yeares to see
Their Poems read in this farre westerne Ile,
Translated from their ancient Greeke, by thee;   20
Each his good Genius whispering in his eare,
That with so lucky, and auspicious fate
Did still attend them, whilst they liuing were,
And gaue their Verses such a lasting date.
Where slightly passing by the Thespian spring,
Many long after did but onely sup;

Nature, then fruitfull, forth these men did bring,
To fetch deep Rowses from Ioues plentious cup.
    In thy free labours (friend) then rest content,
Feare not Detraction, neither fawne on Praise: 30
When idle Censure all her force hath spent,
Knowledge can crowne her self with her owne Baies.
Their Lines, that haue so many liues outworne,
Cleerely expounded shall base Enuy scorne.

Michael Drayton.

Prefixed to Book ij. of Primaleon, &c. Translated by Anthony Munday (1619).

OF THE WORKE and Translation.

If in opinion of iudiciall wit,
Primaleons sweet Invention well deserue:
Then he (no lesse) which hath translated it,
Which doth his sense, his forme, his phrase, obserue.
And in true method of his home-borne stile,
(Following the fashion of a French conceate)
Hath brought him heere into this famous Ile,
Where but a stranger, now hath made his seate.
    He liues a Prince, and comming in this sort,
    Shall to his Countrey of your fame report.

M.D.

From Annalia Dubrensia (1636).

TO MY NOBLE Friend Mr. ROBERT DOVER, on his braue annuall Assemblies vpon Cotswold.

Douer, to doe thee Right, who will not striue,
That dost in these dull yron Times reuiue
The golden Ages glories; which poore Wee
Had not so much as dream't on but for Thee?
As those braue Grecians in their happy dayes,
On Mount Olympus to their Hercules
Ordain'd their games Olimpick, and so nam'd
Of that great Mountaine; for those pastimes fam'd:
Where then their able Youth, Leapt, Wrestled, Ran,
Threw the arm'd Dart; and honour'd was the Man   10
That was the Victor; In the Circute there

The nimble Rider, and skill'd Chariotere
Stroue for the Garland; In those noble Times
There to their Harpes the Poets sang their Rimes;
That whilst Greece flourisht, and was onely then
Nurse of all Arts, and of all famous men:
Numbring their yeers, still their accounts they made,
Either from this or that Olimpiade.
So Douer, from these Games, by thee begun,
Wee'l reckon Ours, as time away doth run.   20
Wee'l haue thy Statue in some Rocke cut out,
With braue Inscriptions garnished about;
And vnder written, Loe, this was the man,
DOVER, that first these noble Sports began.
Ladds of the Hills, and Lasses of the Vale,
In many a song, and many a merry Tale
Shall mention Thee; and hauing leaue to play,
Vnto thy name shall make a Holy day.
The Cosswold Shepheards as their flockes they keepe,
To put off lazie drowsinesse and sleepe,   30
Shall sit to tell, and heare thy Story tould,
That night shall come ere they their flocks can fould.

                    Michaell Drayton.

NOTES

These notes are not intended to supply materials for the criticism of the text. So freely, indeed, did Drayton alter his poems for a fresh edition, that the ordinary machinery of an apparatus criticus would be overtasked if the attempt were made. All that has been undertaken here is to provide the requisite information in places where the text followed seemed open to suspicion.

It may be added that the punctuation of the originals has in general been preserved; in a few flagrant instances, where the text as it stood was misleading, it has been modified. Such changes are not noted here.

2,	1,	l.	14	vertues] vertuous 1619
3,	3,	l.	1	Ioue] loue 1599, 1602, 1605
		l.	3	them forth,] them, forth 1599. But the 1619 version supports the reading in the text.
5,	8,	l.	8	men] ones 1599: women 1619
		l.	9	to 1599, 1619: of 1594
6,	9,	l.	11	in] on 1602
	10,	l.	12	her] his 1602: their 1619
8,	14,	l.	14	anatomize 1599. But there is ground for believing that anotamize represents a current pronunciation.
9,	15,	l.	10	She'st] ? She'll
10,	17,	l.	9	Were] Where 1594
	18,	l.	5	Elizia] Elizium 1599
11,	20,	l.	10	whir-poole] whirl-poole 1602
		l.	12	Helycon] Helicon 1602
14,	26,	l.	5	Thy 1599 etc.: The 1594
15,	27,	l.	4	Thus] This 1594
		l.	12	depriued] ? depraued

18, 33, l.   3   Wishing] Wisheth 1599

19, 36, l.   13   And others] And eithers 1599

20, 37, l.   4   euer-certaine] neuer-certaine 1602

28,   1, l.   4   song] sung 1613

31, 10, l.   2   bids] bad 1619

         l.   12   my…his] his…my 1619

37, 30, l.   14   hollowed] halowed 1605: hallow'd 1619. But cf. 94, l.
                     18.

38, 43, l.   3   Wherein 1602, 1605: Where, in 1619: Wherein 1599

39, 44, l.   4   Paynting] Panting 1608

         l.   8   Wherein 1602, 1605, 1619: Where in 1599

40, 55, l.   7   forces heere,] forces, here 1619

         56, heading A Consonet] A Cansonet 1602

41, 57, l.   13   yet] then 1595

42, 17, ll. 4, 13 Promethius] Prometheus 1605

43, 27, l.   2   Who can he loue? 1608: Who? can he loue: 1619

         l.   12   They resolute,] They resolute? 1608, 1619

44, 31, l.   4   appose] oppose 1608, 1619

         l.   9   They 1619: The 1602, 1605, 1608

48, 47, l.   8   a 1619: and 1605, 1608

49, 51, l.   1   to 1608: omitted in 1605

53, 21, l.   11   soe] ? loe

         l.   13   Troth] Froth 1619

71,   l.   16   scowles] scoulds 1606

       l.   37   whome 1606: whose 1619

       l.   41   rage 1606: age 1619

74,   l.   25   he 1619: shee 1606

77,   l.   34   some few 1606: some, few 1619

79,   l.   10   their] ? there.

83,   l.   72   Stuck] The emendation Struck is tempting (the form
                  is somewhat uncommon but not unparalleled);
                  especially in view of l. 80.

94,   l.   18   hollow'd] cf. 37, 30, l. 14

96,   l. 120   the] no doubt a printer's error for they

97,   l. 125   be lowe] belowe 1627

97,   l. 126   whether] whethet 1627

98,   l.   37   it] omitted in 1627

101,   l.   62   be] ? been

104,   l.   88   him] ? them

       l.   94   ceaze 1620: lease 1627

106,   l.   37   his] omitted in 1631

       l.   56   warnd] warne 1627

110,   l. 105   Neat] Next conj. Beeching

118,   heading Chaplaine] Chapliane 1627

120,   l.   81   extirpe 1631: extipe 1627

146,   l.   90   fett] sett and frett have been conjectured.

153,   l.   92   debate] delate 1627

154,   l. 115   claue] ? cleaue

156,   l. 220   euery] euer 1627

174,   l. 225   wither] whither 1630

177,   l. 343   rawe] taw 1748

192,   l. 18   there] they 1630

232,   l. 12   vnto] vp to 1619

233,   l. 53   fame] faire 1606

234,   l. 66   moue] mock 1606

238,   l. 25   feature] features 1619

240,   l. 99   long] loue 1606

242,   Ecl. ij, l. 21 moane 1600: moans 1605

243,   l. 55   But it if the Male doth want 1619

244,   l. 37   along she went 1619: she went along 1606

245,   l. 43   lowe] loud 1600, 1619

247,   l. 37   glories 1619: glorious 1606

ERRATA

Page 94, l.   5   for of said read said

" 173, l. 170   for you read your

Lightning Source UK Ltd.
Milton Keynes UK
06 April 2011

170449UK00002B/36/A